RELEASED
—— FROM ——
BONDAGE

DR. NEIL T. ANDERSON, DR. FERNANDO GARZON,
AND JUDITH E. KING

Publishers Since 1798

THOMAS NELSON PUBLISHERS®
Nashville

A Division of Thomas Nelson, Inc.
www.ThomasNelson.com

Published in Nashville, Tennessee, by Thomas Nelson, Inc.

Scripture quotations noted NASB are from the NEW AMERICAN STANDARD BIBLE, © Copyright The Lockman Foundation 1960, 1962, 1963, 1968, 1971, 1972, 1973, 1975, 1977. Used by permission.

Scripture quotations noted NIV are from the HOLY BIBLE: NEW INTERNATIONAL VERSION, Copyright © 1973, 1978, 1984 by the International Bible Society. Used by permission of Zondervan Publishing House. All rights reserved.

Scripture quotations noted NKJV are from THE NEW KING JAMES VERSION, Copyright © 1979, 1980, 1982, Thomas Nelson, Inc., Publishers.

Scripture quotations noted KJV are from the KING JAMES VERSION.

Diagrams on page 187 and revised material on page 250–51 taken from *Christ Centered Therapy*. Copyright © 2000 by Neil T. Anderson, Terry E. Zuehlke, and Julianne S. Zuehlke; chapter written by Judith E. King. Used by permission of Zondervan.

Library of Congress Cataloging-in-Publication Data

Anderson, Neil T., 1942–
    Released from bondage / Neil T. Anderson.
      p. cm.
    Originally published: San Bernardino, CA: Here's Life Publishers, 1991.
    ISBN 0-7852-6527-9
    1. Spiritual warfare. 2. Pastoral Counseling. 3. Suffering—Religious aspects—Christianity. 4. Anderson, Neil T., 1942– . I. Title.
    [BV4509.5.A53 1992]
    248.8'6—dc20

                                                                92-41366
                                                                CIP

Printed in the United States of America

02 03 04 05 06 PHX 17 16 15 14 13

We dedicate this book
to the courageous people who have shared their stories.
May the Lord protect them and use their faithful service and
testimony to help many live a victorious life in Christ.
They have proved themselves to be disciples:
"By this is My Father glorified, that you bear much fruit,
and so prove to be My disciples" (John 15:8 NASB).

Contents

PART ONE

How the Truth Set Them Free

Introduction

When I graduated from seminary, I was looking forward to being the captain of a "gospel ship." I would sail off into the eternal sunset, rescuing people from the watery abyss. We would have Bible classes, clubs for the kiddies, and sports for the athletically inclined (for the purpose of outreach, of course). Everybody would love one another.

Off I sailed on my first pastoral assignment, but it wasn't long before I noticed a dark ship sailing alongside. On that ship were people struggling with alcohol, sex, drugs, panic attacks, eating disorders, fear, anger, depression, and abuse of every conceivable kind. I can almost tell you the day that I realized I was on the wrong ship. God had called me to minister on the dark ship. Through a series of life-transforming events, I changed ships—only to discover it was the same ship!

Our churches are filled with hurting people. Many wear masks, frightened that someone will discover who they really are and expose their inner turmoil. They cling to what little hope they have, and long for some affirmation and legitimate help.

This book is about resolving personal and spiritual conflicts through discipleship counseling and Christ-centered therapy. You will read actual accounts of courageous people who have agreed to tell their stories from their perspectives. They were looking for help with the hope that Christ would be their answer and that the truth of His Word would set them free. Some are in full-time ministry.

Their names, occupations, and geographical references have been changed to protect their identities.

What's at stake isn't my reputation or transient ministry, but the integrity of the church. Countless millions are counting on the church to take its rightful place in God's kingdom program of setting captives free. I pray that you will find great personal help in reading these pages, but beyond that, it is my prayer that you will be better equipped to help others. I hope that you will be able to say, "Christ is the answer, and the truth of His Word will set us free!"

HOPE FOR THE HOPELESS

I received a call from a friend in the pastorate. We chatted about what God was doing in our respective lives and ministries, then he shifted to the real intent of his call. "Neil," he began, "I recall your saying that a husband can get caught in a role conflict if he tries to counsel his own wife. I have had the privilege of helping others find their freedom in Christ, but trying to help my wife is another matter. Could you possibly find time to see my wife? She is a wonderful lady, and people see her as competent and composed, but she struggles inwardly on a daily basis."

I met twice with this dear woman. The first session was a "get-acquainted" time. The second session I led her through the "Steps to Freedom in Christ." A week later I received this letter from her:

Dear Neil,

How can I say thanks? The Lord allowed me to spend time with you just when I was concluding that there was no hope for me to ever break free from the downward spiral of continual defeat, depression, and guilt. I did not know my place in Christ or recognize the enemy's accusations.

Having literally grown up in church and having been a pastor's wife for twenty-five years, everyone thought I was as put together on

Note: The Steps to Freedom in Christ is a comprehensive tool to help Christians resolve their personal and spiritual conflicts. They may be purchased at Christian bookstores or obtained directly from Freedom in Christ Ministries.

the inside as I was on the outside. On the contrary, I knew there was no infrastructure on the inside and often wondered when the weight of trying to hold myself together would cause my life to fall apart and come crumbling down. It seemed as if sheer determination was the only thing that kept me going.

When I left your office last Thursday, it was a beautiful, crystal-clear day with snow visible on the mountains, and it felt like a film had been lifted from my eyes. In the tape player was a piano arrangement of "It Is Well with My Soul." The words of the song fairly exploded in my mind with the realization that it *was* well in my soul . . . for the first time in years.

The next day at work my immediate response to "How are you today?" was "I'm doing great! How about you?" In the past I would have mumbled something about being almost alive. The next comment I heard was, "Boy, something must have happened to you yesterday."

I have heard the same songs and read the same Bible verses as before, but it is as if it's all totally new. There are underlying joy and peace in the midst of the same circumstances that used to bring defeat and discouragement. For the first time, I have wanted to read my Bible and pray. It is hard to contain myself—I want to shout from the rooftops what has taken place in my life, but my real desire is for my life itself to do the shouting.

Already the deceiver has tried to plant thoughts in my mind that this won't last, that it's just another gimmick that won't work. The difference is that now I know those are lies from Satan and not the truth. What a difference freedom in Christ makes!

With gratitude,

Mary

What a difference indeed! Is there something special about Neil Anderson that made this counseling session so effective? Do I have some unique gift from God or special anointing? No, I don't think so. In fact, there are people all over the world using the same message and method I use, with similar results.

While I was conducting a "Living Free in Christ" conference in

Grand Rapids, Michigan, Judy King, a licensed Christian therapist, decided to do some informal testing on those who were in need of personal counseling. The subjects of her study were those who attended the conference and requested a Freedom Appointment. They were given a questionnaire before their appointment and then again three months later. The counseling appointment was for one extended session conducted by a lay encourager who was trained to take a person through the "Steps to Freedom in Christ." The results showed a 52 percent improvement in depression, 47 percent improvement in anxiety, 57 percent improvement in tormenting thoughts, 48 percent improvement in personal and spiritual conflicts, and 39 percent improvement in negative habits or behavior. An independent research group led by Dr. George Hurst from the University of Texas Medical Center has found similar results after conferences. More extended testing is in process. No attempt was made to determine what the counselees' individual problems were before the pretest was completed. In other words, some of the people asking for appointments may not have been depressed or overly anxious, which makes the results even more impressive.

COGNITIVE THERAPY

In January 2000, I taught a doctor of ministry class at Regent University. Dr. Fernando Garzon, who taught in their psychology department, requested permission to conduct research on the students. The class was a one-week intensive session, meeting eight hours every day. The students were working on their master of divinity, doctor of psychology, and doctor of ministry degrees. Dr. Garzon used Judy King's questionnaire, plus the students took a pretest and posttest using the Rosenberg Self-Esteem Inventory, the Beck Anxiety Inventory, and the Symptom Checklist 90-R. Dr. Garzon's results were published in the *Journal of Psychology and Theology*. In summary, he wrote:

> Statistically significant reductions were found in several scales of the SCL-90-R (global severity index, anxiety, depression, obsessive-

compulsive, interpersonal sensitivity, hostility, somatization, paranoid ideation, and psychoticism). Anxiety was reduced as measured by the Beck Anxiety Inventory, and statistically significant increases in self-esteem and spirituality items were also found.[1]

I think you will agree that most students at that level of education don't take a class to have their lives changed, but in effect that is what happened.

How does one explain such significant results? I can assure you that the results we are seeing routinely in our ministry have little to do with our personal skills as counselors. The editors of the *Journal of Psychology and Theology* asked the critical question: What is Freedom in Christ Ministries doing that is different from standard cognitive therapy, which is well accepted by both Christian as well as secular counselors? In other words, if Neil taught a class (or conducted a conference) and the students experienced significant positive changes in their lives, isn't that just cognitive therapy being conducted on a group? The answer is yes, cognitive therapy is a part of the process, but no, cognitive therapy alone would not fully explain the results.

From a Christian perspective, *cognitive therapy* is very similar to the biblical concept of *repentance*, which literally means "a change of mind." People are doing what they are doing and feeling what they are feeling because of what they are choosing to think or believe. Therefore, what needs to change is what people think or believe. That is the basic theory behind cognitive therapy. The cognitive therapeutic process could be summarized as follows:

1. First, the client is helped to see the connection between negative thoughts and beliefs, the emotions they create, and the behaviors that follow.

2. Then the client is taught to recognize and monitor negative thoughts or distortions of reality. Thoughts or beliefs leading to negative feelings and improper responses to life are identified as ineffective or dysfunctional.

3. Next, the client examines the evidence for and against such distorted thinking or perceptions of reality. What does the evidence indicate? Is the client going to continue to think in this way, to believe what is being thought, and to act accordingly—or will the client change? This is decision time.

4. If the client concludes that what has been believed is not true and that his or her perception of reality was not right, then the client must substitute new ways of thinking/believing and responding.

5. Finally, the client is helped to identify and change the inappropriate assumptions that predisposed him or her to distort the experience in the first place.

Such a process is not only appropriate for Christian pastors and counselors; it is extremely helpful for those seeking answers for their lives. Biblical preaching and teaching can accomplish the same thing, although the process is less personal and interactive. However, cognitive therapy as outlined above is not enough by itself to produce the kind of fruit that we believe every pastor and Christian counselor can bear in Christ.

BEYOND COGNITIVE THERAPY

While researching for the book *Freedom from Fear*, I came across another book by Dr. Edmund Bourne entitled *Healing Fear*, which was published in 1998. Dr. Bourne wrote an earlier book, entitled *The Anxiety and Phobia Workbook*,[2] which won the Benjamin Franklin Book Award for Excellence in Psychology. A second edition was published in 1995, after which he went through the worst period of anxiety he had ever experienced. It caused him to reevaluate his own life and approach to treatment. In the foreword to his latest book, Dr. Bourne wrote:

The guiding metaphor for this book is "healing" as an approach to over-coming anxiety, in contrast to "applied technology." I feel it's important to introduce this perspective into the field of anxiety treatment since the vast majority of self-help books available (including my first book) utilize the applied technology approach. These books present—in a variety of ways—the mainstream cognitive behavioral methodology for treating anxiety disorders. Cognitive behavioral therapy reflects the dominant zeitgeist of Western society—a worldview that has primary faith in scientifically validated technologies that give humans knowledge and power to overcome obstacles to successful adaptation . . . I don't want to diminish the importance of cognitive behavioral therapy (CBT) and the applied technology approach. Such an approach produces effective results in many cases, and I use it in my professional practice every day. In the past few years, though, I feel that the cognitive behavioral strategy has reached its limits. CBT and medication can produce results quickly and are very compatible with the brief therapy, managed-care environment in the mental health profession at present. When follow-up is done over one- to three-year intervals, however, some of the gains are lost. Relapses occur rather often, and people seem to get themselves back into the same difficulties that precipitated the original anxiety disorder.[3]

I don't want to diminish the role of Cognitive Behavioral Therapy (CBT) either, but I also believe that CBT by itself is not enough for three reasons. First, giving people the words of Christ without possessing the life of Christ will prove insufficient. Christianity is a righteous relationship with God, not just an intellectual exercise. The truth will set you free, and Jesus is the Truth. Dead orthodoxy is just that: dead! Jesus came to give us life, and without the life of Christ we lack the power to live a righteous life. The Christ-Centered Therapy (CCT) approach to counseling is based on the need to help people get right with God by resolving personal and spiritual conflicts through genuine repentance and faith in God. The Steps to Freedom in Christ (Steps) is just a tool to help people submit to God and resist the devil. The Steps don't set you free. *Who* sets you free is Christ, and *what* sets you free is your response to Him in repentance and faith. The Steps, like any tool, can be used rightly or wrongly.

Second, discipleship counseling is primarily an encounter with God as opposed to some applied technique or learned procedure. Jesus is the Wonderful Counselor and only He can set a captive free, only He can bind up the brokenhearted, only He can make us new creations in Christ, and only He can transform a sinner into a saint. Nobody can fix our past, even God doesn't do that, but we can be free from our past if we are new creations in Christ. According to the gospel, it is the birthright of every believer to be alive and free in Christ. The pastor, Christian counselor, and properly equipped layperson are facilitators in the ministry of reconciliation. When one Christian attempts to help another, there are not just two people present. God is omnipresent and each person has a role and a responsibility, which cannot be usurped by another person and still be effective.

Third, CBT will not be effective if the counselor does not take into account the reality of the spiritual world and the possibility that the suffering person could be paying attention to a deceiving spirit. The apostle Paul made it very clear when he wrote, "The Spirit clearly says that in later times some will abandon the faith and follow deceiving spirits and things taught by demons" (1 Tim. 4:1 NIV). Paul also wrote, "I am afraid that just as Eve was deceived by the serpent's cunning, your minds may somehow be led astray from your sincere and pure devotion to Christ" (2 Cor. 11:3 NIV). Such obvious scriptural passages and years of experience have helped us to understand that many people considered to be mentally ill are actually experiencing a spiritual battle for their minds. We are admonished in Scripture to take every thought captive to the obedience of Christ (2 Cor. 10:5), put on the armor of God (Eph. 6:10–17), and choose to think upon that which is true, pure, and lovely (Phil. 4:6–8).

We were all born dead in our trespasses and sins (Eph. 2:1), i.e., we were born physically alive but spiritually dead. During those early and informative years of our lives we had neither the presence of God in our lives nor the knowledge of His ways. So we all learned to live our lives independent of God. Then one day we were born again spiritually, but nobody pushed the *clear* button in our memory bank. That is why we still struggle with many of the same things we did before our conversion. The apostle Paul explains what must happen: "Do not conform any longer to the pattern of this world, but be transformed by the renewing of your mind" (Rom. 12:2 NIV). CBT contributes to that process, but not without the presence of Christ, who gives us life, nor without the Holy Spirit, who leads us into all truth.

CHRIST-CENTERED THERAPY

I had the privilege to co-author a book with Dr. Terry and Julie Zuehlke, entitled *Christ Centered Therapy* (Zondervan) and subtitled *The Practical Integration of Theology and Psychology*.[4] Both Terry and Julie have secular degrees. Terry has a doctorate in psychology and Julie has her master's degree in psychiatric nursing. They both began their practices in the marketplace as religious nonbelievers. Then they both came to Christ and struggled with integrating their newfound beliefs into their secular practices. Finally, Terry founded his own Christ-centered practice in the suburbs of Minneapolis with offices around the state of Minnesota. Julie is on staff at Crystal Evangelical Church, overseeing their ministry of pastoral care. More than three thousand people have found their freedom in Christ through the ministry of that church. They have the working model that Freedom in Christ Ministries is encouraging other churches to adopt. Our passion is to see that churches and Christian therapists consider how to work together and integrate the above three issues into their practice along with a biblical use of cognitive behavioral therapy so that God's children can live free and productive lives in Christ.

This book is written for laypeople as well as pastors and Christian therapists. Part One is composed of seven chapters, which are testimonies of people finding their freedom in Christ. They are essentially the same as the first edition of this book; however, I have updated and expanded the notes. By anyone's standards they are remarkable testimonies, but in no way are they unusual or unique. They were chosen because they afforded a great opportunity for instruction. Not only will you be blessed by these testimonies, you will learn from their experience.

For most Christians, testimonies speak for themselves because we will be known for our fruit, according to Jesus (Matt. 7:20). There is no reason to apologize for using testimonies to illustrate truth and glorify our Lord and Savior Jesus Christ. The apostle John explained how victorious Christians have overcome: "They overcame him [Satan] because of the blood of the Lamb and because of the word of their testimony" (Rev. 12:11). Those who give great credence to the scientific method of investigation, however, believe that using testimonies is too anecdotal and does not constitute valid research. It is disappointing to discover that those who protest the loudest usually have no anecdotal experiences of their own to share. Actually, applying treatment and measuring results does constitute valid research. Admittedly, one-shot research designs are not the most reliable and represent the most basic of research designs. However, having a research doctorate myself, I can appreciate and respect the need that some have for scientific validation. For that purpose, Judy King and Fernando Garzon have teamed up to add a second part to this second edition.

Beyond Judy King's informal research reported above, which was conducted following our conferences, Fernando and Judy have worked together to research the use of Freedom In Christ Ministries' message and method as applied to therapy. They share their own perspectives in the second introduction and explain their research methodology. This second part reads differently. In the first part of the book, you will read testimonies from the counselees' perspectives with commentary from myself. In Part Two, Judy will take you through the therapeutic process in three case studies. It is an example of true integration. Dr. Garzon has independently done the research and analysis.

If you are teaching in higher education or have an advanced degree as a pastor or therapist, you will be most interested in the second part of this book. Judy is a gifted therapist and Fernando is an articulate researcher. They don't have any particular desire or need to promote Freedom in Christ Ministries and neither do I. All three of us desire deeply that Christ be exalted and become the focal point for all our ministries. We simply want to see God's people be established alive and free in Christ so they can be all that God created them to be. I close with some final words from the book *Healing Fear* by Dr. Bourne:

> In my own experience, spirituality has been important, and I believe it will come to play an increasingly important role in the psychology of the future. Holistic medicine, with its interest in meditation, prayer, and the role of spiritual healing in recovery from serious illness, has become a mainstream movement in the nineties. I believe there will be a "holistic psychology" in the not too distant future, like holistic medicine, [that] integrates scientifically based treatment approaches with alternative, more spiritually based modalities.[5]

CHAPTER 1

Molly:
Freedom from the Cycle of Abuse

I often start a conference by asking the people, "In the short time that I am here, if I really got to know you, would I like you? I mean, if I *really* got to know you?" I asked my seminary class that question and before I could go on, one of my students responded, "You'd feel sorry for me!" It was said in humor, but it captured the perspective of many who live a life of quiet desperation. Lost in their loneliness and pain, they cling to a thin thread of hope that somehow God will break through their fog of despair.

The system has not been kind to them. The parents who were to provide the nurturing love and acceptance they needed were, instead, often the cause of their plight. The church they clung to for hope didn't seem to have the answers.

Such is the case of our first story. I had never met Molly before I received a rather lengthy letter sharing her newly found freedom in Christ. Then, months later on a conference tour, I had the privilege to meet her. I expected to see a broken-down, dumpy human being. But instead, the person who had lunch with my wife and me was a thoroughly professional, intelligent, and attractive woman.

You will form your own mental picture as you meet her yourself. Her story is important because I didn't personally counsel her. She found her freedom by watching the videos of our conference on

"Resolving Personal and Spiritual Conflicts" in Sunday school. Her story is representative of those who suffer because of a dysfunctional family and an inept church. I believe that many living in bondage would step into freedom if they knew who they are in Christ and knew how to resolve their personal and spiritual conflicts as Molly did.

～～～

MOLLY'S STORY

I was born to the two meanest people I have ever met.

My whole life has changed since I became involved in the video series "Resolving Personal and Spiritual Conflicts." The source of my lifelong bondages became clear to me for the first time. I am forty years old, and I feel that I have just now reached the "promised land."

I was born in a rural area, grassroots U.S.A., to the two meanest people I have ever met. My father was a farmer with very little education who married my mother very young. My father was one of fifteen children in a family plagued with mental illness. There is a lot of instability in my mother's family as well, but they simply deny there is a problem.

The bright spot among my relatives was my grandmother. I'm sure I would have gone over the edge long ago if it had not been for her. She was a saint and I knew she loved me.

I was the firstborn of my parents, but that was after they had been married for twelve years. My first memory of them together is that of my mom locking my dad outside at night. I can still see the fierce expression on his face as he looked at me through the door and yelled, "Molly! Open the door and let me in." My mom, who was standing directly behind me, screamed, "Don't you dare open that door!"

My mother and father divorced when I was four, and my mother moved us out of the house. Sometime before the divorce, I remember one evening when my mother and father were planning to go out. My one-year-old sister and I were in their bed, probably waiting for a baby-sitter, when suddenly I saw an evil appearance that was *exactly* like the classic red devil, dancing at the end of the bed. I was petrified with fear and felt compelled not to tell anyone exactly what I was seeing.

I called for my mother, crying as I told her only that there was something in the room. She turned on the light and said, "There's nothing here; there's nothing here." I pulled up the covers so I couldn't see the end of the bed as she turned out the light and left the room. I stayed hidden under the bedcovers for a long time, afraid to look out. When I did, the presence was still there, laughing.

Those words felt like a knife going through my heart.

After my mother and father divorced, I remember the two of them meeting on the street, stopping to chat, and my daddy asking my mother if he could have my sister. Those words felt like a knife going through my heart because they meant that my father did not want me.

The voices probably started right then: "Your father doesn't even want you." And it was true. He told me all through my life that I was "just like my mother." I knew what that meant since I knew he hated her. She was a "rageaholic," and I was terrorized by her outbursts of anger.

Once when I was about six, I was at my dad's house and an aunt said to him, "Molly looks exactly like you." Instantly, his whole demeanor changed, and he stood up and screamed at her, "She looks exactly like her mother! I lived with that woman for sixteen years and she looks like her mother!" With that, he stomped out of the house, and I felt a sharp pain shoot through my chest.

Members of our family thought my mother might harm us. Once when my mother was really bad, an aunt came to our home and stood outside one of our windows. She was watching over us because she worried about our safety. Mother cursed us a lot of the time and totally controlled our lives. She had no friends, no love or tenderness, and often said that her life would have been a lot better without me. I felt she resented us and we were a bother to her.

In the next couple of years, Mom became even more bitter and mean. For the remainder of my years with her, I feared for my life. Though I didn't know much about the spiritual world, I felt, even then, that Satan was involved in our home life.

A time came when I would not eat my food unless my mother ate hers first because I was so afraid she would poison us. I can't describe the terror of being a child who always lived with a foreboding threat of danger. Though some of our relatives feared for us as well, they feared her more, so they never did anything about it.

When I was fourteen, my mother decided that I'd lost something and she refused to listen when I tried to tell her that I never had it. She beat and cursed me from six in the evening until one in the morning, making me go from room to room and even outside in the dark to go through the trash, searching over and over again for this item. I guess she finally got tired and went to bed. I was looking for the top to the toothpaste tube!

Right after that, my dad came for his monthly visit. He probably would have seen us more, but his new wife ranted and raved the whole time they were with us, treating us much the same way our mother did. On the way home that day, my mind suddenly blanked out. I could not remember who I was or who all the people in the car were. A huge lump welled up in my throat, and I was so scared that I couldn't talk. Then, just as suddenly, when Dad turned onto our street, my memory came flooding back. Oh, how I hated walking back into the "hell" of my home, but there was nowhere else to go.

Through all of this, I desperately wanted the love of my father and mother. All the way into my thirties, I called my mom every day even though she would often slam the phone in my ear. I was still trying to get her to love me.

When I was quite young, one of my uncles, who had a number of children of his own, would come over to our house and take me out. Apparently, it never occurred to my mother to be cautious and question why he would do that. From the time I was four until I was seven, I remember him fondling me and threatening to tell my mother that I was smoking cigarettes if I told her what he did. I remember feeling tremendous guilt, thinking that I should have said "no," but I was afraid.

After that I became addicted to masturbation, a problem that I never could control until I found my freedom in Christ. That sexual desire has tried to come back, but now I know what to do about it. I just proclaim aloud that I am a child of God and tell Satan and his evil emissaries to leave me. The compulsion is gone, instantly.

Recently I wanted to tell someone about that sexual addiction so that I would be accountable. When I did tell one of my friends who went to the Bible study I was attending, she said, "I've always had that problem too." We cried together and I told her of my victory over that demonic influence and all the violent sexual thoughts that went along with it. I rejoice now that I no longer have to be subject to the evil presence associated with that act and its overwhelming power. In Christ, I am free to choose not to sin in that way.

I was molested again at age nine by a business acquaintance of my mother. She let him take my sister and me for drives in his car, and he would kiss me and put his tongue in my mouth. One time, I was so scared of what he might do that I crawled up in the back window of his car and begged him to take us home. After that, he stopped taking us out.

I had seen movies in which people lost touch with reality.

Life got even worse as I grew older. I don't remember when, but I started to pray that God would not let me lose my mind and end up in an institution. I knew that could happen very easily because I had been hearing voices as long as I could remember. I had seen movies like *The Three Faces of Eve* in which people lost touch with reality, and I could see how that could happen to me.

We had no spiritual life. My mother totally rejected Christianity and wouldn't let me talk about it with her. My dad went to church every Sunday, but was extremely legalistic—a trap I later fell into. I began to attend a neighborhood church as a teenager and became very legalistic, doing everything they told me to do—everything—to make sure that I would be happy when I was older.

At the age of fourteen, I asked Jesus Christ to be my Savior, and I was so thrilled I couldn't wait to learn all I could about Him. The first time I went to a youth group, they distributed some books and gave us an assignment to do. By the next week, I had answered all the questions and purchased a notebook. Someone saw that I had completed the work and yelled out, "Look, everybody, she even answered the questions." The whole group laughed and I never did another assignment.

Sunday school was worse. There were a lot of girls in our church who were wealthy, and everyone in our Sunday school class was in a sorority except me and one other girl. We would call each other every Sunday morning to be sure we would both be there because the others didn't talk to us, and neither of us wanted to be there alone.

All during this time the voices were saying, "You're ugly. You're disgusting. You're unworthy. God couldn't possibly love you." My life seemed to have a way of making me believe that about myself.

When I got married, God would let me find happiness.

The oppression, depression, and condemning voices continued, but no one knew. There was no one I could talk to. I thought I deserved it. When I tried to tell people what my mother was like, they either didn't understand or responded inappropriately. Once I confided in a Sunday school teacher and she said, "Let's go talk to your mother." That struck icy fear in my heart because I knew what I would get from my mother after the teacher left, so I wouldn't do it. I was too terrified.

I lived by a code of self-effort, trying to please my mother to keep her from becoming angry. I believed that God put me where I was, and if I could stand the suffering, be obedient, live a good life and not sin, then when I got married He would let me find happiness. My goal was to have a Christian home and a Christian husband so I could find happiness and a secure place where no one would abuse me.

The summer after my senior year I ran into a man I had met at high school graduation, and it was love at first sight. He was the man I would marry for happiness ten months later, when I was nineteen. We were in church every Sunday and every Wednesday night, and we went to everything else there was to attend. But we had no friends and were never invited to anyone's home.

They didn't offer premarital counseling at our church and marriage was a big shock. I had saved myself for marriage, but I hated sex. Within a week, my husband began staying away, sometimes for a weekend. We moved into an apartment, and with the boxes still unpacked he simply left to play golf and be with his friends.

That was the final straw after a lifetime of never having felt loved by anyone. My self-esteem was so low that when I realized my husband didn't care anymore, I just went to bed and sank into a deep depression. Three weeks later, I felt convicted and got up. I thought, *How could he love me? He couldn't respect someone who clung to him and tried to hold on for dear life to his every move.* So I tried to change and make our marriage work. Somehow, we managed to stay together for fifteen years—fifteen years of conflict, rejection and pain. We vacillated between living a legalistic pretense of Christianity and completely turning our backs on God.

I hoped that having a child would bring happiness, and when I couldn't get pregnant I started seeing doctors. When my fifty-year-old doctor was kind and held my hand, I felt he was just being fatherly. But then he fondled me while I was on the examination table. Later, when I developed a lump in my breast, I went to another doctor, and he did something similar.

I wasn't the kind of woman who was flirty; I could hardly look another person in the eye. I believe that is just the way Satan works, using others to bring his evil into our lives when we are vulnerable. I felt so very uncomfortable while these things were happening, but then I was used to being uncomfortable. Later, one of my friends who worked in a law firm called and told me that one of those doctors had done the same thing to someone else and was being sued. That's when I finally knew that it wasn't me, and I was relieved of some of the doubts about myself. Right was wrong and wrong was right. My thought processes were so wrong that I just didn't know what was right.

I finally got pregnant and was catapulted into motherhood. Not very long after that, my husband came home one night and said, "All the guys at work talk about are girls and sex, so I spend most of my time with Linda. She goes to our church and she's a Christian and I go on breaks with her." He asked if I minded, and I said, "No, I don't mind."

My friends had warned me that he was seeing other women, but I wouldn't believe it. I just said, "He wouldn't do that." That was my way of dealing with it because I wanted to avoid the pain of finding out that he was unfaithful. Eventually he left me for Linda.

When my husband finally walked out and left me with two babies, I gave up on God and blamed Him for all the pain. I learned in church that the way to happiness for a single girl is to marry a Christian, and I had done that. Now I was angry at God, and for six years I ignored Him.

My mother urged me, "Do something. Don't just sit there with your life. Do something, even if it's wrong."

The people from work wanted me to go to the bar with them, and though I had never been to a bar, I went and soon got into that lifestyle. I never intended to date seamy people, but the lowest class of people would make me feel better. I even went to bars where some of the people had no teeth! I guess that was the only place I felt okay about myself because they were worse off than I was.

I was still bound by legalism and sometimes would try to go to church, but it took a herculean effort. On Friday evenings I would go to the bar, and when my kids came home from visiting their father on Saturday, I would go back to being a good little mother. On Sunday I would try to take them to church, but when I did I felt like a nail was being driven into my temple. I had always had a lot of headaches, but this pain was excruciating. Sometimes I would get sick and have to leave, and once I threw up in the car, so I finally quit going to church.

I would go to the bar and someone would say something nice to me.

I remember one of the last sermons I heard. The preacher said, "There is a downward spiral. When it starts, the circle is really big and things are moving slow at the top. As it goes down, things are closer and closer together and go faster and faster until they are out of control. But you can stop the downward spiral by not taking that first step."

I had already taken that first step. Things did get out of control and I couldn't stop. When I got depressed, I would go to the bar and someone would say something nice to me. I would have a drink and, temporarily I didn't feel so bad. I found acceptance at the bar but very little at the church. I had been in church regularly since I was fourteen, but never had a close friend. I was so withdrawn and it seemed like people didn't reach out, so I just sat there, miserable and alone.

I was in such a bad place in my life. In those bars, people would get into knife fights and sometimes somebody would pull a gun. But as time passed I got to the place where I would even go in to drink by myself and ignore the danger. I really didn't care anymore what happened to me.

I had a brush with cancer, which frightened me, and I thought maybe God was stomping on me to get my attention. So I quit the bars and went back to church. But after a year I forgot my cancer scare and slipped into the old lifestyle. I was living such a lie that it was inevitable. I had always had a strong conscience before, but at that time I remember thinking, *I don't even feel bad about this.*

I was miserable and thought of suicide, but I was such a chicken I couldn't do it. My life was so out of control that when I met a man at a bar who wanted to marry me, I rushed headlong into it. I didn't ask God what He thought about it, because I knew what His answer would be and I didn't care. The guy was still married when I met him and was a client where I worked. I was so afraid he would mention that he knew me from the bar—I wanted to keep that part of my life secret. I married him out of desperation to find happiness, but we were only together for two years.

Even before that marriage, I had slipped back into a legalistic cycle in which I tried to control everything. We went to church, and I made sure my husband read everything I wanted him to read. But he was more sick than I was and very weak, with no sense of his own identity. In the beginning, I could control everything. But when his two daughters came to live with us, "all hell broke loose." Their mother had been in a mental hospital and was now living in a lesbian relationship. The girls were totally without discipline and I decided I was going to "save" them, but my efforts blew up in my face.

I asked my husband to leave because I knew he was planning to leave me anyway, and I wanted to get the jump on him. I filed for divorce, but then I couldn't sleep at night and I stopped the proceedings. I knew it was wrong. I told him that he could get the divorce if he wanted to, but I never heard from him again.

We had gone to counselors, but nobody helped us.

My second husband and I did go to counseling, but no one was able to help us. They didn't deal with the reality of spiritual conflict, so how could they help us? They just patted us on the hand and said everything would be all right.

Finally, my last counselor did acknowledge that I was having a spiritual problem. I told him repeatedly about the fear of dying . . . about the suicide thoughts . . . about never being able to feel loved by God . . . about the cloud that overwhelmed me when I came home . . . but he didn't seem to know how to help me.

He asked me if I loved God, and I said, "I don't know." He responded, "Well, I know you do." I told him that the only God I knew was up in the heavens with a hammer waiting to beat me. He argued with me that God was not like that, but it didn't help.

I didn't tell him about the big black spider I saw as I woke up in the mornings, because after I started the day I forgot about it. It's incredible that this went on for ten years and I never thought about it except while it was happening. I convinced myself I was having a nightmare with my eyes open.

I got to the point where I couldn't stand pretending anymore. I would cry all weekend and pray, "God, I can't pretend anymore that I'm okay." I would get up when the kids came home from their weekend and put on my good-mother face. The truth was that all weekend I lay on the couch in utter blackness. I didn't open the windows and I never went out. And I never talked to anybody because there were always the voices in my head: "They don't want to talk with you. They don't like you." I never realized that I was paying attention to deceiving spirits.

I would do okay at work, but the second I walked in the door at night a cloud was waiting there to engulf me. I would usually just lay on the couch again, feeling miserable. Menial things like going to the grocery were really difficult because people were out there, and I felt they all hated me.

I kept going to the last counselor because I was desperate and couldn't keep up the pretense any longer. I was even crying at work. I told the counselor, "I'm losing my mind. I'm miserable. I can't go on."

He gave me a book to read, but it never got to the core of the problem. Although it spoke of Christ, there was no resolution; there was only hope if you could go to one of the clinics it described. However, the book did refer to *malignant codependency* and I knew that was me: no friends, totally isolated, living a lie, not knowing who I was. That petrified me.

After I read the book, I went to my counselor and said, "This is me." I was on the verge of suicide, but he simply told me to come back in two weeks. I tried to get into the clinic but couldn't because I didn't have the money they required.

My sister was also going through serious problems at the time, but she couldn't go to the counselor at our church because she wasn't a member. They were so overloaded they couldn't take nonmembers. My counselor recommended a class for children of dysfunctional families at another church. I wanted to go too, but it was hard to start over with a new group of people.

When the weekend came, my children went away and I spent all Friday night and all day Saturday on the couch, totally depressed and eating nothing but popcorn. By Sunday the thought came that I should attend the class. Nothing in the world could have been harder to do, but somehow I gathered the courage to go. When I walked into that class, I felt totally at home. I attended regularly and it helped a lot. It was so good to have friends even though they were sick themselves.

As I viewed the video, my mouth fell open.

One of my new friends invited me to a different class where they were showing the video series by Neil Anderson. As I viewed the video, my mouth fell open and I found myself saying repeatedly, "This is the truth." After the first visit, I wouldn't have missed that class for anything. Once I even went when I was sick because nothing in my life had given me such hope.

When I heard Neil talk about people hearing voices, I was so excited because I'd finally found someone who knew what I was experiencing. Then he talked about Zechariah 3, where Satan is accusing the high priest and the Lord says, "I rebuke you, Satan." That truth set me free. I thought, *I can do that.*

I realized that I had been deceived by the father of lies. He had been accusing me all my life and I did not stand against him. I learned that because I am alive in Christ and seated with Him in the heavenlies, I have authority to rebuke deceiving spirits and reject Satan's lies. I left that evening floating on air.

The depression is gone . . . the voices are gone . . . the huge spider-like object that I have been seeing in my room for the past ten years when I first wake up is gone!

My employer gave me the "Resolving Personal and Spiritual Conflicts" tape series for Christmas, and I have been listening to them over and over again. There's light in my mind where there was darkness before. I love the light now and open the curtains and windows to let it shine in. I really am a new person! I have people into my home for a Bible study with the tapes, something I couldn't have done before.

As I look back over my life, I see that the messages I got from my family were negative. I can't remember really feeling love in my life until I heard the videotapes and realized, God loves me just as I am.

Before I found my freedom in Christ, I was behaving just as my mother before me, going into rages with my kids and then hating myself afterward. That is so rare now, and my children feel comfortable with me.

I'm not like I was; I'm being healed. When I see myself falling back into old habit or thought patterns, I know what to do. I don't have to grovel in self-pity. At each point of conflict I can look for the particular lie Satan wants me to believe and then stand against it by deliberately choosing what I now know to be true.

My goal is to be the kind of parent God wants me to be, and I believe He will make up for all the years the locusts have eaten (Joel 2:24–25).

❦

How People Live

Nobody can consistently behave in a way that is inconsistent with what they believe about themselves. Molly believed she wasn't any good, that nobody wanted her, that she wasn't worthy of love. She was living a distorted life, foisted on her by abused and abusive parents. The cycle of abuse would have continued except for the grace of God.

When I hear a story like this—and I hear a lot of them—I just wish people like Molly could be hugged by someone in a healthy way for every time they have been touched wrongly. I want to apologize to her for her parents. I want to see people have a chance. They are sitting in bars near your church. Some sneak in the back door of the sanctuary and sit in the last row. Others become clinging pests whom we seek to avoid. They are children of God, but they don't know it and most have never been treated as such.

STOPPING THE ABUSE CYCLE

As believers, we have all the power we need to live productive lives and the authority to resist the devil. People like Molly are not the problem, they are the victims—victimized by the god of this world, abusive parents, a cruel society, and legalistic churches.

How do we stop this cycle of abuse? We lead them to Christ and help them establish their identity as children of God. We teach them the reality of the spiritual world, and encourage them to walk by faith in the power of the Holy Spirit. We care enough to confront them in love and stand by them when they fall. We do it by becoming the pastors, parents, and friends that God wants us to be. We pay attention to the words of Christ in Matthew 9:12–13:

> It is not those who are healthy who need a physician, but those who are sick. But go and learn what this means, "I desire compassion, and not sacrifice," for I did not come to call the righteous, but sinners.

The video series she watched is condensed from my first two books, *Victory Over the Darkness* and *The Bondage Breaker*, and both books and tapes (audio or video) can be purchased from your local Christian bookstore or from the office of Freedom in Christ Ministries.

THE PATH TO GOD

In no way am I advocating a quick fix for difficult problems. Processing the Steps to Freedom can take hours, and that is not the end. In fact, it only affords a new beginning of growth. There are a million ways to go wrong. The road to destruction is broad, the paths numerous, and their explanation complex. But the path back to God is not broad. Jesus is the Way that is narrow, the Truth that is simple, and the Life that is transforming. No wonder Paul said, "I am afraid, lest as the serpent deceived Eve by his craftiness, your minds should be led astray from the simplicity and purity of devotion to Christ" (2 Cor. 11:3 NASB).

Helping a person recognize deception and counterfeit guidance and choose the truth isn't simple. Knowing how to get a person in touch with the emotional pain of the past and work through forgiveness isn't easy. Confronting a person about pride, rebellion, and sinful behavior requires a godly love and acceptance.

Some are able to process these steps on their own as Molly did because truth is what sets us free, and the Holy Spirit will lead us into all truth. However, many need the assistance of a godly encourager. Prerequisites for the pastor/counselor are the character of Christ and the knowledge of His ways. This type of counseling requires the presence and leading of the Holy Spirit, who is the Wonderful Counselor.

We are suffering from a paralysis of analysis. If I were lost in a maze, I wouldn't want someone to explain to me all the intricacies of mazes and then give me coping skills so I could survive in the maze. I certainly wouldn't need someone to tell me what a jerk I was for getting in there in the first place. I would desire and desperately need clear directions out of there. God sent His Son as our Savior, provided the Scriptures as a road map, and sent the Holy Spirit to guide us. People all over the world are dying in a lifeless maze, for want of someone to gently show them the way out.

CHAPTER 2

Anne:
Freedom Through Stages of Growth

God's will for our lives is our sanctification (1 Thess. 4:3). As believers we are in the process of conforming to His image. If we are working with God, then every Christian pastor and counselor should be contributing to that process. Many people are not growing for lack of knowledge. Others are not even able to receive the truth because of unresolved conflicts in their lives (1 Cor. 3:1–3). That was the case for Anne. Before I get to her story, I need to lay a foundation for the path of sanctification.

BORN DEAD

Paul writes, "As for you, you were dead in your transgressions and sins, in which you used to live when you followed the ways of this world and of the ruler of the kingdom of the air, the spirit who is now at work in those who are disobedient" (Eph. 2:1–2 NIV). Since Adam, we are all born physically alive but spiritually dead (i.e., separated from God). During our formative years, we learned how to live our lives independent of God. We had neither the presence of God in our lives nor the knowledge of God's ways.

This learned independence from God is characteristic of the flesh or old nature. And one of the ways the flesh functions is to develop defense mechanisms whereby we learn how to cope, succeed, and survive without God. *Defense mechanisms* are similar to what some call "mental strongholds" or "flesh patterns."

ETERNALLY ALIVE

We are spiritually alive the moment we are born again. That means our souls are in union with God. That carries the same meaning as being *in Christ.* Eternal life is not something we receive when we die; we are eternally alive *in Christ:* "The witness is this, that God has given us eternal life, and this life is in His Son. He who has the Son has the life; he who does not have the Son of God does not have the life" (1 John 5:11–12 NASB).

REPROGRAMMED

At the moment of conversion, all of God's resources are available to us. Unfortunately, nobody pushes the *clear* button in our previously programmed minds. Until God's transformation process begins in our lives, we live in a state of being conformed to this world and regimented by it. That's why Paul writes, "Do not conform any longer to the pattern of this world, but be transformed by the renewing of your mind. Then you will be able to test and approve what God's will is—His good, pleasing and perfect will" (Rom. 12:2 NIV).

Therefore:

- The major task of Christian education is to disciple previously programmed people, living independent of God, into a dependent relationship with Him.

- The major task of discipleship/counseling is to free people from their past and eradicate old defense mechanisms by substituting Christ as their only defense.

BECOMING TRANSFORMED

Truth and obedience are key issues in living a Christ-dependent lifestyle. But truth can only be believed if it is understood, and commandments can only be obeyed if they are known. As the Holy Spirit leads us into all truth, we must respond by trusting and obeying: "The one who says, 'I have come to know Him,' and does not keep His commandments, is a liar, and the truth is not in him" (1 John 2:4 NASB). We give Satan an opportunity when we fail to believe the truth and act in disobedience. According to Ephesians 2:2, that spirit "is now at work in those who are disobedient" (NIV).

The process of sanctification begins at our new birth and ends in glorification. In the New Testament, sanctification is presented in the past, present, and future tenses. We have been sanctified, we are being sanctified, and someday we shall fully be sanctified. Past-tense sanctification is often referred to as *positional sanctification*, and present-tense sanctification is referred to as *progressive sanctification*. Positional sanctification is the basis for progressive sanctification. As born-again believers, we are not *trying* to become children of God. We *are* children of God who are becoming like Christ. It is important to understand this, because every defeated Christian I have worked with didn't know who they were in Christ nor did they understand what it meant to be a child of God. Our identity and position in Christ are the basis for our growth in Christ.[1]

DIFFUSING THE PAST

In many cases, traumatic childhood experiences continue to have a debilitating effect upon present living. I have come to understand that people are not so much in bondage to past abuses as they are in bondage to the lies they have believed as a result of the abuses. In the previous chapter, recall that Molly believed a lot of lies about herself because of her abusive parents. It is common to have many of these experiences blocked from memory. Secular psychologists are aware of this and attempt to get at hidden memories through hypnosis. Some try a hospitalization program using drugs to induce memories. While their sincerity is commendable, I am unequivocally opposed to both procedures for two reasons. First, I don't want to do anything to bypass the mind of a person; and second, I don't want to get ahead of God's timing.

You will find no instruction in Scripture to dwell on yourself or direct your thoughts inward. Scripture argues for the active use of our minds and for our thoughts to be directed outward. We invite God to search our hearts (Ps. 139:23–24). All occult practices will try to induce a passive state of the mind, and Eastern religions will admonish us to bypass it. God never bypasses our minds. He works through them for our transformation. Scripture requires us to think and assume responsibility for taking every thought captive to the obedience of Christ (2 Cor. 10:5).

If there are hurtful ways within us, and hidden memories of our past, God will wait until we reach enough maturity before He reveals them. Paul wrote:

> I care very little if I am judged by you or by any human court; indeed, I do not even judge myself. My conscience is clear, but that does not make me innocent. It is the Lord who judges me. Therefore judge nothing before the appointed time; wait till the Lord comes. He will bring to light what is hidden in darkness and will expose the motives of men's hearts. At that time each will receive his praise from God. (1 Cor. 4:3–5 NIV)

The above passage clearly indicates that God has knowledge of us that we do not possess. We will never have perfect knowledge of ourselves in this lifetime. In our ministry we frequently encounter people who can't recall periods of their lives. I believe that God allows them to dissociate while being abused. It is an extreme defense mechanism that allows the person to develop somewhat normally. Like any defense mechanism, it breaks down over time and is no longer necessary when we come to Christ. That is why some people start to recall early childhood traumas later in their lives.

PURSUING GOD

What should we do if we know something in our past is still affect-ing us and has never been resolved? I believe we should continue the pursuit of knowing God, learn to believe and obey that which is true, and commit ourselves to the sanctifying process of developing our character. When we have reached enough security and maturity in Christ, He reveals a little more about who we really are. As Christ becomes the only defense we need, He weans us of our old means of defending ourselves.

Stripping off old defense mechanisms and revealing character deficiencies is like taking off layers of an onion. When one layer is removed, we feel great. We have nothing against ourselves and we are free from what others think about us, but we have not yet fully arrived. At the right time, He reveals more in order that we may share in His holiness.

Our next story is about this progressive process of sanctification. Anne wrote the following letter and handed it to me halfway through a conference. She heard who she was as a child of God, learned how to walk by faith, and saw the nature of the battle for her mind. She was so excited that she jumped ahead and processed the Steps to Freedom on her own.

ANNE'S STORY

I was taught not to think for myself.

Dear Neil:

Praise God, I think this is the answer I've been searching for. I'm not crazy! I don't have an overactive imagination as I have been told and believed for years. I'm just normal like everybody else.

I have struggled through my whole Christian experience with bizarre thoughts that were so embarrassing I usually never told anyone else. How could I admit to someone in the church what had crossed my mind? I tried once to honestly share part of what I was struggling with in a Christian group. People sucked in their breath, there was a stiff silence, then someone changed the subject. I could have died. I learned quickly that these things are not acceptable in the church, or at least they weren't at that time.

I didn't know what it meant to take every thought captive.[2] I tried to do this once, but I was unsuccessful because I blamed myself for all this stuff. I thought all those thoughts were mine and that I was the one who was doing it. There has always been a terrible cloud hanging over my head because of these issues. I never could accept the fact that I was really righteous because I didn't feel like it.

Praise God it was only Satan—not me. I have worth! The problem is so easy to deal with when you know what it is.

I was abused as a child. My mother lied to me a lot and Satan used the things she said, like, "You're lazy. You'll never amount to anything." Over and over he has been feeding me so much junk—preying on my worst fears. At night I would have nightmares that the lies were true, and in the morning I would be so depressed. I have had a difficult time shaking this stuff.

Being abused, I was taught not to think for myself. I did what I was told and never questioned anything for fear of being beaten. This set me up for Satan's mind games. I was conditioned to have someone lie to me about myself, primarily my mother. I feared taking control of my mind because I didn't know what would happen. I believed I would lose my identity because I wouldn't have anyone to tell me what to do.

In actuality, I have gained my identity for the first time. I am not a product of my mother's lies; I am not a product of the garbage Satan feeds me. Now I'm finally me, a child of God! Through all his junk, Satan has terrorized me. I have been living in fear of myself, but praise God, I think it's over. I used to worry whether a thought came from Satan or myself. Now I realize that's not the issue. I just need to examine the thought according to the Word of God and then choose the truth.

I feel a little unsure writing this so soon. Maybe I should take a "wait and see" attitude, but I am sensing such joy and peace that I feel in my gut it must be real. Praise God for the truth and answered prayer! I am free!

With a heart full of thanks,
Anne

One layer of the onion was exposed. The critical first part of the Epistles, which speaks of our identity in Christ, was made known to Anne. She was no longer just a product of her past; she was a new creation in Christ. With that foundation laid, she was able to face and repudiate the lies she had believed for so many years. When she had tried to share some of her struggles in the past, she felt rejected, probably because others in the group were struggling in a similar fashion but were unable to reciprocate.

Oh, how I long for the day when our churches will help people firmly establish their identity in Christ and provide an atmosphere where people like Anne can share the real nature of their struggles. Satan does everything in the dark. When issues like this arise, let's not suck in our breath and change the subject. We buy Satan's devious strategy by keeping everything hidden. Let's walk in the light, and have fellowship with one another in order that the blood of Jesus will cleanse us from all sin (1 John 1:7). God is Light, and in Him there is no darkness at all (1 John 1:5). Let's lay aside falsehood and speak the truth in love, for we are members of one another (Eph. 4:15, 25).

Now Anne knows who she is and understands the nature of the battle going on for her mind. She must be totally free, right? Wrong! She was free of what she processed, but God wasn't through with her yet. One layer doesn't constitute the whole onion. Two weeks after the conference she wrote a second letter.

⟪⟫

Dear Neil:

Good night! Where do I start? Let me just say that I came to your conference for academic reasons. I could not have fathomed in advance what the Lord had in store for me. In fact, I probably wouldn't have believed it anyway. I guess I should start where I left off with you a few days ago.

I wrote you a letter explaining that I had been freed from obsessive thoughts. A few months ago, I had specifically asked the Lord to help me understand this problem. When I heard the information in the conference at the beginning of the week, I was thrilled. It was exactly what I had asked the Lord for. At home I prayed through all of the prayers in the Steps to Freedom. It was a struggle, but the voices stopped. I felt free; thus, I thought I was done. Little did I know!

You talked to me one evening after a session and told me that I probably needed to forgive my mother. I didn't buy it very well because I had tried it once before and it didn't work. I now realize that I was pushed into it by some well-meaning Christians who said that my feelings didn't matter. In fact, they said I shouldn't even have any angry feelings. To them, the kind of rage I was feeling was very sinful. So I grudgingly went through the motions of saying that I forgave the people who had hurt me. As a result of that phony effort, I became very bitter and sarcastic. I tried not to be, but the truth is that I was. God showed me later that my bitterness resulted from denying that I was angry while going through the motions of forgiving.

A year ago I attended a support group for abuse victims. The leader of the group told me that I was bitter because I had tried to forgive before I was ready. She said that I needed to work through all my feelings about each incident. After that, I would be able to forgive.

When you talked to me that evening, I thought you were coercing me into another ritual prayer of forgiveness that would mean nothing. All I knew was that I couldn't return to the bitterness trail. I decided to just take the information that I received at the beginning of the conference as what God wanted me to receive and put the rest of the information on the academic shelf.

Thursday evening, when you spoke on forgiveness, I was miserable. I had a horrible time sitting through the meeting, feeling bored and angry. I felt very misunderstood and thought I was wasting my time. I knew I couldn't leave or everybody would think I was possessed or something. So I struggled with staying awake and couldn't wait to get out of there.

That night I started working on an assignment for a class. I couldn't process anything because the forgiveness issue hit me square in the face again. I felt angry, but something in my gut told me that there had to be something more to what you were saying. I decided that I should be open and willing to try anything. I figured it couldn't hurt, although I really doubted that it would help since I had been trying to forgive my parents for years.

So I made a list of people and offenses and worked through them as you had suggested that night. During that time, God showed me that I had been hanging on to their offenses in anger because it was my way of protecting myself against further abuse. I didn't know how to scripturally set boundaries around myself to protect myself from them. I was taught by the church that I must keep turning the other cheek and keep letting them slap it. When you spoke of what it really meant to honor your parents, I knew that was my ticket to freedom.

God showed me that it was okay to stick up for myself and that I didn't need an unforgiving attitude to protect myself. He showed me that the abuse support group was right in telling me to focus on my emotions; however, there was never any real closure because they never taught us to come to a decision about forgiveness. That was always down the road—when you felt better. I see now that both Christian groups were emphasizing one aspect about forgiveness, but not both.

After forgiving, I felt exhausted. Interestingly, though, I immediately had a real love jump in my heart for you, Neil. It hadn't been there before. I went to sleep feeling pretty good.

An hour later, I woke up with cold sweats and my heart racing. I had just had another one of my awful nightmares. I hadn't had one in several months, so I was kind of surprised. For the first time in my life, it occurred to me that maybe this wasn't all a result of my abuse as I had been taught in the past. I prayed that the Lord would help me figure it out and went back to sleep. At 2:30 A.M., my roommate woke me up with her screaming. I jumped out of bed and woke her up. We compared notes and realized we both had had similar dreams. After praying together and renouncing Satan,[3] we went back to bed and both slept fine the rest of the night.

In those early morning hours as I was drifting back to sleep, God showed me that I had been having similar dreams since third grade—dreams that I had met the devil and he had put a curse on me. I can't believe I forgot all that. I asked the Lord what happened in the third grade and remembered that I had started watching *Bewitched* at that time. It was my favorite TV show and I watched it religiously.

Because of that show, I became very interested in spiritual powers. Along with many of my school friends, I read books on ghosts, ESP, palm reading, and even a book on spells and curses. It also was an "in" thing to play with magic eight balls, Ouija boards, and magic sets. Another TV favorite was *Gilligan's Island,* where I got the idea to use my dolls as voodoo dolls to get back at my mother. I considered putting a curse on her. By the time I was in sixth grade, I was so depressed. I started reading Edgar Allan Poe and it became the only thing I craved. *I can't believe I had forgotten all this.*

In high school the dreams came back and I became suicidal. By the grace of God, I invited Jesus Christ into my life soon after that. The biggest thing God showed me was that I knew when I was very young that there was evil power out there, and I had desired to have it.

When Saturday came, you can bet I was all ears. This wasn't hocus-pocus to me anymore. So as you led us through the Steps to Freedom, I prayed all the prayers again and renounced all the lies that have been going on in my family for years. I acknowledged my own sin and lack of forgiveness.

The best way I can describe what happened to me this week is this: You know how it is when somebody has been in a cult for a long time, and they get taken in for deprogramming? That's the way it was for me. It was like God locked me in a room and said, "Give Me your brain. We're not leaving here until you do." It's taken an intensive week to get me to see the lies I have been believing. I had no idea.

Since I have returned home, the lying thoughts—*You're no good. You're stupid. No one likes you*—have been coming out in great numbers. I told my husband everything, so every time I have a lying thought I tell him and we both laugh about it and talk about what's really true. Praise God! I was too embarrassed to tell him before.

Last night one of my nightmares started up again. I felt the oppression coming on as I was drifting off to sleep. I said "Jesus" right away. Neil, I could feel the oppression lifting off my heart, quickly, almost like it had been torn away. Praise God!

Because of counseling through the years, I have quite a few notebooks filled with accounts of the pain from my past. This pain pile has been sitting in my drawer and has been an eyesore every time I have looked at it. I now know that my identity isn't in the past anymore; it's in Christ. I burned all the notebooks.

Thank you for telling me the truth even if I didn't understand it at first. The joy I feel is the same joy I felt when I first received Christ! Finally, I understand what it means to be a child of God.

Joyfully,
Anne

⟋⟋⟋⟋

Three layers of the onion peeled off in a week is rather remarkable. Anne understood her identity in Christ, was able to forgive from her heart, and learned to stand against Satan. She may have more going for her than most, having a Christian education and a loving, understanding, and supportive husband to go home to. That is not to say that others can't resolve the same issues, but for some it may take longer.

FORGIVENESS BRINGS FREEDOM

Several issues need to be expanded on. Every person in this book has had to face the need to forgive. It drives legitimate counselors up a wall when well-meaning Christians suggest that somebody who expresses feelings like anger and bitterness shouldn't "feel that way." Bypassing feelings will never bring resolution to problems. If you want healing, you will have to get in touch with your emotional core. God will surface the emotional pain in order that it may be dealt with. Those who don't want to face reality will try to shove it down, but that will only result in prolonging the bitterness.

Forgiveness is what sets us free from our past. We don't do it for the other person's sake; we do it for our sake. We are to forgive as Christ has forgiven us. There is no freedom without forgiveness. "But you don't know how bad they hurt me," says the victim. The point is, they're still hurting you, so how do you stop the pain? You need to forgive from the heart—acknowledge the hurt and the hate and then let it go. To not forgive from the heart is to give Satan an opportunity (Matt. 18:34–35; 2 Cor. 2:10–11).

Going over the past and reliving all the pain without forgiveness only reinforces it. The more you talk about it, the stronger the hold it has upon you. The assumption seems to be that you have to heal first, then you will be able to forgive. Not true! You forgive first, then the healing process can begin. The painful feelings may take time to heal, but forgiveness is primarily a choice. It is a crisis of the will and the reward is freedom.

STAND AGAINST SIN

Many, like Anne, see their anger as a means of protecting themselves from further abuse. Secular counselors see Christian forgiveness as codependency and argue, "Don't let that person shove you around anymore. Get mad!" I say, "Don't let that person shove you around anymore. Forgive!"

Then take a stand against sin. Forgiveness does not mean tolerating ways in which others may be sinning against you. God forgives, but He doesn't tolerate sin. It grieves me that some pastors will hear of abuse and tell the child or wife to just go home and submit, saying, "Trust God to protect you." I want to say to that pastor, "Why don't you go home in their place and get knocked around?" But doesn't the Bible say that wives and children are to be submissive? True, but it also says that God has established government to protect abused children and battered wives. Read Romans 13:1–7, and then turn abusers in as the law even requires you to do in many states. I'm not saying this because I am vindictive. I am encouraging you to confront the abusers for their sake and if necessary turn them in to the law. You will never help abusers by allowing them to continue in their abuse.

If a man in your church abused another woman in your church, would you tolerate it? If a man or woman in your church abused another person's child, would you tolerate that? It is not only wrong to tolerate abuse in our homes, it is doubly wrong. Family members are not only getting abused, they are also losing their protection. Husbands and parents are charged by God to love, protect, and provide for their wives and children. Never are they given a license to abuse, nor should it ever be tolerated. Turn them in, for everyone's sake, or the cycle of abuse will just continue to the next generation.

One mother of three children shared with me in tears one evening that she knew exactly who it was that she needed to forgive. It was her mother. But if she forgave her that evening, what was she to do that Sunday when she had to go over to her house? "She will just bad-mouth me all over again." I said, "Put a stop to it. When you go to her home next Sunday say: 'I want to love and respect you, but you have been bad-mouthing me all my life. It isn't doing you any good and it certainly isn't doing me any good. For the sake of my husband and children, I really can't be a part of that anymore. If you can't stop treating me that way, then I am going to have to keep my family from visiting here.'"

Her response was typical: "Doesn't the Bible say that I am supposed to honor my mother?" I explained that letting her mother systematically destroy her and her present family would certainly not honor her mother. Eventually it would dishonor her. "Honor your mother and father" is better understood as taking financial care of them in their old age. The need to obey one's parents no longer applies to this woman since she had left her mother and father and was now an adult.

LIVING WITH CONSEQUENCES

The major decision you are making in forgiveness is to bear the penalty of the other person's sin. All forgiveness is efficacious. If we are to forgive as Christ forgave us, how, then, did He forgive us? He took the sins of the world on Himself. He suffered the consequences of our sin. When we forgive the sin of another, we are agreeing to live with the consequences of his or her sin. You say, "That's not fair!" It may not be fair, but the truth is you will have to anyway, whether you forgive or not. Everybody is living with the consequences of somebody else's sin. We are all living with the consequences of Adam's sin. The only real choice is whether we will do it in the freedom of forgiveness or the bondage of bitterness.

Some victims have asked, "Why should I let them off my hook?" That is precisely why you should forgive. If you don't forgive, you are still hooked to them. One man exclaimed, "That's why moving away didn't resolve it." When you let them off your hook, are they off God's hook? Never! God says, "Vengeance is Mine, I will repay" (Heb. 10:30 NASB). God will deal justly with everyone in the final judgment, which is something we cannot do.

GET GOD INTO THE PROCESS

God has to be involved in the process. Step 3 in the Steps to Freedom addresses bitterness versus forgiveness, and begins with a prayer asking God to reveal "to my mind those people I have not forgiven in order that I may do so." I have had many look at me in all sincerity and say they don't think there is anyone they need to forgive. But I ask them to share with me names that are coming to their minds anyway.

Within minutes, I often have a full page of names because the Lord is faithful to answer that kind of prayer. Then we spend the next hour (or sometimes hours) working through forgiveness.

I encourage them to pray, "Lord, I forgive (name) for (the offense)," and to go through every remembered pain and abuse. God will bring to their minds many painful memories in order for them to forgive from their hearts. He probably has been trying to for years, but they have been suppressing them. One person said, "I can't forgive my mother. I hate her!" "Now you can," I said. God never asks us to lie about how we feel. He only asks us to let it go from our hearts so He can free us from our past.

I encourage people to stay focused on the person they are forgiving until every painful memory has surfaced, and then go on to the next person. I have seen experiences surface that they have never talked about or remembered before. Some may respond, "My list is so long, you don't have enough time." I reply, "Yes, I do. I'll stay here all night if I have to." And I mean it. One man started to cry and said, "You're the only person who has ever said that to me." Once you start the step on forgiveness, finish it.

LAYERS OF THE ONION

It is not uncommon for a person to leave a counseling session feeling free, only to struggle a few hours, days, or weeks later. They may conclude it didn't work, but if you check the issues they are dealing with now, they are probably working on another layer of the onion. In many cases, like the stories in this book, freedom is best maintained if they know who they are as children of God and understand the nature of the battle for their minds. As long as we are on planet Earth, we will have to pick up our cross daily and follow Jesus. This means putting on the whole armor of God and resisting the world, the flesh, and the devil.

The "onion effect" is more pronounced for those who have been ritually abused. The Lord begins with early childhood and works forward. I believe that we are to help these people become firmly

established in their identity in Christ and then assist them in resolving the conflicts of their past as God slowly reveals it to them.

Freedom in Christ is a prerequisite to growth. You can observe this
by the rapid growth that will take place in people's lives when they
experience their freedom. However, these people will have to deal
with many other issues in the sanctifying process, and we all have to
take our stand against the god of this world. For instance, Anne
sensed an oppression come on her one evening, but she had learned
how to take a stand against the devil by verbally expressing the name
of Jesus. She was depending on Him to defend her. As other schemes
of Satan surface, she is learning to recognize and expose them in the
light of the truth, and the truth continues to set her free.

CHAPTER 3

Sandy:
Freedom from Cultic and Occult Bondage

When I first met Sandy, she was fleeing from a conference session in fear. She is a lovely lady in her early forties, and she has a bubbly personality with enough energy for two. She has a committed Christian husband, five children, and she lives in a beautiful suburban community.

Sandy masked very well the battle that had been raging in her mind for most of her life. Few people, if any, suspected the war going on inside until she mysteriously started withdrawing from church and friends eighteen months before we met. Here is her story.

~~~

SANDY'S STORY

I lived mostly in a very tiny corner of my mind.

At last I am able to believe I am a child of God. I am now sure of my place in my Father's heart. He loves me. My spirit bears witness with His Spirit that it is so. I no longer feel like I am outside the family of God—I no longer feel like an orphan.

Since the time we spent together at the conference, the evil presence inside me is gone, and the many voices that haunted me for thirty-five years are also gone. It feels clean, spacious, and beautiful inside *all* of my mind.

Before I found my freedom in Christ, I lived mostly in a very tiny corner of my mind. Even then I could never escape the commanding voices or the filthy language or the accusing anger. So I tried to separate myself from my mind altogether and live a life disassociated from it.

I became a Christian in 1979, but I have struggled continually to believe that God actually accepted me, wanted me, and cared about me. At last this lifelong struggle has come to an end. Before, I could never hear that still, small voice of God in my mind without being punished for it by the other voices. Today, only the still, small voice is there.

It all started when I was very young. My father professed to be an atheist and my mother was very religious, so there was a lot of conflict and confusion in our home. I went to religious schools, but when I came home I heard from my father that religion was all a lot of nonsense for weak people. I actually hoped that he was correct and that there wasn't any God because I was afraid of my mother's religion. I was afraid that God would get me if I didn't behave correctly. I was looking for spiritual answers, even though I rejected both of my parents' beliefs.

I would communicate with the ball,
using it as a fortune-telling device and
believing that it was magic.

My family, both parents and grandparents, was riddled with superstitious beliefs and good-luck charms. I remember visiting my grandparents on my mother's side and feeling that their house was a quiet place to get away from the chaos of the home I was growing up in. Grandma didn't have any toys for me to play with, only a black Crazy 8 ball. There was a window in the ball and little chips inside with many different answers. I would ask the ball a question like

"Will it rain tomorrow?" One of the answers would float up to the top such as "Probably."

I grew very attached to that ball and spent a lot of time at my grandmother's house playing with it and believing that it had magic power and answers for everything. I would communicate with the ball about my parents and what was happening in my life, using it as a fortune-telling device. Many of the answers the ball gave me were correct, reinforcing my belief that the ball had power.

I suppose the grown-ups thought it was just a toy for the grand-children to play with. When I had problems, though, I would store them up until I got to my grandmother's house and try to solve them with the magic ball. When I visited my father's parents, they would take me to their very legalistic church and I became terrified of hell. Being fearful of God and religion, I turned to the magic ball to try to predict events. That way I could be prepared in advance for any disasters God was going to send my way.

I would become explosively angry over anything. At the same time, I felt like a lonely, sad, scared little girl.

By the time I was fourteen I had become very religious in the Catholic Church where, for some reason, I felt safe. At home, my dad's alcoholism and my parents' fighting intensified and there was no peace. My parents would probably say that I was the problem, and that I was a problem child. My mother tried to keep my father and me separated because he was very abusive and I was not pas-sive. I loved to fight and I would always get in between him and anyone he was angry with. He would throw me out of the house whenever he saw me, so eventually I only came home when he was away or asleep.

I was angry and rebellious and hated everyone in authority to the extent that people would walk carefully around me because of my explosive anger. What they didn't know was that inside I felt like a sad, lonely, scared little girl. I just wanted someone to take care of me, but I could never share this. When someone attempted to get close to me, I hid my insecurity by becoming argumentative.

I was a problem at school and in the community, and I became sexually promiscuous—basically doing anything I could that would break the Ten Commandments. Once I went into a Catholic church, looked at the crucifix and said, "Everything You hate, I love; and everything You love, I hate." I was daring God to strike me, and I wasn't even afraid that He might.

At nineteen I went to a major city and lived with two other girls for two years. In a bar at 2:00 A.M., a bartender gave us a small calling card and asked, "Why don't you girls go to my church? Maybe you'll find answers to some of your problems and won't have to be out here in the middle of the night." I felt that I might as well try the "church" one more time, believing that all churches were the same. I just wanted to be in a family and feel safe, so the next day we went to that church. I had no idea it was a cult, and for ten years I was involved in it!

Initially, I felt loved; it was my "family." They took an interest in my life. No one had paid that much attention to me before. No one had taken enough notice of me to say, "We want you to get nine hours of sleep. We want you to eat three meals a day. We want to know where you are." They held me accountable for my lifestyle, and I interpreted their interest in me as love and concern for my well-being. I would have died for them.

I accepted their philosophy that we are all gods. This fit in with my father's atheistic views that there really is no supreme God and that religion is just somebody's invention to control people. They also explained who Jesus Christ was and, to me, that seemed to satisfy my mother's religion. They said that He was just a good teacher like Muhammad or Buddha, but that He wasn't supreme or God, or else He could have prevented Himself from having to die on the cross.

The more I got involved, the more the cult consumed my life. I believed everything they said and that anything I read in the newspapers or heard on TV was a lie. So I read nothing unless the cult wrote it, and I believed nothing unless their signature was on it. My whole world revolved around its teaching.

I went through a lot of personal instruction where they told me what to do to become a "totally free spiritual being." Because they taught reincarnation, I believed that I'd had hundreds of past lifetimes. I "learned" previous names, how many children I had, even the color of my hair. This included lives on other planets. Because I trusted them, I believed them. The reason no one else knew this "truth" about themselves was because they weren't willing to know the truth.

I tried to live in two worlds. Ever since I was seven years old I had heard voices in my head and had invisible friends. I would live in one world at school but in another world at home. The voices in my head continued speaking to me. The cult leaders said the voices were from my past lifetimes. My ill-fated hope was that they would be put to rest and not bother me anymore when I was fully instructed.

While this was happening, my family moved to another state and my mother was invited to a neighborhood Bible study where she became a born-again Christian. She didn't tell anyone because my father was still an atheist and wouldn't have let her go to the study. But she asked her friends to pray for the conversion of her husband and her kids. Had I known they were praying for me, I would have tried to stop her.

> *I went to visit my mother on her deathbed with the idea from a cult member to try to convert her.*

When my mother became ill with cancer, I visited her on her deathbed with the idea from a cult member to convert her so that we could have her spirit to care for in the next lifetime. In the next lifetime, she would live in the cult and I could become aware of her. Then she would have a better life than the one she'd had with Dad.

While visiting her, I felt total hatred for her friends who came into her room and talked about Jesus and prayed for her healing. I ridiculed their attempts, but was astounded by the strength of my mother's convictions. It was a battle between her mind and mine, but one night she was in so much pain, and so worn down emotionally, that she went through a commitment prayer with me to give her spirit to my cult. Satisfied, I went home the next day, and she died several days later.

I remember playing Scrabble that day with a neighbor at three o'clock one afternoon when suddenly I sensed the presence of my mother in the room. I said, "What are you doing here? You should go to headquarters where you are supposed to be." Later, my brother called and told me that my mother had died around that time in the afternoon.

My friend in the cult told me that everything was fine—they had received my mother's spirit. Eventually, they would call me when the baby was born who would receive my mother's spirit, so that I could go to see this baby.

That made me so angry that I stole a Bible to highlight all of the lies.

About a week later, I received a letter from one of my mother's friends who had been with her when she died. She said that my mother had gone to be with Jesus. That made me so angry that I went to a local church and stole a Bible. I was going to highlight all of the lies and then send it to this lady to show her how confused she was and to convert her to the cult.

I opened the Bible to the middle and began reading in the book of Isaiah. Instead of highlighting the "lies," I found myself highlighting phrases like, "Come let us reason together says the Lord . . . If you will turn to Me, I will turn to you." I discovered the book is filled with passages about not getting involved with mediums and astrologers. By the time I was finished, I was confused about what the truth was.

I had never read a Bible before, much less owned one, so I turned to the back to see how it ended. When I read the book of Revelation, I was scared because the cult taught the book of Revelation backward. They said that people were really "gods" who go back and take their rightful place in heaven.

I sat there trying to get in touch with my mother's spirit.

I went to the church where I stole the Bible and tried to get in touch with my mother's spirit. I figured that if she was a Christian, then I should be able to go to a Christian place and contact her. When I got to the church, a middle-aged couple approached me and asked if they could help me in any way. When I told them I was trying to get in touch with my mother, they lovingly said that they didn't think I would find her there, but they invited me to have breakfast with them and talk about it. It turned out to be a Christian fellowship breakfast where, for the first time in my life, I was with a group of people whose lives seemed special because of their relationship to Jesus Christ.

The next several months my confusion continued as I went back and forth between reading my Bible and my cult books. I visited the church where I had met the couple, and they would come over to my house just to read Scripture with me. I consider them my spiritual mother and father. They never made me feel evil or bad; they just loved and accepted me. Every month they would pick me up and take me to their Christian breakfast and other church services.

During this time I remember praying and telling God that wherever my mother went was where I wanted to be. If I caused her to lose heaven because of what I did, then I didn't want to be a Christian. I wanted to be with her. But if she had really gone to be with Jesus, as her friend who wrote me had said, then I wanted to be there too. I just couldn't choose.

One night I had a dream in which I saw my mother walking

toward me with another person in white, and she said, "I forgive you for what you did, and I want you to forgive yourself and to pray for your father." That woke me like a shot. I awakened my husband and said, "I know where she is." I was angry that she had asked me to pray for my father, but that's how I know it was my mother. No one else would dare ask me to do that.[1]

The next week I went to church with that couple, gave my life to the Lord, and renounced my cult involvement. I gave them all of my cult books and paraphernalia and they took it out of the house. For the next two years I was discipled by them and their fellowship group.

Six weeks after becoming a Christian I found out that I was pregnant. I was angry with the Lord. I had already had three abortions and decided that I shouldn't have to go through with the pregnancy just because I was a Christian. But my husband said, "I thought you were a Christian and that Christians don't believe in abortions." It angered me that God would speak to me through my husband who wasn't even a Christian, but God seemed to say to me, "Listen, your home is big enough for a baby. How about your heart? Is it big enough?" I decided to keep the baby.

Nine months after the baby was born my husband gave his life to the Lord. He said, "When you decided against an abortion, I was impressed by God's intervention and impact in your life."

I wondered if I should become a Catholic as my mother had been. My spiritual parents said it would be all right to go to the Catholic church, so I went to a charismatic Catholic prayer group. When the priest learned of my background, he suggested that I probably needed deliverance, so I met with him. He started talking to whatever was inside me, asking its name. The "thing" would give him a name and become angry and violent; I became frightened and beat up the priest.

It scared me so much I decided to keep all of this a secret. I wanted to believe that if I were really a Christian, God would make that horrible presence go away. Because it didn't, I couldn't believe I had a relationship with God. People would tell me I was saved since I had given my heart to the Lord, but no one could provide the assurance I was looking for. I felt half evil and half good, and I couldn't see how half of me could go to heaven.

I would go to church, but when I came home the voices tormented me. They were no longer my friends.

We moved again, had more children, and got involved in a new church and Bible studies. I still had this separated life. I would go to church, but when I came home the voices tormented me. They were no longer my friends. They were accusing, screaming, angry, and profane. They told me, "You think that you're a Christian, but you're not. You're dirty and sinful." The more involved I became as a Christian, the worse the voices became.

I became legalistic, thinking that I had to go to every Bible study and church activity. I went Sunday morning and Sunday evening and Wednesday evening, believing that being present every time the church was open was the only way I could prove that I was a Christian.

I went on mission trips and taught Sunday school. When I taught Bible studies and shared the dangers of cults with others, everything inside me became intensified. Anger became rage, the pain became torment, and the accusations made me feel suicidal. I thought, *Why don't I just kill myself? I can't ever be good enough to be a real Christian.*

When I went on a radio program and talked about the dangers of cults, I was plagued with fear that my kids would be killed. I became paranoid about even sending them to school, so I dropped everything. When I withdrew, I temporarily felt better and the voices lessened, but I became a loner—not going anywhere or talking to anybody, just wanting to be by myself all the time. I felt more and more bound, and my internal life became a prison where no light could shine.

I went to Christian counseling, and it did help me to sort out my abusive childhood and put some things together. I was diagnosed as having a dissociative disorder because of the voices and MPD (multiple personality disorder), because many times I would say, "Well, we feel this way." My counselor would ask, "Why are you saying 'we'?" I would say, "I don't know."

This frightened me, but I was also relieved to know that someone believed there were voices inside me. I went to counseling two days a week trying to relieve the pain and the torment. If at any time there was an apparent look in the right direction, I was fearful, and then I felt the need to punish myself by doing anything dangerous or painful. Nothing quieted the rage inside me but worship and praise tapes. Only while listening to them did I feel that I wasn't going crazy, but I could only listen, never sing.

The counselors loved me and were faithfully there for me every week. They prayed for me and promised to stay with me for the journey. They felt it would take a long time for me to become integrated. They gave me hope, assuring me that God wanted me to be whole and that He would bring it about. I vacillated between hope and despair like I was on a roller coaster. The Christian counselors were a lifeline for me. I felt God's love and acceptance through their listening, understanding, and caring.

However, when I was seven years old a traumatic event had occurred in my life that resulted in such tremendous fear that even in counseling I could never progress beyond that point. I would get to the age of seven and then be too afraid to go on. I reasoned, *If it's that bad, I don't want to know what it is.* A voice in my head told me that I would be harmed if I remembered.

My neighbor was my friend and knew about my struggle. One day she asked me if I would help her prepare for a "Resolving Personal and Spiritual Conflicts" conference that was coming to her church in about six weeks—visiting churches, putting up posters and selling the books. I didn't want to do it. I was sure the conference was just one more meeting like the ones I had already tried. Every time I went I came home so lonely and discouraged, knowing my punishment waited for me for even trying to find a cure. I was afraid it would make my life more miserable, but I halfheartedly said that I would help.

After watching ten minutes of the first video, I decided that I hated Neil Anderson.

My neighbor gave me videos of the conference to preview so that I would be able to answer questions about the materials. After watching only ten minutes of the first video, I decided that I hated Neil Anderson and that he didn't have anything to say. I felt like telling people not to go and said to my neighbor, "I don't like him. Are you sure you want him to come and give this conference? I think there's something wrong with him." She replied, "Well, you're the only one who has told me that and I've talked to about thirty-five people."

At the conference my resistance increased and I didn't hear all of what was said. I couldn't remember the nights Neil talked about our identity in Christ, and I sat in the second row, unable to sing any of the hymns. He would speak and a part of me would say, *That's not new. We all knew that anyway.* Another little voice inside of me would say, *I sure wish that everything he said is true and that this man could help me.* But I never revealed that hopeful part, only my critical part. Talking with others I would say, "So what do you think of the conference? It's really not that great, is it?"

Near the end of the week, a two-hour taped counseling session was shown. I could not watch the woman on the video finding her freedom. I felt fear and anger all at the same time. I started choking, felt sick, and headed for my car to go home, determined not to show up again on Saturday. But Neil was in the hallway between me and my car.

We went into a side room and Neil walked me through some renunciations where I verbally repeated a series of statements, taking a stand against Satan and all of his influences in my life. I also prayed that God would reveal to me whatever it was that prevented me from sitting to watch the video, and that's when I remembered what happened when I was seven years old. It was like the clouds rolled away and I saw myself as a little girl, terrified of a dark, black presence.

I was playing with dolls in the back bedroom of our home. It was daytime and nothing frightening was happening and no one else was present in the room. But suddenly I felt total fear. I remember stopping my play and lying down, facing the ceiling and saying, "What do you want?" to a huge, black presence that was over me. The presence said to me, "Can I share your body with you?" And I said, "If you promise not to kill me, you can."

I actually felt that presence totally infiltrating me from head to toe. It was so oppressive to have this thing go into every pore of my body that I remember thinking, *I am going to die.* I was only seven, but it was so sexual and so dirty that I felt I had a big secret I had to hide and that I could never tell anyone. From that time on I felt that I had more than one personality, and it seemed natural to share my body with unseen others. Sometimes I would do things and not remember them when people would tell me. And I would think, *Well, that wasn't me. That was my invisible friend who did that.*

I never played with the black ball again. I only spoke with my invisible friend who would suggest things that I should do. Sometimes the suggestions were bad, but sometimes they were good. Because I needed companionship in my abusive childhood, I never thought the voice was anything other than a friend.

Whenever I would tell him what the voices were saying, Neil would say, "That's a lie." And he gently went through the Steps to Freedom.

Neil led me by giving me the words to speak, and I specifically renounced all satanic guardians that had been assigned to me. At that point I was startled by the presence of evil and afraid we would both be beaten up. It reminded me that I had played with that magic ball for years.

Neil told me not to be afraid and asked what the presence was saying to my mind. Whenever I told him what the voices were saying, he would say, "That's a lie," and he gently led me through the Steps to Freedom. I can remember the very moment the presence wasn't there anymore. I felt like the small person that was really me was being blown up like a balloon inside me. Finally, after thirty-five years of fractured living, I was the only person inside. The place that evil presence vacated I have now dedicated to my new occupant: the clean, gentle, quiet Spirit of God.

Saturday morning I was afraid to wake up, thinking, *This isn't real.* I didn't want to open my eyes because usually the voice would say something like, "Get up, you stupid little slut. You've got work to do." So I would get up and do whatever it said. But that morning there were no voices and I lay in my bed, thinking, *There's no one here but me.*

When I went back to the conference and walked in the door, people noticed that I looked different. I told them how I had always felt like an orphan in the body of Christ but now I felt free and part of the family of God.

I thought that as soon as Neil left, this thing was going to come back. But the peace lasted, because Jesus Christ is the One who set me free. Whenever that fear would come I would go through the Steps to Freedom by myself, something I did at least four or five more times. I became convinced that God wanted it gone as much as I did, and it's never been there since.

A week later, my family had a head-on car collision. I was afraid the voice would be there to say, "I'm going to crush you because you think you're free." Instead I sensed God saying, "I am here to protect you and I'll always be here like this."

When one of my girls asked me if the wreck was her fault, I wondered why she felt this way. I remembered that one of the Steps to Freedom is breaking the ancestral ties because sins of the parents can be passed on from one generation to the next (Ex. 20:4–5). As we talked, my ten-year-old told me, "Sometimes I know things are going to happen before they happen. And sometimes I look out the window and see things that nobody else sees."

Instantly, I knew that my daughter also needed to be released from bondage. So I took her through the steps, paraphrasing the big words into her language. She renounced all the sins of her ancestors and rejected any way in which Satan might be claiming ownership of her. She declared herself to be eternally and completely signed over and committed to the Lord Jesus Christ. Since then she has never again experienced that demonic presence.

My husband was away during the conference, and when he came home I told him everything that had happened. The next Sunday, in our Sunday school class, the leader asked if anyone wanted to share about the conference. My husband stood and said, "I want to share even though I wasn't there because the Lord gave me a new wife to come home to."

Now I feel God's face toward me and sense His smile.

Before the conference, I didn't have any identity or positive sense of worth. Every day I felt that God had a measure of mercy for me and that some day it would run out, that even God Himself must wonder why He made me. I just knew that someday He was going to say, "I've had enough of Sandy." So every day I would pray, "God, please don't let it be today. Let me get this one last thing done before You do it."

It was so freeing when Neil taught that God and Satan are not co-equal, but that God is off the charts and Satan is way beneath Him, that we should not make the mistake of thinking he has divine attributes. I had always thought that God and Satan were co-equal, fighting it out for us, and that God was basically saying, "You can have Sandy."

I had cried to God constantly since my conversion:

> Create a clean heart in me!
> Renew a right spirit in me!
> Please don't cast me out of Your presence!
> Please don't take Your Holy Spirit from me!

Over and over I had prayed these prayers for myself, agonizing to know the Lord in a warm and personal way, but feeling like I had a relationship with God's back. Now I feel His face toward me and sense His smile.

I don't live in a tiny corner of my mind or outside of my body anymore. I live inside, sharing my mind with only my precious Lord. What a profound difference! There are no words to adequately describe the peacefulness and absence of pain and torment that I now enjoy daily. It's like being blind all these years and now I see. Everything is new, precious, and treasured because it doesn't look black. I'm not afraid anymore that I'll be punished for every move I make. I'm able to make decisions now and have choices. I am free to make mistakes!

The last year and a half I had become unable to have anyone touch me without feeling pain or having horrible sexual thoughts. While having sex I would watch it from outside of my body. When that evil presence claimed to be my "husband" I knew why I had always felt like a prostitute, even as a Christian.

After exposing that lie and renouncing it, I have since come to understand the meaning of "bride" for the first time in my life, after twenty years of marriage. I also feel the love from the Bridegroom I shall someday see.

He has wiped away my tears and answered the cry of my heart. At last I sense a right Spirit inside me, and the departed presence was not the presence of God, but of the evil one. I was fearful that God's presence would leave me. I now feel clean inside. I continue to go to Christian counseling, and I am making progress. I am learning to face and let go of the past abuse. I am learning to live in community and trust others again after feeling betrayed by my cult experience.

I believe God in His lovingkindness met me at my point of need, and ordained the meeting that exposed and expelled the demonic oppression in my life. Now I can continue growing in the family of God. I now am certain I belong to this family, and I'm loved by it. God has shown me that He is faithful and able, not just to call me from darkness to light, but also to keep me and sustain me until the journey ends, when I shall see Him face-to-face. I still face trials, temptations, and the pain of living in a fallen world, but I walk in it sensing the strong heartbeat of a loving Father within. The demonic interference has been removed.

Praise the Lord.

WE CANNOT BE IGNORANT OF SATAN'S SCHEMES

The hideousness of Satan is revealed in Sandy's life story. Would he actually take advantage of a child with dysfunctional parents and grandparents who ignorantly provided occult toys for their grandchildren? Satan would and does.

I have traced the origin of many adult problems to childhood fantasies, imaginary friends, counterfeit guidance, the occult, and abuses. It is not enough to warn our children about the stranger in the street. We need to warn them about the one who may appear in their room. Our research indicates that half of our professing Christian teenagers have had some experience in their room that frightened them. That, more than anything, has prompted Steve Russo and me to write *The Seduction of Our Children*.[2] We want to help parents know how to protect their children and defeat the influence of darkness. I would encourage you to read *Spiritual Protection for Your Children*,[3] which I co-authored with Peter and Sue Vander Hook. Peter is an evangelical pastor who had to deal with his own children coming under attack. In that book, we have age-graded steps for children.

TRUTH, NOT POWER ENCOUNTER

In the ministry of deliverance, the priest's noble but disastrous attempt at an exorcism is one reason why I don't advocate the power-encounter approach. It can be like sticking a broom handle into a hornets' nest, rattling it around and proclaiming, "Hey, there are demons here!" That kind of experience left Sandy terrorized and reluctant to address the issue again. When the spiritual battle is seen as a truth encounter, you need only work with the person and you never have to lose control.

The brain is the control center, and as long as Sandy was willing to share with me what was going on inside we never lost control. Accusing and terrorizing thoughts were bombarding her mind. When she revealed what she was hearing, I would simply expose the deception by saying, "That's a lie," or by asking Sandy to renounce it as a lie and tell it to go away. The power of Satan is in the lie; when the lie is exposed the power is broken. God's truth sets people free. Occasionally, I will have a person ask God to reveal what it is that is keeping him or her in bondage, and it's not uncommon for past events (often blocked memories) to be brought to mind so the person can confess and renounce them. In Sandy's case, she had no conscious memory of what had happened when she was seven.

EXERCISING AUTHORITY IN CHRIST

Her concern about my leaving town is another reason I like to deal only with the person. When she asked me what she was going to do when I wasn't there, I responded, "I didn't do anything. You did the renouncing and you exercised your authority in Christ by telling the evil presence to go. Jesus Christ is your deliverer and He will always be with you." She renounced her invitation to let the demon share her body. Later she renounced all her cult and occult experiences. It cannot be overstated how important this step is. It is a critical part of repentance.

Throughout its history the Church has publicly declared, "I renounce you, Satan, and *all* your works and *all* your ways." Most

Catholic, orthodox, and liturgical churches still make that profession, but for some reason evangelical churches don't. That generic statement needs to be applied specifically for each individual. Any dabbling in the occult, involvement with cults, or seeking false guidance must be confessed and renounced. *All* Satan's works and *all* Satan's ways need to be renounced as God brings them to our memory. All lies and counterfeit guidance must be replaced by "the way and the truth and the life" (John 14:6 NIV). This is done in the first of the seven Steps to Freedom.

SATAN'S BONDAGES

Sandy had never had a "normal" sexual relationship. She perceived herself as a prostitute because the evil presence claimed to be her husband. Freedom from that bondage allowed her to have a loving, intimate relationship with her husband. I will have much more to say about sexual bondages in the following chapters.

The mental battle she suffered is quite typical of those in bondage. Most people caught in a spiritual conflict will talk about their dysfunctional family background or other abuses, but seldom will they reveal the battle going on for their minds. They already fear they are going crazy, and they don't relish the thought of it being confirmed by a pastor or counselor who doesn't understand spiritual warfare. Nor do they like the prospect of taking antipsychotic medication.

Sandy was relieved when her Christian counselor believed her. The secular world has no other alternative than to look for a physical cure, since mental illness is the only possible diagnosis. The tragedy of antipsychotic medication (when the problem is actually spiritual) is the drugged state in which it leaves the recipient. How is the truth going to set someone free when the person is so medicated that he or she can hardly talk, much less think?

Christian counselors with whom I have dialogued are greatly appreciative of being made aware of spiritual conflict and how to resolve it. This makes their counseling practice much more complete and effective.

One lady shared in the middle of a conference that I was describing her to a T. She said she was going to a treatment center for thirty days. I asked if I could see her first, since I knew that the treatment center she was going to would rely primarily on drugs for therapy. She agreed and wrote the following:

> After meeting with you Monday night, I was absolutely euphoric, and so was my husband. He was so happy to see me happy. I was finally able to take my position with Christ and renounce the deceiver. The Lord has released me from my bondage.
>
> My big news is that I didn't wake up with nightmares or screams. Instead I woke up with my heart singing! The very first thought that entered my mind was, *Even the stones will cry out,* followed by, *Abba, Father.* Neil, the Holy Spirit is alive in me! Praise the Lord! I can't begin to tell you how free I feel, but somehow, I think you know!

ASSUMING RESPONSIBILITY

Nightmares and voices may have a spiritual explanation for their origins, and the church bears the responsibility to check it out. I believe that every pastor and Christian counselor should be able to help people like this.

You have nothing to lose by going through or taking someone through the Steps to Freedom. It's just old-fashioned housecleaning that takes into account the reality of the spiritual world. All we are doing is helping people assume responsibility for their relationship with God. Nobody is accusing anybody of anything. If there is nothing demonic going on in someone's life, the worst thing that can happen is that the person will really be ready for Communion the next time it is served!

Sandy's story brings out very well the two most sought-after goals we have with this type of counseling. First, that people will know who they are as children of God, that they are a part of God's forever family. Second, that they will have a peace and quietness in their mind, the peace that guards our hearts and our minds, the peace that transcends all understanding (Phil. 4:7).

CHAPTER 4

Jennifer:
Freedom from Eating Disorders

I received a call from Jennifer asking if I would spend some time with her if she flew out to California. I agreed to set aside one Monday morning and after hearing her story, I led her through the Steps to Freedom. A month later I received the following letter.

Dear Neil,

I just wanted to write and thank you for the time you spent with me. I guess I felt like nothing happened at the time we prayed and that maybe there wasn't a problem with the demonic. I was wrong. Something really did happen, and I have not had one more self-destructive thought or action or compulsion since that day.

I think the process began through my prayers of repentance in the months following my suicide attempt. I don't understand it all, but I know something is really different in my life and I feel free today. I haven't cut myself in a month and that is a true miracle.

I have a few questions I wish you would respond to if you have time. They have to do with my psychological problems. I was told that I have a chronic manic-depressive, schizo-affective disorder, and I am on lithium and an antipsychotic medication. Do I need these? Am I really chronic?

I always felt during my acting-out periods, which is what they based my diagnosis on, that it was not me but rather some strong power outside myself that drove me to act self-destructive and crazy. The last three times I have quit my lithium I have become suicidal and ended up in the hospital. I don't want that to happen again, but was that demonic? I also had a lot of mood swings even on the pills, but since my visit with you I have had none! This makes me wonder if I'm really okay and don't need the pills.

Also, ever since I was a little girl I have never been able to pray; there always seems to be a wall between me and God. I was never very happy and have always felt a sense of fear and uneasiness, like something is wrong.

Jennifer

Jennifer's story is important because it clarifies the need to know who we are as children of God and the nature of the spiritual battle we are in. That one morning we were able to process a lot, and she did achieve a sense of freedom. But does she know who she is as a child of God, and does she know how to maintain her freedom in Christ?

Within six months Jennifer was having difficulty again. Another year passed before she was desperate enough to call. She decided to fly out again, but this time she attended a whole conference. Here is her story.

✕✕✕

JENNIFER'S STORY

Everything around me seemed like a dream and everybody was just an actor.

In seventh grade my eating disorder started—overeating, then starving. I would baby-sit and clean out the refrigerator, and then I wouldn't eat anything for three or four days. My focus became my weight; I was obsessed with the need to be thin.

Everything around me seemed like a dream and everybody was just an actor. I thought, *Someday I will wake up, but I won't know the dreamer.* Nothing seemed real. I lived in a "checked-out" state. I didn't think. When people talked I would look at them in bewilderment because I wasn't in touch with my mind.

During the day I appeared normal and functioned fairly well in school. Nighttimes were weird with a lot of bad dreams and terror. I wept often because of the voices in my head and the images and nonsense thoughts that often filled my mind. But I never said a word to anyone. I knew people would think I was crazy, and I was terrified that nobody would believe me.

My college years were really hard, filled with routine bingeing and purging. I lost thirty pounds and began fainting and having chest pains. Because I was pathetically thin from anorexia, the skin literally hung on my bones. Finally, I agreed to be hospitalized. I was totally exhausted physically, mentally, and spiritually.

I nearly died. My pulse was forty when I was admitted, and they had trouble finding my blood pressure. My parents were very supportive. The hospital was good and I had Christian therapists, but they never touched on the spiritual. I was cutting myself, using razor blades and knives, and I still have scars on my hands from digging holes into them with my fingernails.

I crawled down the hall, trying to get away from the things flying around my room.

The voices in my head and the nighttimes were bad, with demonic visitations and something raping me at night, holding me down so I couldn't move. Sometimes I crawled down the hall, trying to get away from things flying around my room. I was terrorized; thoughts of cutting my heart out dominated my mind. I did actually cut on my chest with knives because I thought my heart was poison and that I needed to get rid of it so I would be clean.

When childhood memories started to surface, I lost it. I was back in the hospital again and absolutely out of control. On some days it required five or six people to restrain me. I would be out of my body watching those people hold me down while I was fighting and kicking, until they would sedate me. I was diagnosed as manic-depressive. I took lithium and continued with antidepressants for the next six years, which did quiet me somewhat.

While I was in the hospital a friend suggested that I talk with Neil Anderson, but I told her no. The thought of there being something demonic was terrifying to me, and I told her, "God said if two or more people pray He would listen. Why can't several people just pray with me here in the hospital? Why do I need some man to come?" I talked with my Christian counselors and they said, "Your associates just want to make this spiritual because they don't want to deal with the pain in your life." The counselors had gained my trust that year, so I believed them and refused to see Neil. That's the first time I ever heard Neil's name. I did not meet him for three years. I was too afraid; the whole idea freaked me out.

Somehow I graduated and started working. I would do a fantastic job at work, then get in my car, pull out my razor blades, and live in a different world for the next sixteen hours. Then I would go back to work. I was talking with all of my "friends" in my head and ritualistically cutting on myself for the blood. I just wanted to feel; I knew I was not in touch with reality.

At night I would often lie awake, hoping I would die before morning. I wrote suicide notes and knew every empty house around. These were houses that were for sale, where I could drive my car into the garage, leave the motor running, and kill myself. I also knew the gun shops in town and their hours, so if I needed a gun I could get one. I kept two or three hundred pills at home so I always had an "out" for when I could bear it no longer. I had many plans to commit suicide.

I kept thinking, *The Lord has got to get me through this*. I knew He was my only hope and that there was a reason to live, so I kept crying out to Him. I remember crawling into a corner of my room at night and sleeping there on the floor. I was trying to get away from it all and praying to God that I could get through one more night. I prayed that He would give me strength and protect me from myself. I blamed myself for all of this.

I feared for my life and so did many of my friends. I went to see a pastor and told him that I thought I had a spiritual problem and I also felt I was going to die. He said, "You have one of the best psychiatrists in town; I don't know why you're talking to me." Then he asked, "Are you taking your medicine?" He was scared of me and he didn't know how to help me.

Once I spent several hours talking with some caring friends. One suggested, "Jennifer, you just need to go into the throne room of Jesus." The voices inside me said, "That's it!" To me, "going into the throne room" meant to die. I drove to a hotel, went to a room, and took two hundred pills. I lay down by my simple note that read, "I'm going home to be with Jesus. I just can't take it anymore."

I didn't want to be alone when I died.

I called someone because I didn't want to be alone when I died. I felt that if there was someone on the other end of the phone it would help. At first I wouldn't give the phone number to my friend, but later I was so sleepy and out of it that I gave in so I could go to sleep and my friend could call me back later. Two and a half hours later they found me and took me to a hospital where my stomach was pumped. I was placed in the intensive care unit. I should have died, but by a miracle of God I didn't.

I was hospitalized again in a different Christian clinic. The possibility of my problem being spiritual was never addressed. I was diagnosed as being schizo-affective and bipolar depressive. They told me I didn't know reality and that I needed to base my confidence on what others said and not on what was going on in my head. They told me I would be dependent on medication for the rest of my life. The side effects of the antipsychotics and antidepressants were horrendous. The tremors were so bad that I had trouble even using my hand to write my name, and my vision was blurred. I was so drugged I couldn't even hold my mouth open.

In counseling I told them I was hearing voices, but they never explored the possibility of them being demonic. They did tell me that since I'd had a lot of therapy already, they wanted to deal with me on the spiritual level. They brought in a godly man who was good, but I couldn't hear or remember a word he said. As soon as he opened his Bible and started to talk, I began listening to other things and planning to kill myself. I felt that if I could just get out of there I would do it, and this time I would be successful.

One day a friend called me at the clinic and honestly addressed the sin in my life. He basically told me I was being manipulative, dishonest, hateful, attention-seeking, and selfish. That was heavy stuff, but he spoke kindly and I was at a point where I was ready to hear it. I got on my knees and wrote a letter to God in my journal asking forgiveness. Those sins were a part of me that I was ashamed of and I had lived with the guilt of them all my life. I did experience some release, and I know that was the beginning of my healing.

The voices were talking so loud I couldn't hear a word he said.

Friends invited me to California for a visit, and I decided I wanted to meet Neil Anderson. I went to his office and we talked for about two hours. He opened his Bible and was going through the Scriptures, but the voices were so loud I couldn't hear a word he said. It was like he was talking gibberish—his words were like another language. That's how it always was with me when people were using the Bible.

I got through the Steps to Freedom, but I didn't feel any different when I left. I wondered if the words just went straight from my eyes to my mouth without my internalizing anything I was reading. But two areas improved. The struggle with food was better, and I never cut myself again. The voices were also gone for a couple of weeks, but then they came back. I didn't remember Neil saying what to do when the voices and thoughts came back, and it never occurred to me that I didn't have to listen. I didn't know I had a choice, so I got hit worse than ever.

Six months later I was in the hospital again, both suicidal and psychotic. I was out of it and did everything the voices were telling me to do. I was encouraged to see Neil again, but if that didn't work I knew I was going to die. All of this had been going on for seven terrible years, and the side effects of the drugs were so bad that all I did was work four hours and then sit in front of the TV or sleep. I couldn't carry on a meaningful conversation with anybody, and I really didn't care about anything anymore. I felt hopeless, exhausted, and discouraged.

I went to the conference on Resolving Personal and Spiritual Conflicts. I again met with Neil, and at one point I got so sick that I threw up. He introduced me to a lady with a past similar to mine. She sat beside me and prayed for me, so I was more able to hear and comprehend what Neil was saying.

I learned a lot about the spiritual battle that was going on for my mind and what I needed to do to take a stand. Once that part became clear, I was free. I knew what to do and how to do it. Previously, I didn't know how to stay free and walk in my freedom, although I was raised in a good Christian home. Even though I accepted Christ when I was four, I never knew who I was in Christ, and I didn't understand the authority I had as a child of God.

I told my psychiatrist that I was free in Christ now and wanted to get off my medication. He said, "You've tried this before and look at your history." I said, "But it's different now. Will you support me in this?" When he said, "No, I can't," I replied, "Well, I'm going to do it anyway; I'll take responsibility for myself."

He said he would see me in a month. I came back in a month and was functioning on half of the prescription, and in two months I was off completely. He asked how I felt and when I told him I was fine, he shook my hand and said I wouldn't need to come back anymore. It was like I was discovering life for the first time, and I felt impressed to write the following letter to Neil:

Dear Neil,

I was reading back over my journals from years past and was harshly reminded of the darkness and evil in which I was engulfed for so many years. I often wrote about "them" and the control they had of me. I often felt that rather than be torn between Satan and God, I would rather rest in the darkness. What I did not realize was that I was a child of God and alive *in* Christ, not hanging between two spirits. So often I felt that I was being controlled and was crazy, having lost all sense of self and reality. I think in a way I had learned to like the darkness. I felt safe there and was deceived by the lie that if I let go of the evil, I would die and God would not meet my needs or care for me the way I wanted.

This is why I would not talk with you the first time. I didn't want you to take away the only thing I had. I felt sheer terror at the thought. I guess the evil one had something to do with those thoughts and fears. I was so deceived. I really tried to pray and read the Bible, but it all made little sense. Once I tried to read *The Adversary* by Mark Bubeck, and I literally could not make my hand pick it up. I just stared at it.

Psychiatrists tried many different medications and doses (including large doses of antipsychotics) to make things better. I took up to fifteen pills a day just to remain in control and somewhat functional. I was so drugged I couldn't think or feel much at all. I felt like a walking dead person! The therapists and doctors all agreed I had a chronic mental illness that I would deal with for the rest of my life—a very defeating prognosis to hear!

At the conference, I saw the total picture. Just weeks before, I had made the decision that I did not want to entertain the darkness any longer and that I really wanted to get well, but I had no idea how to take that step. Well, I learned, and once again my head became quiet. The voices stopped, the doubts and confusion lifted, and I was free. Now I know how to stand.

I feel like a small child who has been through a horrible and terrifying storm, lost in confusion and loneliness. I knew my loving Father was on the other side of the door and that He was my only hope and relief, but I could not get through that strong door. Then someone told me how to turn the knob and told me that because I was God's child, I had all the authority and right to open the door. I have reached up and opened the door and run to my Father, and now I am resting in His safe and loving arms. I know and believe that "neither death, nor life, nor angels, nor principalities, nor things present, nor things to come, nor powers, nor height, nor depth, nor any other created thing, shall be able to separate us from the love of God" (Rom. 8:38–39 NASB).

I am working in ministry now, taking tons of time to read and pray and be loved by the God I had heard so much about but never experienced. I am giving and sharing and serving in ways I have always dreamed of doing. In bondage, I could never reach beyond my desperate self. Now I feel peaceful and full inside, somewhat childlike, with purpose and direction, joy and hope.

Now when I get accusing or negative thoughts, they just bounce off because I have learned to bind Satan with one quick sentence, ignore his lies, and choose the truth. It works! Because of my strong Savior, Satan leaves me alone almost instantly. I've had a few pretty down days, but then I choose to remember who I am and tell Satan and his demons to leave. It's a miracle; the cloud lifts!

My sadness has come when I realize I have lived most of my life in captivity, believing lies. I try to remember, "For this purpose I have raised you up, that I may show My power in you, and that My name may be declared in all the earth" (Ex. 9:16 NKJV). I know God will use my experiences mightily in my own life as well as in others'. The chains have fallen off. I have chosen the light and life.

Because of the obvious changes in my countenance, people have been seeking me out for light and truth. I can't keep up with who has which of your tapes. I have shared them a lot with others who find themselves in bondage and need.

I am still seeing a Christian counselor, and this has been very helpful. It's horrendous coming out of my past, and it's a struggle learning how to live. My biggest temptation is to be sick because I got a lot of strokes from that. I needed to see that the sick person is not who I am, but that I am a child of God and He desires for me to be free. It was difficult for me to accept that new identity. A few times I have had "crazy" days. But I realize that this is not what I want, and I call my friend to pray with me and renounce the darkness with her encouragement.

My biggest fight is to stay single-minded because my tendency is to let my mind split off. My prayer every day is that He will help me to stay focused and that I will love Him with all my heart and soul, not just a part of it.

Another important friend is a woman who was set free five years ago from being a medium in New Age. She has been a tremendous help, but my main support is the friend I met at your conference. Our phone bills are huge, and we see each other three or four times a year. I really don't think I would have made it and stayed free those first couple of months without her.

My family and the treatment I received were the best. They did everything they knew to love me, help me, and save my life. I have been so loved throughout my life by so many friends and family members. I feel it is because of their prayers, consistent love, and support that I am alive today.

I firmly believe that the prescription drugs were what kept me from being able to think or fight. They left me in such a passive, semi-alert state that I couldn't concentrate. I couldn't write because of horrible hand tremors . . . I couldn't see at times because of blurred vision . . . I couldn't pray because there was no concentration . . . and never did I have the energy to discern thoughts or remember truths in Scripture . . . and I couldn't follow conversation. It was like being on twelve to fifteen antihistamine tablets at one time, leaving me in a very helpless condition, with no quality of life.

I have written out a ton of truth verses on cards that I carry everywhere. There have been times when the dark cloud of oppression is so crushing. That's when I pull out my cards and read them aloud until the light dispels the darkness and I'm able to pray again. Then I can find the lie I've been believing, claim the truth, announce my position in Christ, and renounce the devil. The process has become so routine that I find myself claiming and renouncing under my breath, almost without thinking.

My friend and I have talked often of an active surrender. How do I acknowledge my total dependence upon God and fight at the same time? I don't totally understand it, but it is an active surrender that sets us free.

My most difficult struggle to this day is to want to be free. I'm tempted to use my dissociative "alters" or friends. They occupied the places in my split-off self where I used to go to escape reality and find relief. Satan takes advantage of those mental escapes, playing havoc in my mind and life.

I actually buried stones in the ground representing each split-off piece of my mind that I had held on to. In one sense, it was a huge loss. In another, I knew I had to do that because those identities and psychotic-like splits were homes where Satan and his workers resided. I still am tempted, and even have returned to those states when I am under stress, but I fight it and I am able to bounce back. I'm grasping for God's love and strength in a way I never have been able to before. I now desire to find my safety in Him.

I cannot express the difference in my heart and life. Where my heart used to reside in pieces, now it is whole. Where my mind was void, now there is a song and an intellect beyond anything I could have previously comprehended. Where there was a life of unreality and despair, now there is joy and freedom and light. To God be the glory because all I have done is to finally say "yes" to His offer of freedom. I am grateful to be alive!

Jennifer

〰〰

GETTING AND STAYING FREE

When Jennifer saw me the first time, I led her through the Steps to Freedom. The fact that there was some resolution was clear from the first letter she sent. However, in a short three-hour counseling session, neither I nor anyone else has enough time to educate sufficiently regarding our identity in Christ, much less the nature of the spiritual battle. Plus, I didn't have the experience base then that I do now. Since Jennifer lacked this knowledge, she slipped back into her old habit patterns. In her second visit, she sat through a whole conference designed to give her the information she needed to experience her freedom in Christ and maintain it.

Most pastors can't afford the time to sit one-on-one with people for extended teaching sessions. I usually ask a person to read *Victory Over the Darkness* and *The Bondage Breaker* before we meet for our first session. If they struggle with reading, as Jennifer did (which is often a symptom of demonic harassment), then I take them through the Steps to Freedom first and follow up with assignments, such as reading the books or listening to the tapes on the same subject. Some prefer to listen to the tape series instead of reading the books. It is important that they have a faith base for their walk with Christ.

I don't assume anything regarding spiritual conflicts. What is needed is a safe means to spiritually check out possibilities. It is no different from going to a medical doctor and having your blood and urine checked. The church needs to assume the responsibility for spiritual diagnosis and resolution.

Seeing counseling as something you do for another person will usually not be very effective. You may even be successful in casting out a demon, but it is very possible that it will return and the final state could be even worse. When Jennifer did the confessing, renouncing, forgiving, etc., she learned the nature of the battle by going through the process. Instead of bypassing her mind where the real battle was, I appealed to her mind and helped her to assume responsibility for choosing truth.

Jennifer's comments on prescription drugs are appropriate. Using drugs to cure the body is commendable, but using drugs to cure the soul is deplorable. Her ability to think was so impaired that she couldn't process anything. I often see people in this condition and it is extremely frustrating. However, I never go against the advice of a medical doctor. I strongly caution people not to go off prescription drugs too fast, or serious side effects will occur. Jennifer did go off too quickly after her first visit with me, and that may have contributed to her subsequent relapse.

Some People Don't Want Freedom

Spiritually healthy people will have a hard time understanding that others may not always want to get free from their lifestyle of bondage. I have come across many people who don't want to get rid of their "friends." Once, after walking through the Steps to Freedom with a pastor's wife, I sensed that her freedom wasn't complete. She looked at me and asked, "Now what?" I paused for a moment and said, "Tell it to go." A quizzical look came to her face and she responded, "In the name of the Lord Jesus Christ, I command you to leave my presence." Instantly she was free. The next day she confided that the presence was saying to her mind, "You're not going to just send me away after all the years we have been together, are you?" It was playing on her sympathy.

One young man said a voice was pleading not to make him go because he didn't want to go to hell. The demon wanted to stay so he could go to heaven with him. I asked the young man to pray, asking God to reveal the true nature of the voice. As soon as he had finished praying, he cried out in disgust. I really don't know what he saw or heard, but the evil nature of it was very obvious. These are not harmless spirit guides; they are counterfeit spirits seeking to discredit God and promote allegiance to Satan. They are destroyers who will tear apart a family, church, or ministry.

Bingeing and Purging

Eating disorders are a plight of our age. The sick philosophies of our society have given godlike status to the body. Young girls are often obsessed with appearance as the standard of their worth. Instead of finding their identity in Christ, they find it in their appearance. Rather than focus on the development of character, they focus on appearance, performance, and status. Satan capitalizes on this wrong pursuit of happiness and self-esteem.

Compounding the problem is the rise of sexual abuse and rape. Many girls and young women who are addicted to eating disorders have been sexually victimized. Lacking a gospel, the secular agencies have no way to completely free these people from their past. Knowing who they are in Christ and the necessity of forgiveness is what brings freedom, but they still have to deal with the lies Satan has been using on them.

One young lady was taking seventy-five laxatives a day. Being a graduate of an excellent Christian college, she wasn't dumb. Yet reasoning with her had proved futile. Eating disorder units had stemmed the tide of weight loss by using strong behavioral controls. When I talked with her I asked, "This has nothing to do with eating, does it?" "No," she responded. Then I said, "You're defecating to purge yourself from evil, aren't you?" She nodded in agreement. I asked her to repeat after me, "I renounce defecating in order to purge myself of evil, and I announce that only the blood of Jesus cleanses me from all unrighteousness." As soon as she prayed that prayer, she began to sob. After she regained her composure several minutes later, I asked her what she was thinking. "I can't believe the lies I was believing," she replied.

Another woman said she had purged all her life, just as her mother had. She said she did not consciously plan to do it, and that it was a little joke with her teen daughters that she could vomit into a paper cup while driving and never cross over the line on the road. When I asked her why she was throwing up, she said she felt cleansed afterward. I asked her to repeat after me, "I renounce the lie that throwing up will cleanse me. I believe only in the cleansing work of Christ on the cross." Afterward she immediately cried out, "Oh my God, that's it, isn't it? Only Jesus can cleanse me from my sin." She said that she saw in her mind a vision of the cross.

That is also why people cut themselves, excessively defecate, and purge. They are trying to purge themselves of evil. It's a spiritual counterfeit, a lie of Satan, that we can be the god of our lives and effect our own cleansing. It also illustrates what Paul is teaching in Romans 7:15–25. Paul says there is evil present in me even though

I want to do good. Cutting, purging, and defecating will not get rid of the evil.

Remember the 450 prophets of Baal who came up against Elijah? They cut themselves (1 Kings 18:28). Travel around the world and you will still witness many pagan religions in which they cut themselves during religious ceremonies. It is necessary to reveal that lie and renounce it. In many cases the person isn't aware of why they do it, so asking may be counterproductive. Jennifer was trying to cut out her heart, believing that it was evil. She also shared that she was cutting herself to get in touch with reality, believing that live people bleed.

It is important to note that not all of those who cut themselves have eating disorders, and many who have eating disorders don't cut themselves.

I received an insightful letter from a lady who found tremendous release by going through the Steps to Freedom, but the pastor had not addressed her eating disorder at that time. She wrote:

Dear Neil,

I just finished reading *The Seduction of Our Children*, which I found very eye-opening in many areas. In chapter 13, I was reading through the steps for children when I noticed a separate section for eating disorders. As I was reading, my heart was pierced with a severe pain, yet there was also a sigh of relief. Your words described what my life has been like since grade school.

Earlier this year I went through the Steps to Freedom with a pastor, and I was a totally different person. Yet, the one thing that didn't seem right was the struggle I was continuing to have with my physical appearance. That subject hadn't come up during my counseling session.

As I read your description of a typical person with an eating disorder, I just wept before the Lord. It started for me by cutting myself, then I became anorexic, then bulimic, and eventually a mixture of all three.

I read through the renouncing and announcing that you stated and agreed with a friend in prayer about it. God is so good to me. For whatever reason it was overlooked in earlier counseling, the enemy meant it for evil to keep me in bondage to an area that had run most of my life. God used your book to add this step of freedom in my life. Thank you so much.

THE NEED TO BE BELIEVED

These people are desperately looking for someone who will believe them, who understands what is going on. They know enough not to share too much of the bizarre thoughts and images with people who don't understand. In Jennifer's case, when she finally did share part of her story, people didn't really believe her and some don't to this day. They see her wholeness as a fluke. Pastors and counselors must recognize the reality of the spiritual world and come to terms with the truth that we do not "fight" against flesh and blood, "but against the rulers, against the powers, against the world forces of this darkness, against the spiritual forces of wickedness in the heavenly places" (Eph. 6:12).

AFTERCARE

Jennifer's thoughts on aftercare are on target. The need to have a friend to call and be accountable to can't be stressed enough. We were never intended by God to live alone; we need each other. And Jennifer needed to continue with counseling to help her adjust to a new life. In many ways, she had not developed as others do and needs now to mature into wholeness. Freedom does not constitute maturity. People like Jennifer are developing new habit patterns of thought and it takes time to reprogram their minds.

Her counselors provided her with the support she needed to survive, and they are good people who would have done anything to help her. Nobody has all the answers. First and foremost, we need the Lord, but we also need one another.

EFFECTIVE PRAYER FOR OTHERS

I think of the pastors who try to help people like Jennifer. Most pastors haven't had formal training in counseling, and few have had seminary training that equipped them to deal with the kingdom of darkness. Desperate people come with overwhelming needs, knowing that their only hope is the Lord. Sometimes the only pastoral weapon at their disposal is prayer, so they pray. But often they see very little happen in response to their prayer of faith. That can be very discouraging.

Most Christians are aware of the passage in James that instructs those who are sick to call the elders, who are to pray and anoint with oil. I believe the church should be doing this, but I think we have overlooked some very important concepts and the order implied in James: "Is anyone among you suffering? Let him pray" (5:13). Initially, the person who needs to pray is the sufferer. Hurting people asked for prayer when I was a pastor. Of course, I prayed for them but I saw very few answers to prayer. When it comes to resolving personal and spiritual conflicts, the only effective prayer is the prayer of a repentant heart.

After leading a social worker through the Steps to Freedom, the change in her countenance was so noticeable that I encouraged her to visit the rest room and take a good look in the mirror. She was glowing when she returned to my office. As she reflected on the resolution of her spiritual conflicts, she said, "I always thought somebody else had to pray for me." That is a very common misconception. In the Steps to Freedom, the counselee is the one doing most of the praying.

We can't have a secondhand relationship with God. We may need a third party to facilitate the reconciliation of two personalities, but they won't be reconciled by what the facilitator does. They will only be reconciled by the concessions made by the principal parties. In spiritual resolution, God doesn't make concessions in order for us to be reconciled to Him. The Steps to Freedom lay out the "concessions" we have to make in order to assume our responsibility.

"Is anyone among you sick? Let him call for the elders of the church" (5:14). Notice that the responsibility to take the initiative is placed upon the one who is sick. We will never see victory in our churches unless our people assume the responsibility for their physical and spiritual well-being. We will never be effective in trying to heal a hurting humanity that doesn't want to get well. The Steps to Freedom only work if the counselees want to be well and will assume their own responsibility.

Mark records the incident when Jesus sent His disciples on ahead of Him in a boat. The wind came up, and the disciples ended up in the middle of the sea, "straining at the oars." As Jesus walked on the sea, "He intended to pass by them" (Mark 6:48 NASB). I believe that Jesus intends to pass by the self-sufficient. If we want to do it ourselves, He will let us. When the disciples called upon Jesus, He came to them. When the sick call the elders, they should also come.

James continues, "Therefore, confess your sins to one another, and pray for one another, so that you may be healed. The effective prayer of a righteous man can accomplish much" (5:16 NASB). I believe our prayers will be effective when people confess their sins. The Steps to Freedom are a fierce moral inventory. I have heard people confess incredible atrocities as they go through the steps. My role is to give them the assurance that God answers prayer and forgives His repentant children.

I am most confident in prayer after I have taken a person through the Steps to Freedom. John writes, "The one who practices sin is of the devil; for the devil has sinned from the beginning. The Son of God appeared for this purpose, that He might destroy the works of the devil" (1 John 3:8). I believe we are perfectly in God's will when we ask Him to restore a life damaged by Satan. That damage could be physical, emotional, or spiritual.

The order is "seek first the kingdom of God," then all the other things will be added unto us (Matt. 6:33 NASB). A young lady approached me in a conference with a cheerful "Hi!" "Hi," I responded. She said, "You don't recognize me, do you?" I didn't, and even after she reminded me that I had counseled with her a year earlier, I still didn't recognize her. She had changed that much. Like Jennifer, her appearance and countenance were totally different, a beautiful demonstration of change in a person "seeking first the kingdom of God." What a difference freedom in Christ makes!

CHAPTER 5

Nancy:
Female Sexual Abuse and Freedom

Many defeated Christians are caught up in the sin, confess, sin, confess, sin, confess, sin, "I give up" cycle, and it is most common in sexual bondages. This cycle of defeat is destined to continue downward and is incomplete for two reasons. First, confession is the initial step toward repentance, but it is not complete repentance. Second, God and the individual are not the only two players in this eternal struggle between good and evil. Satan and his evil workers are very active players to the point that the whole world lies in the power of the evil one (1 John 5:19).

Suppose there is a talking dog on the other side of a closed door, saying, "Come on, let me in. You know you want to. Everybody does it. Nobody will know. You will get away with it." On the other side of the door, he is the tempter. As soon as you yield to that temptation, you open the door. The dog's jaw is now clamped around the calf of your leg and he changes his role to that of an accuser: "You opened the door. You opened the door." If you could see the true picture, would you beat on yourself or the dog? If we don't understand the spiritual battle, we will buy his accusations and condemn ourselves, and a few well-meaning Christians may also strike a few blows.

Painfully aware that we left the door open to sin, we cry out to God for forgiveness. Guess what God does? He forgives us! Actually, we are already forgiven. Confession doesn't mean asking for forgiveness; it means ackowledging "I did it." It is critically important that we confess to God and admit that we opened the door (sinned). But that is not enough because the dog is still there and the door is still open. Rather than the "sin, confess" routine, the complete biblical perspective is: sin, confess, *resist*, and *repent*: "Submit therefore to God. Resist the devil and he will flee from you" (James 4:7 NASB).

If you and God are the only two players, then either you or God will have to take the rap for an awful lot of havoc in this world. Certainly God is not the author of confusion and death. In fact He is the author of life. The god of this world is the chief architect of rebellion, sin, sickness and death. He is the father of lies (John 8:44).

However, "the devil made me do it" is not a part of our theology or practice. There will be no victory for those who will not admit that they opened the door and assume responsibility for their own attitudes and actions. It is our responsibility not to let sin reign in our mortal body (Rom. 6:12). But treating those in bondage as the principal culprits, and throwing them out because they can't get their act together, is the height of pharisaic judgment and human rejection. Tragically, those most inclined to judge are usually those most incapable of helping.

If you witnessed a little girl being sexually molested because she left the door open and evil intruders took advantage of her carelessness, would you overlook the abusers and confront only the girl? If you did, the little girl would conclude that there was something evil about herself and that there was nowhere to turn for help. That's what Nancy and many others like her have experienced. Let's learn from her story.

~~~

NANCY'S STORY

We looked like a normal, happy family.

Both my parents were young and non-Christians. They had been married two years, and their marriage was rocky when I was born. Later, two brothers and a sister were added, and photos from that time show that we looked like a normal, happy family. My dad was handsome and my mother was attractive. Mostly the pictures are of the family all dressed up for church on Easter Sunday—we never went any other time.

We moved a lot, and I attended eight different schools before attending two different high schools.

My father would tell me that I was his special girl. Then he would touch me.

My father had a drug and alcohol problem and was in and out of jail for stealing to buy the things he needed in order to feed his addiction. He even broke open my piggy bank for whatever money I had and once sold all the lamps in the house. He would leave for a couple of days at a time and then come home smashed and abusive, breaking furniture, pictures, and glassware. This was not an uncommon thing; whenever my father got mad, things were destroyed.

My father told me when I was three years old that I could sleep in his room while my mother was at work. I remember lying in my parents' bed and my dad talking to me like I was his wife. He would tell me that he loved me more than he did my mother and that I was his special girl. Then he would touch me sexually. I really had no idea what was going on, only that this made Daddy happy and then he would be nice to me. He told me that I should never tell my mother about this because she wouldn't understand. It was then that I started masturbating, usually several times a day.

This was a confusing time for me. Sometimes I was torn between my parents, but on other nights, when my mother was home, my father would beat me and throw me against the wall. One night he took a blanket and threw it over my entire body and then sat on the blanket. I couldn't breathe or see any light. At first my mother just laughed, but then she yelled at my dad and told him to get up. That experience was one of the first times I remember being outside of myself and watching what was going on.

Another time, my dad got my baby brother and me drunk. He would give us tastes of whatever he was drinking and then spin us around and watch us walk funny.

About every two or three months my mom would leave my dad and we would spend some time at my grandparents' home until my dad would say, "I'm sorry; I won't ever do it again." So we would move back in with him. During those times of separation I would always be with my mom, and I was glad. I was so afraid of being totally alone with my father.

One time when I was about five, Dad came home and there was the usual broken furniture and pictures, but this time was different. It was late at night and Mom and I were up, but we were not packing to leave as we often did. On this particular night we were crouched in a corner of their bedroom. The house was totaled, worse than usual, and my dad was standing over us with a gun pointed at my mother's head. He said, "This is it, I'm going to pull the trigger." My mom hugged me tightly and pleaded with him not to kill her. I was crying, and I heard the trigger snap, but no explosion. Mom had thrown away the bullets and the gun that my dad thought was loaded was empty, although Mom wasn't sure whether he had gotten more bullets or not.

At that, my dad became even more angry and picked up my mom and threw her across the room. Mom told me to run next door, so I did. The police came and took my dad away, and I stayed at the neighbors' house, sleeping in a strange bed all alone and crying like I had never cried before. I wanted my mom to hold me, but she wasn't there. I don't know where she went, but whenever things got really bad I always had to stay somewhere else without my mom. I still don't understand where she went and why she didn't want me with her.

Another time, my dad had a knife and my mother had a broken bottle and they were fighting. I remember battling in my mind about which one I wanted to win. I loved my mom, but I never felt that she loved me. I knew my dad loved me, but he scared me. That time, Dad did cut Mom's throat and beat her up, and a neighbor had to take her to the hospital where she stayed for several days. I was, of course, at a friend's house . . . alone again.

I thought my parents loved animals more than people. One time my dad brought home a dog that had been mistreated. My parents felt so bad for this dog—they loved him, fed him extra and talked about how awful his past owners had been. I remember being jealous of the dog, wishing that my parents would be good "owners" of me.

By the time I was six, my dad had been in and out of jail several times and my mother finally left him. We moved in with my grandparents for a couple of years and then into another house in the same town.

I talked to myself constantly, saying how much I needed to masturbate in order to feel better. I would dream of boys in class at school and pretend we were making love. One time I was masturbating while watching television and my mother came into the room and watched. I didn't see her at first, but when I did, she just smiled at me and told me this was normal.

There were times in the bathtub when I would travel outside of myself and dream I was drowning myself. It felt both good and scary all at the same time. I'd fill up the tub as high as I could, get in and see myself under the water, face up, and dead.

Shadows would come out of Grandma's closet. I would hear voices and things would move around the room.

I spent as much time as I could at my grandmother's house and saw strange things: shadows coming out of Grandma's closet, voices and noises, and things moving around the room. Once my toy broom flew across my bedroom. These things startled me at first, but after a while I enjoyed trying to make things move myself.

My grandmother gave me a Ouija board, and my brother and I played with it. It was about this time that I asked my brother to sleep with me, and we kissed and held hands. I loved him so much and felt there was no other way to really show him that I cared (Oh, how I hate you, Satan!).

I was given a dog and would look at him and think, *I love you truly.* I would let him lick me and for a while it would feel good, but then I would get depressed. One day, I looked at him and wondered what it would be like for him to be dead. Only a few minutes later, he ran out in the road and was hit by a car and killed instantly. I remember having other dreams come true as well.

When I was about seven, I attended a neighborhood church. I enjoyed the songs and the people seemed so nice, but I can't remember anyone ever asking who I was or why I was there by myself.

My grandmother and grandfather didn't sleep together. I learned later that my grandfather had an affair and my grandmother had said that he could stay, but they never slept together again. So I would sleep with my grandmother. She wrote stories and would tell them to me, usually stories about friendly ghosts. So I thought the ghosts I was seeing in her house were good.

My grandfather loved me and told me I was his favorite grandchild. I slept with him, too, but he never touched me inappropriately or yelled at me or hurt me in any way. We would talk together at the dinner table and play games together, and he would play his guitar and sing for me. Even though there were strange things at their house, this was the closest thing to a happy family in my experience.

My mother remarried and we moved away. The first few years of their marriage seemed normal. We got spankings, but not beatings. I was in Brownies, tap dancing, and gymnastics, and I did well at school. I still heard voices saying, "You're ugly and stupid. This is going to end and your real father is going to come and get you."

I started having dreams about dying and would lie in bed crying out to God for help, "Please let there be something other than death, something beyond death." I dreamed that my grandparents were going to die, that I would never see them again. I dreamed my mother would die. It became such an obsession that I couldn't get to sleep unless I thought of someone in my family dying, and then I would cry myself to sleep.

I went to a church with a Christian friend and went forward during the altar call, wanting so much for someone to love me and help me, but this was not the time or the place. The counselor said that I needed to be "slain under the cross" so that I could speak in another language. My friend said that I would fall over afterward and that I shouldn't be afraid.

There were about thirty people around me who all started to pray, some in tongues and some not. It was hot and I just wanted to go home, so I thought I would talk some gibberish and fall over, which I did. Everyone was so excited that I was now a "Christian." I knew I had fooled them and was confused, wondering if Christians were fakes.

> *We would play in the greenhouse, and*
> *we would hold hands and kiss.*

While in grade school, I had a baby-sitter only a few years older than me who would take off her clothes and my clothes, and we would lie on each other on the living room floor. Sometimes I spent the night at her house and she would play with me, naked.

In the summers I visited my grandparents' home. The summer after I finished fifth grade, I took a friend with me. I had never had homosexual desires before, but that summer it was different. We played in the greenhouse and I told her she was my wife, or I hers, and we would hold hands and kiss. One thing led to another and we would end up on the floor rolling around together until I would end up masturbating. I don't think she ever did and she seemed scared, but she was always willing to play the game several times a day.

When we returned home, we went into the bushes and tried the game again, but this time it didn't seem right and we never did it again. We stayed friends throughout our school years but never again mentioned our summer together.

The next year I took another friend to Grandmother's house. This time we stayed in the bedroom and read magazines and acted out the stories in them.

By the time I was in junior high, my mom and stepfather were fighting more and more. I felt guilty about their fights, but mostly about my masturbation problem. I couldn't tell anyone or ask if this was normal, though I already knew it couldn't be. I tried my hardest to stop, but there was always that voice saying, "No, it's all right. Everyone does it." Then, afterward, the same voice would say, "You fool. You are so stupid and ugly, no one will want you."

When I was in high school, lying became a big part of my life. I wanted to have friends and fun, but I saw myself as stupid and inferior, so I would make up stories to make myself look and feel better.

I dated a lot and would let the boys do whatever they wanted with me, up to the point of actually having intercourse—I could finish that feeling at home. Of course, the guys didn't know that, so I became known as a big tease. Several told me that I drove them crazy for sex and that made me feel so down on myself: guilty, dirty inside and out, ugly, and again a failure.

Finally the inevitable happened. I did have intercourse with a boy in the front seat of his car outside a drive-in. It wasn't really painful; it wasn't anything. We drove back to his house because his dad was an alcoholic and never at home. We took a shower together and I did sex dances for him.

When I got home, my stepfather was waiting up for me as he always did. We didn't talk much, just looked at each other, and I went to bed, feeling numb as I fell asleep thinking about all that had happened that night. The next morning I called the boy and told him I never wanted to see him again, and I told everyone at school what a loser he was.

Later I asked my mom if you could wear white to your wedding if you were not a virgin. She just said, "You can wear whatever you want." I felt so rejected—I wish she would have asked me what had happened.

After one of our family moves I rode the bus to my new high school. I had decided I would not make friends with anyone because I hated it there and I hated my stepfather for making us move again. A blonde, bubbly cheerleader got on the bus and sat next to me, holding a trophy and smiling from ear to ear. I just glared at her. I was into cheerleading and pep week at the school I just moved from, and I didn't need her to remind me of what I had left behind.

She talked all the way to school and ended up inviting me to her church youth group. I had no idea what a church youth group was, and I certainly wasn't going to make friends with her. However, we rode the bus together for several weeks and finally I agreed to go.

I was surprised to find a group of kids singing, laughing, and reading Bibles. I remembered how good it felt in church when I was a child and felt that way again. My voices told me, "No! These kids won't like you. You are stupid for being here." But the girl I met on the bus continued to be my friend, and by the end of that school year I asked Christ to come into my life and was baptized.

I was so on fire for the Lord. I had finally found someone who would never leave me, hit me, or make me do bad things—someone who would always love me. I told everyone about Jesus and walked around the house with my Bible, quoting verses. I began a Bible study with my brothers and we would pray together and talk about Christ's love.

Then when I was in my senior year of high school, my mom and stepfather had a very violent fight. I was frozen with fear and felt that I couldn't stand to see what had happened with my birth father reenacted, so I took all the money I could find in the house and ran away. I drove to another state and moved in with a boy I had met earlier. The voices within me started up again, saying, "You slut! You call yourself a Christian?"

After a while, my boyfriend and I broke up and I went back home, but my stepfather didn't want me to stay. One night I attended a ball game at a local Bible college. Through all that had been happening, I wore a facade and told people that I was a Christian and that God is great.

However, during the game, I was thinking about my situation: how I had been living with a guy, had come back from running away, and now had no place to live. Just then, a girl next to me asked if I needed a place to live. I asked if she could read my mind and told her that I did. I moved in with her and two other girls and found out

that she was a lesbian and thought I was cute. But that was one relationship I never did pursue.

---

*Some of the things in my life were
hard for him to take, but he told
me that he loved me anyway.*

One of the girls I lived with had a brother I liked, but she was
trying to guard his innocence and really didn't want me to date
him. However, we started to go out together, and it was a different
relationship than I'd ever had before. I knew Jim cared about me—
really cared!

Shortly after we were engaged, I cheated on him. I felt so guilty
that I gave back the engagement ring, but he wouldn't break off the
relationship. I was all mixed up, still masturbating and not eating
well. In my heart I wanted him to love me and stay with me, but I
was mean to him.

I decided that the man I would marry would have to know the
truth about me, so I shared my past with him. He had come from a
very strict, sheltered Christian home, and some of the things in my
life were hard for him to take, but he told me that he loved me anyway. Seven months later we were married.

We never slept together before we were married, but afterward we
had a very abnormal sexual relationship. I was addicted to sex, not
only with my husband but also with masturbation. This created tension, so we fought and I began to feel dirty and alone again.

Our first ten years of marriage were turbulent. Jim attended Bible
college, worked for a major company for seven years, and then offi-
cially went into ministry. I was excited to be a minister's wife and put
high expectations on myself to be perfect and always available to
help others.

We had two children, but I wasn't much of a mom. I hit them
a lot and was easily depressed. I felt like my life was a waste; suicide was a daily thought. I would alternate between fits of rage

and asking forgiveness. I wanted to be close to God but never felt that I was.

When I became pregnant a third time a big part of me wanted to have an abortion, but a small part of me said, "Love this child." My husband was excited about that pregnancy, but we fought even more and my mood swings went out of control. The baby came and I didn't know how I could possibly take care of another child. All I wanted was to be out of this life. I was depressed and bored, and felt ugly and stupid, unwanted and lonely.

Meanwhile, at church and in meetings everyone seemed to like me. I was usually the life of the party, but that was a cover. No one really knew me.

I came very close to having an affair with one of the deacons who was married to my best friend. We never got beyond the talk stage, but I was very tempted and so confused. A voice inside me said, "Go for it. No one will ever know." But another part of me said, "Be faithful to your husband." After that I became disinterested in sex with Jim, but still had the problem with masturbation.

I could see shadows darting across the hall. I tried to kill myself.

My stepfather died and we brought his favorite chair home. When I sat in the chair and looked down our hallway, I could see shadows darting from the kids' rooms to the bedroom across the hall. At first I thought I was just tired, but then I learned that my husband and others saw them too.

One night a figure stood at the end of my bed and stared at me. It was tall and dark with a short-looking child standing beside it. These apparitions occurred off and on for several months. I got more and more depressed and tried to kill myself several times with pills. I talked about death and sang songs about dying. I told my husband that was the only way I would ever have peace—then things would be quiet and I would be with God.

As I became increasingly morose, Jim began staying away at night and would take the kids away for the weekend. He didn't know what to do, so he ran and hid from it all. I would stay in bed for two or three days at a time with the door locked and a sign on the door telling everyone to go away. Meanwhile, Jim would make excuses for me at church, telling everyone I was sick.

Several times our oldest child called for an ambulance, thinking that I was dying. They would take me to the emergency room, run some tests, tell me I was fine, and send me home again. Once a minister's name came to mind and I cried out in desperation for someone to get him to help me. Jim wasn't home, but our baby-sitter was there and she called him. He prayed with me and referred me to a Christian counselor whom I saw for three months.

The counselor began by saying I was a Christian and he was a Christian, but that this was not a spiritual problem. He said I had been abused by several men in my life, I was too busy, and I wasn't facing the child inside me. A small voice inside me said, *But where is Christ in all this?* I knew the answers must be in Him, but I just couldn't get there. I finally stopped going to the counselor.

One day I decided it was time for action, so I took my stepfather's chair to a flea market and sold it. After that, we all stopped seeing ghosts in our home. I quit my job because I had been seeing ghosts there too. At this point I started having a daily Bible study.

Jim and I started to get along better and things became nearer to normal, though I still really wanted to die so he could find a better wife and our kids could have a good mom who didn't cringe when they said, "I love you, Mom." Then Jim was offered another job and we moved, desperately hoping this fresh start would help us.

In our new location, one of our children began seeing "things" and having terrible dreams. He wouldn't be left alone. He would see a blond man run through his room and out the door. One night when he was four, he said, "I need the Lord to live in me." He asked Christ into his life and not only did the apparitions and dreams go away, he was also instantly healed of serious asthma attacks and went off all of his medicine and a breathing machine! If you ask him about that today, he will say, "God healed me."

After that brief time of near normalcy, the new job turned into a disaster. I started masturbating again, fighting and lying. My husband was fired and we moved to another location where God wonderfully provided a home and another job on the staff of a church. With the excitement of the new situation we were fine for a while, but then depression set in again. I couldn't function and I just wanted to die. I had no friends; there was no one I could talk to. Who would understand voices, ghosts, deep depression, and an obsession with dying? I lived a double life—trying to help at church, even introducing some to the Lord, while at home I was a hysterical, raging person. I was fooling everyone but my family. I felt like I was going crazy.

A doctor diagnosed my problem as PMS and said there was a new pill that would help. I believed that a Christian could have physical problems, but in my case the problem was in my mind and I knew that somehow I needed to end this mental torment.

I was afraid to take a shower for fear that the shower curtain would wrap itself around me and kill me . . . afraid to answer the phone, not wanting to talk with anyone . . . afraid to take responsibility, no longer being the person who loved to plan and organize and conduct big events . . . afraid of the faces in the mirror in my bedroom . . . and afraid to drive at night because figures and snakes would appear in the headlights.

At a Bible bookstore, I found a prayer notebook and Jim bought it for me. He was so desperate for me to get better that he would do anything. All through this time, he was telling me that God would bring us through this, was praying for me constantly and, this time, not running away to his work.

I brought the prayer binder home and began to have daily morning Bible studies. I had preached having daily Bible study to others, but had never been able to keep it up myself. I began a regular time with God and it was wonderful. The negative voices stopped, and for a while I stopped masturbating. Prayers were being answered and our ministry at the church was growing.

---

*I felt so scared and sick that I
wished Neil would cancel.*

In preparation for a "Resolving Personal and Spiritual Conflicts" conference at our church, a film was shown in which Neil spoke and some people gave testimonies. As I watched, I started getting sick and wanted to run out, but I stayed because of what people would think. On the way home that night I told Jim that I didn't want to go to the conference and that I was better now. I felt that as long as I studied and prayed every morning I would be fine. We talked about it and then dropped the subject. Since the conference was still two months away, I felt safe.

In the weeks before the conference there was a lot of excitement at church. Everyone was talking about how great it sounded and they were inviting friends. I decided that I would go just to learn how to help others and to support Jim. Then the turmoil started again—I couldn't pray, I became angry easily, and I started masturbating again. I felt so scared and sick that I wished Neil would cancel.

The first night of the conference I sat there acting cool, taking notes and pretending it didn't affect me. By the third night I couldn't concentrate and nothing made sense. I felt that I would either throw up or dissolve in tears. I heard voices, had terrible thoughts and was going downhill fast, especially when Neil mentioned rape.

Jim made an appointment for me with Neil, and when he told me about it I started shaking. When the morning of the appointment came, I told Jim there was no way I was going to see some conceited speaker who would just say that I was lying and needed to snap out of it.

Jim prayed a lot and convinced me to go with him to the conference and then to the appointment. That morning I cried through the sessions. Finally, I could take it no longer and went out to sit in the car. This was by far the worst internal struggle of my entire life. I found myself saying, "Why did he come? Doesn't he know that I don't need his help? I like being this way. I'm just fine. Why can't he go away? He will ruin everything." I especially kept hearing that last thought, *He will ruin everything.*

Then another part of me said, "What could he ruin?" I felt such fear that I thought of driving my car right through the fence in front of me and escaping, but I didn't. I had no place to hide. I wanted help so badly but doubted that Neil would have any answers. Then I got mad. I hated Neil; he was the enemy. I would go to this stupid appointment, but I would win.

I told Neil that I didn't like him and that this wasn't going to work.

Jim found me in the car and we went to lunch with a friend. Then we went back to the conference and before I knew it, I was sitting in a room with Neil and a couple from his staff. What happened during the next two hours I will never forget, and I will never be the same.

First I told Neil that I didn't like him and that this wasn't going to work. I told him some of the things about my family in a very matter-of-fact way. Then I went through the first prayer in the Steps to Freedom with no problem, even though I didn't know what I read. But when it came time to renounce all my cultic, occult, and non-Christian experiences, I couldn't pray. I felt like throwing up, my vision went in and out, and I felt like I was choking and couldn't breathe. I remember Neil quietly telling Satan to release me, affirming that I was a child of God. I felt calmed and continued to go through the prayers.

When we came to the forgiveness part, I told Neil I had no one to forgive, that I loved everyone except him right now. He told me to pray and ask God to bring to mind people I needed to forgive. Names came to mind I hadn't thought about in years. When I started praying to forgive them, I cried and cried, and this time the tears felt good. It felt like a heavy block was being lifted from my chest and head.

We went through the other prayers and I felt progressively better. I could breathe and I felt loved. When we had finished, Neil suggested that I go into the rest room and take a good look at myself in the mirror. I did, and for the first time in my life, I liked what I saw! I said, "I like you, Nancy. In fact, I love you." I looked into my eyes and was happy. I felt that because of Jesus, there was a truly good person there. That was the first time I have ever looked in the mirror without feeling disgust for myself.

That night I had to drive a three-hour distance to a brother's graduation. Jim couldn't join me because of his responsibilities at the conference.

I had not driven much in the dark because of the images I would see, usually white snakes jumping up at the car. One time I saw a burning car engulfed in flames, but when I got to the spot there was nothing. I have seen people hitchhiking and then suddenly there was no one there. So driving at night brought great fear. But that night, during the entire three-hour drive, I saw nothing. Praise God!

The next day, along with 28,000 others, I attended the graduation ceremony. Before this, crowds would cause me to panic. I would feel like I was trapped and couldn't get out, like I was choking, like I couldn't breathe, and it was as though the sky was falling around me. That day, however, I felt none of those symptoms. In fact, it wasn't until I was walking out of the stadium with people all around me that I realized the fear was gone. I looked up at the sky and said, "Praise God, I really am free!"

When I was praying with Neil, what I appreciated most is that it wasn't a typical counseling appointment—it was a time with God. Neil guided me through the prayers and kept me going, but it was God who delivered me from Satan's clutches; it was God who cleaned house in my mind.

The first morning in our home after the conference, I looked around our bedroom and listened. It was quiet, really quiet . . . no voices, and they haven't come back! Occasionally I have felt frustrated, but now I know how to deal with it.

Since then, our youngest child has had some fears and bad dreams. Instead of praying in fear, we talked about who he is in Christ. Our son said, "Hey! Satan's afraid of me. He had just better watch out 'cause I'm a child of God."

My husband and I took a couple
through the Steps to Freedom.
They, too, are now free.

A few months later some missionary friends stayed with us for a week. The wife had been harassed in various ways including depression and thoughts of suicide. Jim and I took them through the Steps to Freedom and they, too, are free!

Since I found my freedom in Christ, I can say, "I love you" to my husband and not hear thoughts of *No you don't*, or *This marriage will never last*. For a long time now, I have not had depression. I haven't yelled uncontrollably at my children. I'm not afraid of the shower curtain. And masturbation is no longer a problem. Jim and I have been able to lead many of our friends at church through the Steps to Freedom, and we are enjoying seeing freedom spread. Praise God, I really am free!

DO THEY HATE YOU?

You may be wondering why Nancy, Sandy and others expressed hatred toward me. Obviously, the hatred is not coming from them. Satan isn't pleased with what I'm doing. If we are not experiencing some opposition to what we are doing in ministry, then maybe we aren't doing much. If someone expresses hatred when you're trying to help them, just ignore those comments and continue. After they complete the steps and are free, they often express a great love toward you. Remember Anne's comment in Chapter 2? She said, "I immediately had a great love jump in my heart toward you, Neil."

DEMONIC TRANSFERENCE

Satan will take advantage of illicit sex more than any other sin that I am aware of. Every sexually abused person I have worked with has had major spiritual difficulties. Compulsive masturbation from the age of three is not "normal" sexual development, especially for girls. But it is a common stronghold for those who have been sexually violated. These women feel a deep sense of condemnation when there is no condemnation for those who are in Christ Jesus (Rom. 8:1).

The stronghold is greater if the sexual abuser is a parent. Parents are the authority in the home. They are supposed to provide the spiritual protection that every child needs in order to develop spiritually, socially, mentally, and physically. They are passing their iniquity to the next generation. When they become the abusers, they directly open the gates for spiritual assault in their children. Instead of being the spiritual umbrella of protection, they are opening the floodgates of devastation.

GUARDING WHAT GOD ENTRUSTS TO YOU

The underlying principle is stewardship. We are to be good stewards of whatever God entrusts to us (1 Cor. 4:1–2). Every parent should know what it means to dedicate their children to the Lord and how to pray for their spiritual protection. As parents we have no greater stewardship than the lives of the little children God has entrusted to us.

SEXUAL UNION/SPIRITUAL BOND

Every church has a story of a lovely young lady who gets involved with the wrong man. After having sex with him, she can't seem to break away. Friends and family try to convince her that he isn't any good for her. Even she knows the relationship is sick because he treats her like dirt. Why doesn't she just tell him to take a hike? Because they have bonded or become one in the flesh (1 Cor. 6:15–17).

A pastor called me one day and said, "If you can't help this young girl I've been counseling, she will be hospitalized in a mental ward." For two years she'd had a sick relationship with a boy who was deal- ing drugs and generally treating her as a sex object. The mental assault she was experiencing was so vivid that she couldn't understand why others couldn't hear the voices she was hearing. After hearing her story, I asked her what she would do if I required her to leave this guy and never have anything to do with him again. She started to shake and said, "I would probably get up and leave." From experience, I knew she would respond that way, but I wanted the pastor to hear her.

I took her through the Steps to Freedom. In Step 6, she prayed and asked the Lord to reveal to her mind every sexual use of her body as an instrument of unrighteousness, and the Lord did (Rom. 6:11–13). As each one came to her mind, she renounced the use of her body with that person and asked God to break that bond. Her newfound freedom was immediately evident to everyone in that room. Without any coaching she said she was never going to see that man again, and to my knowledge she never saw him again. That conviction came from the Holy Spirit. Telling our children or friends to break off sexual relation- ships without resolving the bondage first will not prove to be effective.

GOD WANTS HIS CHILDREN FREE

I have found it necessary for all sexual sins to be renounced. I instruct people to pray, asking the Lord to reveal to their minds all the sexual sins and partners with whom they have been involved, whether they were the victim or the perpetrator. It is amazing how experiences will come flooding back to their minds. God wants His children free.

When they renounce the experience, they are specifically renouncing Satan and all his works and all his ways, and breaking those ties. When they confess, they are choosing to walk in the light with God. The power of Satan and sin has then been broken, and fellowship with the Lord is beautifully restored.

CHAPTER 6

Doug:
Male Sexual Abuse and Freedom

Feelings of disgust rise rapidly to the average Christian mind when images of sexual perversion are entertained. Suppose that was your own self-perception, and you were in full-time ministry. To add insult to injury, what if you were an illegitimate child being raised in a racially mixed home with all the social rejection that unfortunately follows?

How would you feel toward yourself? Would you readily accept the fact that you are a saint who sins, or would you see yourself as a wretched sinner? Would you walk in the light, have fellowship with other believers, and speak the truth in love? Or would you live a lonely life, frightened to death that someone would somehow find out what was really going on inside? Such is the case of our next story.

~~~

DOUG'S STORY

Dad never called me "son."

My mother wasn't married when I was born, but when I was two years old she married an Afro-American. He was a decent person, but he never called me "son," and never said he loved me. Whenever I would go somewhere with both of my parents, it was obvious I was not a product of their marriage, and sometimes I was called "Sambo's little kid."

While I was preschool age, a baby-sitter took me to her apartment and played sexual games with me. In the ensuing years I did sexual experimentation with other children, was sexually exploited by older girls and boys, and eventually was raped by young men.

I understood my identity to be a "bastard": I was an unplanned, unwanted accident. Early on I perceived that my craving for love and acceptance might possibly be met through sex, and that by giving fulfillment to others through sex I could show that my love was not selfish. Thus sex became an obsession and eventually led to perversion.

I tried very hard to gain praise and approval in the "straight" world also, and won many awards and honors at school. But my self-image was at zero, and no person or thing seemed to help. At age sixteen I became suicidal.

Then one summer I went to camp and met people who genuinely seemed to care. It was there I learned of Jesus' love for me. The promise of that love, combined with a disgust for myself, drew me to receive Him as my Savior. I then knew that my lifestyle was wrong and that I should turn from it, but I had been programmed to it for years and seemed powerless to change.

Nevertheless, I purposed to follow Christ, praying that somehow, by some miracle, I would become the person I longed to be. I trained for the ministry, graduated from school, and threw myself into my work. I think part of my motivation for going into ministry was to give myself to others so they could love me back.

> *Our marriage relationship was doomed from the start.*

After a few years I married a wonderful woman. Our relationship was doomed from the start because invading thoughts of male images and my own past perversion destroyed any possibility of a healthy sexual life. I continually struggled against going back to previous forms of sex. I turned to masturbation, which I considered "safe" sex because I could control my environment.

My wife was always loyal to me, yet she sensed something was definitely wrong. It wasn't until we were married for ten years that I finally told her a little about my problem. That news was very painful for her, but at the same time she felt relief at finally knowing the truth.

I heard speaker after speaker talk about victory in Jesus and I thought, *That's fine for someone who doesn't have my background. That will work for others, but not for me. I will just have to live with my sin. I'll have heaven later, but for now I'll have to deal with the realities of my past.* I felt locked into a horrible identity; it was a heavy bondage.

If I committed suicide, I hoped it would look like an accident.

I developed a contingency plan in the event that anyone ever found out I had been gay or bisexual. I would drive my car into an oncoming semi-truck. I prepared for that through the years by telling people how I would get very sleepy at the wheel and have to eat snacks to stay awake. If I ever committed suicide, I hoped it would look like an accident and there would be insurance money for my family.

One night in a therapy group, I was hypnotized and told some of my problem—more than I should have. I left with the group's encouragement but did not feel good about what I had shared with them. I looked for semis on the lonely road home, determined to end my life, but there were none. As I drove into the driveway my children came running to me. Their acceptance and love were so wonderful that I clicked back into reality.

After some defeats in ministry, I asked for counsel from some older Christian brothers. One of them said, "I hear you saying you are trying very hard to prove you are worthy." That was hard truth, and I immediately went into my pattern of "pity-partying," saying, "Lord, there has never been a person so rejected as me." Then it was as though God spoke aloud to my mind and said, "The only one I ever turned My back on was My own Son, who bore your sins on the cross." That was a step toward recovery, of moving away from my prison of self-pity.

Little by little there was growth. God was helping me to see things from a different perspective and I wasn't so controlled by my passions. But the reality that our marriage relationship wasn't all that it should be continued to haunt me.

I had an opportunity to sit under Neil's teaching and heard him speak on spiritual conflict. There I learned some new dimensions of resisting Satan and, on a scale of 1 to 10, temptations in my thought life went down to a 2. My prayer life became more vibrant and intense. My need for sexual self-gratification diminished until that addiction of a quarter century stopped altogether.

Finally, I found that I could have a normal relationship with my wife without a videotape playing in my mind of others imposing themselves upon me sexually. It was a wholesome, beautiful thing. All of those changes were taking place without my pursuing them. I happened to sit under Neil's teaching, and the Lord did the rest.

> *I thought that the only way to destroy the sin was to destroy the sinner.*

Then some difficulties arose, and I realized that I was under attack and needed to go back and reinforce what I had learned. The truth that had helped me in such a variety of ways was the truth of who I am in Christ, defined by my Savior and not by my sin. In Romans, I saw the difference between who I am and my activity: "If I am doing the very thing I do not wish, I am no longer the one doing it, but sin which dwells in me" (7:20 NASB). I was finally able to separate the real me from my actions. The reason I was suicidal all those years was because I thought the only way to destroy the sin was to destroy the sinner. There was still an ongoing battle between the authority of my experiences versus the authority of Scripture, but I began to be able to live out my true identity by choosing truth and standing against Satan's lies.

I was able to use the help given to me by Neil when I spoke at a weekend church conference. After the last session, there was a testimony time where people began confessing their faults to one another, like a mini-revival. I had never seen anything like it before; it was beautiful to experience.

But even as I spoke at that conference on spiritual conflict, my wife, who was hundreds of miles away, was startled with demonic manifestations in our home. She had to call in friends to support her and pray for her. That became a pattern for a period of time.

On the plus side: People were being set free through our ministry from bondages that had enslaved them for years. Victims of abuse who had been dysfunctional in their relationships were having their marriages restored; pastors were being freed from problems paralyzing their ministries. At the same time, we found ourselves harassed by Satan and run ragged by a busy schedule.

During that oppression there was a
tidal wave of perverse thoughts.

As I reflect back to the time when I had planned on taking my life but had come home and met my children in the driveway, I realize that many of my memories from the past had been graciously blocked out. During the demonic oppression that came later, there were flashbacks to perverted behavior and tidal wave after tidal wave of perverse thoughts. Then there would be an onslaught of self-destructive thoughts—that suicide was again the easiest way to get out of all the pressure we were experiencing.

I went in and out of reality, unable to control it. I became afraid of losing my mind. In the middle of the night, I would awake in a sweat, having dreamed of incredible horror, of killing loved ones and placing their bodies in transparent body bags.

I shared this attack with my brothers in Christ, and a massive amount of prayer went up. I was weak and vulnerable, and I needed the prayer support of God's people to lift that onslaught of demonic depression. Finally it did lift, and I was again able to think objectively and spiritually about the issues.

From experience, I am convinced that no one is ever so strong that he can stand alone. I have a wife who prays for me, a support group of men with whom I meet once a week, a Bible study group at church, and concerned friends and loved ones. We all need a body of believers for encouragement, people who will stand with us against the attacks of the enemy.

I'm looking forward to the challenges ahead. Our ministry continues. My wife and I are still working on some issues in our marriage that haven't been totally resolved, but there is nothing there that God cannot heal. My acceptance and identity in Christ are my greatest strengths. Because of His unconditional love, I don't have to prove myself worthy. There is nothing I can do to increase His already-proven love for me.

Whereas I used to wear the label of "bastard," Colossians talks about the fact that, in Christ, we are chosen, beloved, and holy. Those are the new labels I now wear, and they establish my identity.

When I was a boy and the others would pick sides for a baseball game, it seemed everyone was chosen before me. It was as though I was a handicap to the team who chose me. But God says that He chose me, and not as the last of the group.

Recently I took my dad's hand and told him that there has never been a time when I loved him more or have been more proud of him than now. Tears came to his eyes and he said, "I never knew you cared. I never knew I was that important to you." He reached over and gave me a hug, and for the first time he said, "Son, I love you." How that penetrated the depths of my heart!

God is in the ministry of repairing our lives. He is changing us into

His likeness, His image. He is putting all the pieces back together, touching all the relationships between father and son, husband and wife, parent and child. He has begun the good work and will continue it until we stand before Him, complete in Christ.

≈≈≈

Where Is Your Identity?

There are a lot of sick ways to identify ourselves, and doing so by the color of our skin or the stigma connected to our physical birth is one of the sickest. If we had only a physical heritage, it would make sense that we get our identity from the natural world. But we have a far more important spiritual heritage in Christ.

Paul repeatedly admonishes the church to put off the old self and put on the new self, "who is being renewed to a true knowledge according to the image of the One who created him—a renewal in which there is no distinction between Greek and Jew, circumcised and uncircumcised, barbarian, Scythian, slave and freeman, but Christ is all, and in all" (Col. 3:10–11 NASB). In other words, our primary identity isn't along racial, religious, cultural, or social lines. We all have a common identity in Christ!

Bondage to Sin

Anybody who would heap more condemnation on this pastor or anyone else who struggles in this way is assisting the devil, not God. The devil is the adversary; Jesus is our Advocate. People trapped by sexual sin would love nothing more than to be free.

No pastor in his rational mind would throw away his ministry for a one-night stand, and yet many do. Why is that? Can we be a bond servant of Christ and at the same time be in bondage to sin? Sadly, many who have been delivered out of the kingdom of darkness and into the kingdom of God's beloved Son are still living in bondage to sin. Even though we are no longer *in* the flesh because we are *in* Christ, we can still choose to walk (live) *according* to the flesh.

Notice that the first deed of the flesh listed in Galatians 5:19 is immorality (fornication).

I surveyed a seminary student body and found out that 60 percent were feeling convicted about their sexual morality. The other 40 percent were probably in various stages of denial. Every legitimate Christian would love to be sexually free. The problem is that sexual sins are so uniquely resistant to conventional treatment. Nevertheless, freedom is attainable. Let me establish a theological basis for freedom and then suggest some practical steps that we need to take. For a more complete understanding, see my book *A Way of Escape* (Harvest House 1998), which deals with freedom from sexual strongholds.

Two Essentials

There are two essential issues that must be resolved in order for a believer to experience freedom in Christ. First, resolve the entrapment of sin that comes from using your body as an instrument of unrighteousness. Second, win the battle for your mind by reprogramming it with the truth of God's Word. Paul summarized both in Romans 12:1–2(NASB):

> I urge you therefore, brethren, by the mercies of God, to present your bodies a living and holy sacrifice, acceptable to God, which is your spiritual service of worship. And do not be conformed to this world, but be transformed by the renewing of your mind, that you may prove what the will of God is, that which is good and acceptable and perfect.

In this chapter I will address the issue of habitual sexual sin as it relates to our physical body. In the next chapter I will deal with the battle for our mind as it relates to sexual bondage.

In Romans 6:12, we are admonished not to let sin reign in our mortal body that we should obey its lusts. That's our responsibility: not to let sin rule in our members, i.e., "your pleasures that wage war in your members" (James 4:1).

DEAD TO SIN

A foundational truth that we need to believe in order *not* to let sin reign in our bodies is given in Romans 6:6–7: "Knowing this, that our old self was crucified with Him, that our body of sin might be done away with, that we should no longer be slaves to sin; for he who has died is freed from sin." I often ask in a conference, "How many have died with Christ?" Everybody will raise their hands. Then I ask, "How many are free from sin?" According to Scripture, it should be the same number of hands.

When we fail in our Christian walk we often reason, "What experience must I have in order for me to live as though I have really died with Christ?" The only experience necessary was the experience that Christ had on the cross. Many try and try to put the old self (man) to death and can't. Why not? Because the old self has already died! You cannot do for yourself what has already been done for you by Christ. Many Christians are desperately trying to become someone they already are. We receive Christ by faith . . . we walk by faith . . . we are justified by faith . . . and we are also sanctified by faith.

We don't always feel dead to sin. In fact we may at times *feel* alive to sin and dead to Christ. Feelings don't always tell the truth. That is why you are to "consider yourselves to be dead to sin, but alive to God *in* Christ Jesus" (Rom. 6:11, emphasis added). Considering this to be so isn't what makes it so. We consider it so because it *is* so. Believing something doesn't make it true. It's true; therefore, we believe it. When we choose to walk by faith according to what Scripture affirms is true, it works out in our experience, but trying to make it true by our experience will never work. As a believer, you can't die to sin because you have already died to sin. You choose to believe the truth and live accordingly by faith, and then the truth that you are dead to sin works out in your experience.

In a similar fashion, I don't serve the Lord in order to gain His approval. I am approved by God; therefore, I serve Him. I don't try to live a righteous life in the hopes that some day He will love me; I live a righteous life because He already loves me. I don't labor in the vineyard trying to gain His acceptance. I am accepted in the Beloved; therefore, I gladly serve Him.

LIVING FREE

When sin makes its appeal, I say, "I don't have to sin because I have been delivered out of darkness and I am now alive in Christ. Satan, you have no relationship to me, and I am no longer under your authority." Sin hasn't died. It's still strong and appealing, but I am no longer under its authority and I have no relationship to the kingdom of darkness. Romans 8:1–2 helps to clarify the issue: "There is therefore now no condemnation for those who are in Christ Jesus. For the law of the Spirit of life in Christ Jesus has set you free from the law of sin and death"(NASB).

Is the law of sin and death still operative? Yes, and it applies for everyone who isn't alive in Christ, those who have not received Him into their lives as Savior. You cannot do away with a law, so you can only overcome it by a greater law. We cannot fly in the flesh because of the law of gravity. But we can fly in an airplane, because there is a power there that is greater than the law of gravity. If you think the law of gravity is no longer in effect, then flip the switch at 20,000 feet and you will crash and burn. If you think the law of sin is not still in effect, then walk by the flesh. You will crash and burn.

The law of sin and death has been superseded by a higher power—the law of life in Christ Jesus. But we will fall the moment we stop walking in the Spirit and living by faith. So we need to "put on the Lord Jesus Christ, and make no provision for the flesh in regard to its lusts" (Rom. 13:14). Satan can't do anything about our position in Christ, but if he can get us to believe it isn't true, we will live as though it's not, even though it is true.

OUR MORTAL BODIES

In Romans 6:12 we're told not to let sin reign in our mortal bodies, and then verse 13 instructs us how to accomplish that: "Do not go on presenting the members of your body to sin as instruments of unrighteousness; but present yourselves to God as those alive from the dead, and your members as instruments of righteousness to God"(NASB). Our bodies are like an instrument that can be used for good or evil. They are not evil, but they are mortal, and whatever is mortal is corruptible.

For the Christian there is the wonderful anticipation of the resurrection when we shall receive an imperishable body like that of our Lord (1 Cor. 15:35–44). Until then, we have a mortal body that can be used in the service of sin as an instrument of unrighteousness, or in the service of God as an instrument of righteousness.

Obviously, it's impossible to commit a sexual sin without using our body as an instrument of unrighteousness. When we do, we allow sin to reign in our mortal body and are being obedient to the lusts of the flesh instead of being obedient to God.

It is hard to understand how a principle (as opposed to an evil personal influence) could reign in my mortal body in such a way that I would have no control over it. Even more difficult to understand is how I could get a principle out of my body. Paul says, "I find then the principle that *evil* is present in me, the one who wishes to do good" (Rom. 7:21, emphasis added). What is present in me is evil—the person, not the principle—and it is present in me because at some time I used my body as an instrument of unrighteousness.

Paul concludes with the victorious promise that we do not have to remain in that unrighteous state: "Who will set me free from the body of this death? Thanks be to God through Jesus Christ our Lord!" (Rom. 7:24–25). Jesus will set us free!

SINNING WITH OUR BODIES

First Corinthians 6:15–20 shows the connection between sexual sin and the use of our bodies:

> Do you not know that your bodies are members of Christ? Shall I then take away the members of Christ and make them members of a harlot?

May it never be! Or do you not know that the one who joins himself to a harlot is one body with her? For He says, "The two shall become one flesh." But the one who joins himself to the Lord is one spirit with Him. Flee immorality [fornication]. Every other sin that a man commits is outside the body, but the immoral man sins against his own body. Or do you not know that your body is a temple of the Holy Spirit who is in you, whom you have from God, and that you are not your own? For you have been bought with a price: therefore glorify God in your body.

Every believer is "in Christ" and is a member of His body. For me to join my body with a harlot would be to use my body to sin, as opposed to using it as a member of Christ's body, the church. "Yet the body is not for immorality, but for the Lord; and the Lord is for the body" (1 Cor. 6:13 NASB). If you are united to the Lord *in* Christ, can you imagine the inner turmoil that will result if you are at the same time united physically to a harlot? That union creates an unholy bond that is in opposition to the spiritual union that we have in Christ. The resulting bondage is so great that Paul warns us to "flee immorality." Run from it!

Paul puts sexual sins in a category by themselves, since every other sin is outside the body. This may have something to do with the ability to create, which we don't have. We can be creative in how we arrange, organize, or otherwise use what God has created, but we don't spontaneously create something out of nothing as only God can do. Procreation is the only creative act that the Creator allows man to participate in, and God provides careful instruction as to how we are to oversee the process of bringing life into this world. He confines sex to an intimate act of marriage, requires the marriage bond to last until death of a spouse, and charges parents to provide a nurturing atmosphere where children can be brought up in the Lord.

Satanic Perversion

Anybody who has helped those victimized by satanism knows how profoundly Satan violates God's standards. The rituals are disgusting sexual orgies. It isn't sex as a normal human would understand it. It is the most ripping, obscene, violent exploitation of another human being you can imagine. Little children are raped and tortured. The satanist's ultimate "high" is to sacrifice some innocent victim at the point of orgasm. The term "sick" doesn't do justice to the abuse. "Total wickedness" and "absolute evil" better epitomize the utter degradation of Satan and his legions of demons.

Satanists have breeders who are selected for the development of a satanic "super-race" who, they say, will rule this world. Other breeders are required to bring their offspring or aborted fetuses for sacrifice. Satan will do everything he can to establish his kingdom while, at the same time, trying to pervert the offspring of God's people. No wonder sexual sins are so repugnant to God. Using our bodies as instruments of unrighteousness permits sin to reign in our mortal bodies. We have been bought with a price, and we are to glorify God in our bodies. In other words, we are to manifest the presence of God in our lives as we bear fruit for His glory.

Homosexual Behavior

While homosexuality is a growing stronghold in our culture, there is no such thing as a homosexual. Considering oneself to be a homosexual is to believe a lie because God created us male and female. There are homosexual *feelings and behavior*, and usually they are developed in early childhood. Every person I have counseled who struggles with homosexual tendencies has had a major spiritual stronghold.

But there is no such thing as a demon of homosexuality. That kind of thinking would have us believe that if we cast out the demon, the person would be completely delivered from any further thoughts or problems. I know of no such cases, although I would not presume to limit God from performing such a miracle. The roots of their homosexual tendencies usually can be traced to early childhood traumas and sexual abuse. They struggle with a lifetime of bad relationships, dysfunctional homes, and role confusions. Their emotions have been tied into their past and it takes time for them to establish a new identity in Christ. They will typically go through an arduous process of renewing their minds, thoughts, and experiences. As they do, their emotions will eventually conform to the truth they have now come to believe.

Thundering from the pulpit that homosexuals are destined for hell will only drive the people who struggle into greater despair. Overbearing authoritarianism only contributes to their demise. Autocratic parents who don't know how to love contribute to a child's wrong orientation, and condemning messages reinforce an already damaged self-image.

Don't get me wrong. The Scriptures clearly condemn the practice of homosexuality as well as all other forms of fornication. But imagine what it must be like to suffer with homosexual feelings that you didn't ask for, and then hear that God condemns you for it. As a result, many want to believe that God created them that way. Militant homosexuals are trying to prove that their lifestyle is a legitimate alternative to heterosexuality and violently oppose conservative Christians who would say otherwise.

We must help those who struggle with homosexual tendencies to establish a new identity in Christ. Even secular counselors know that identity is a critical issue in recovery. How much greater is the Christian's potential to help these people since we have a gospel that sets us free from our past and establishes us alive in Christ! Being a new creation in Christ is what sets us free from our past.

THE PATH FROM SEXUAL BONDAGE

If you are in sexual bondage, what can you do? First, know that there is no condemnation for those who are in Christ Jesus. Putting yourself or others down is not going to resolve this bondage, nor does adding shame and guilt contribute to good mental health. Accusation is one of Satan's tactics. And most definitely, suicide is not God's means to set you free.

Second, get alone or with a trusted friend, pastor, or counselor, and ask the Lord to reveal to your mind every time you used your body as an instrument of unrighteousness, including all sexual sins.

Third, verbally respond to each offense as it is recalled by saying, "I confess (whatever the sin was), and I renounce that use of my body." A pastor told me he spent three hours by himself one afternoon and was totally cleansed afterward. Temptations still come, but the power has been broken. He is now able to say no to sin. If you think this process might take too long, try not doing it and see how long the rest of your life will seem as you drag on in defeat! Take a day, two days, or a week if necessary.

Fourth, when you have finished confessing and renouncing, express the following: "I now commit myself to the Lord, and my body as an instrument of righteousness. I submit my body as a living and holy sacrifice to God. In the name of Jesus, I command you, Satan, to leave my presence." If you are married, also say, "For the purpose of sex, I reserve my body to be used only with my spouse according to 1 Corinthians 7:1–5."

Lastly, choose to believe the truth that you are alive in Christ and dead to sin, and ask the Lord to fill you with His Holy Spirit. There will be many times when temptation will seem to be overwhelming, but you must declare your position in Christ at the moment you are first aware of the temptation. Believe with authority that you no longer have to sin because you are a new creation in Christ. Then decide to live by faith according to what God says is true.

Not allowing sin to reign in our mortal bodies is half the battle. Renewing our minds is the other half. Sexual sins and pornographic viewing have a way of staying in the memory bank far longer than other images. Getting free is one thing; staying free is another. I will address that issue after the story in the next chapter.

CHAPTER 7

Charles:
Freeing the Sexual Abuser

I received a call from a pastor that started with, "Are you required by law to divulge confidential communication?" What he was really saying was, "If I came to see you, could I tell you that I am molesting my child or other children without being turned in to the authorities?" I reminded him that most states still protect clergy confidentiality, but do require licensed professionals and public officials, including teachers, to report any suspected abuse. I said that even though I'm not required to do it by the law in our state, I had a moral responsibility to protect another person in danger.

He took the chance and shared his story with me. It all started with back rubs on his daughter to get her awake in the morning, but it soon led to inappropriate fondling, though no intercourse was ever attempted. "Neil," he said, "I didn't have a great battle with sexual temptation before this, but as soon as I walk through the door of her room it is as though I have no control." When I talked with his daughter, I understood why.

What was happening reminded me of Homer's depiction of the sirens (sea nymphs) whose singing lured sailors to their death on rocky coasts. Every ship that sailed too close suffered the same disastrous end. In the story, Ulysses ties himself to the mast of the ship and orders the crew to wear earplugs and ignore any pleas he might make. The mental torment of trying to resist the sirens was unbearable.

I'm not excusing this pastor, but there is a line in temptation that, when stepped over, will result in losing rational control. This pastor crossed that line when he stepped through the door of his daughter's room. As I learned later, the daughter had major spiritual problems stemming from having been molested by a youth pastor in a former ministry, and this abuse was never resolved spiritually. It wasn't the daughter who was actually sexually enticing this father; it was the demonic stronghold in her life. The "sirens" lured the father to do the unspeakable. When I met with the daughter, she couldn't even read through a prayer of commitment to stand against Satan and his attacks, which is a definite signal of enemy oppression. The father shared his struggle with his wife and, together, they sought the help they needed and worked toward resolution.

The story that follows is different from this in at least one respect. Charles's daughter had never been molested; she was never seductive and there was no apparent demonic stronghold in her life. But at some point in the pursuit of sexual gratification, Charles crossed a line beyond which he lost control. His life became dominated by a power that led him to his daughter's bedroom and caused his world to disintegrate around him. Eventually, he almost lost his life.

Charles is a successful professional who was abused as a child and who then became an abuser. Thankfully, his story doesn't end there, for after the shipwreck there was recovery.

CHARLES'S STORY

God molds those He chooses.

My story is one of God's redemption and the freedom that comes from resting in His grace, a story of being chosen for His work in spite of the opposition of His adversary, Satan. As I write this, I marvel at how little of me and how much of God is revealed in what has happened. I can only praise Him for His transforming work.

I am free from bondage to a vicious assortment of sinful attitudes and habits that cost me the respect of my family, my coworkers and my church. This bondage put me on a relentless path of personal destruction that, if left unchecked, would have taken my life as well. This freedom was bought at a terrible price that I did not pay. The suffering, death, and resurrection of my Lord Jesus Christ bought my freedom, not my own efforts or my suffering. The life I live is Christ's life, God's Son in me, not my own. And I rejoice that I am able with the help of the Holy Spirit to bring my emotions in line with what I know to be true about myself in Christ. However, this has not happened instantly, and the story of how God molds those He chooses is one of struggle and defeat as well as victory.

I ran for my life while my son loaded his pistol.

"Put down your gun! Don't do it! Jesus, help me! Jesus, help me!" My wife's anguished screams echoed in my ears as I ran for my life while my son loaded his pistol, preparing to hunt me down and kill me. I reached my car in the driveway, fumbled with the keys (*He's coming to shoot me!*) and opened the car door. Throwing my briefcase into the car, I slid behind the wheel and started the engine. I backed out of the driveway and sped down the hill, leaving my wife to struggle with my enraged son, not knowing whether he might shoot her instead, not caring enough to stay and face his wrath.

I raced down the street imagining my son pursuing me in his car, ready to run me off the road and finish the job. The side streets beckoned as a way to evade pursuit; I made several turns, finally coming to a stop under a grove of trees. My pounding heart was so loud I was sure everyone in the quiet neighborhood could hear it. My shame was so immense that I thought the end of life as I had known it was imminent. I prayed, but all that would come out were groans and hot tears, and they were all for me. I had lost my family in an instant; I was sure my career, my freedom, and perhaps my life would follow in rapid succession.

What had happened to me and to my family? What terrible fate had intervened in our affairs, threatening life itself? Where was God when I needed Him most? In my despair there were no answers, just questions and accusations. Thoughts of suicide fleetingly intruded, overcome quickly by my instinct for survival. After the initial fear of pursuit faded, I called a psychiatrist I had just met a couple of weeks before. Tearfully, I explained the situation.

I told my wife why our daughter was depressed; I had sexually molested her.

"Do you remember my telling you I felt depressed about my daughter being in the psychiatric ward for the last month?" I began. "She was committed for observation after she ran away and tried to commit suicide. Well, tonight I told my wife why our daughter was depressed; I had sexually molested her. While my wife was still reeling from the revelation, our adult son came in from work and she told him as he walked through the door. He became like a wild man, striking the walls, calling me a monster, and then he went for his gun. I ran for my life. When I left, my wife was struggling with him to keep him from shooting me. I don't know what happened after I left." I finished my confession and broke down and wept.

"Find yourself a place to set up housekeeping for a few days while we work this out," my counselor said. "Obviously, you can't go back there just now. And call me when you get settled in so we can talk."

For hours I drove aimlessly, tortured by thoughts of failure, of gross sin, of condemnation and rejection. I felt utterly dejected, despised by everyone—especially by God. I prayed and prayed but there was no answer. I phoned my supervisor at work, telling him I wouldn't be in until the next day because of a family emergency. Then I started looking at rock-bottom motels that seemed to fit my current status.

Each flea trap reminded me of how low my life had fallen, but my pride kept me from turning in to one of these and registering.

Finally, I settled on a "respectable" motel, as if to deny the power of the events that had turned my world on its head. The desk clerk asked no questions, but I was sure that the disgust must have been lurking behind his calm facade. Once inside the room, fear ran through me, unchecked, drenching me with sweat. I had lost my family, my self-respect, my cockiness, and there was nothing to replace it. I sensed only anger, rejection, condemnation; there was no hint of hope. I prayed, weeping bitterly over my loss, but not facing the sins that led to this moment. I wanted to read the Bible, but it wasn't included in the things I'd grabbed when I fled my home. The motel didn't have a Gideon Bible and I didn't think to ask the desk clerk.

There was very little sleep for me that night. I kept waking, reliving the night before, trying to figure out what I had done wrong, how I could have protected myself better. I was focused on my own feelings of rejection and unworthiness, but not on my hurting family.

What events had led to such feelings of remorse and despair? Nothing mitigates the terrible fact that sin results from the decision to disobey God. You and I are both responsible for our own decisions and actions. Sometimes it's easier to learn from others' mistakes, though. Some background may be helpful in understanding how Satan established beachheads in my life through my responses to life situations.

I was the first child, followed by a brother and two sisters, in a nonreligious family. My parents were married almost forty years until my father's premature death. Ours was a traditional family according to external appearances. My father held a succession of occupations but we didn't move very often, and material needs were always taken care of. In later years my parents were well-to-do and many luxuries were provided for us children. I felt loved and cared for (by the criteria I knew), but I really didn't know much about other kids' home lives, so comparisons were infrequent. One of the characteristics of our family was that we didn't discuss how we got along, how the family was running, or our emotional response to anything. My siblings and I didn't discuss our personal lives with one another, much less with the outside world.

One of my earliest memories was of being spanked for having a toilet-training accident on the bathroom floor. Something I had regarded with childish amusement was suddenly transformed into a time of shaming, scolding, and intense pain. I didn't know what I had done to call down such wrath; at that young age I was only aware of shame because I had disappointed my mother.

Someone had to be caught, blamed, shamed, and punished in order for everyone else to feel worthwhile.

This episode was followed by many others in which accidents, careless or not, were met with punishment and shaming. Things didn't just happen; someone had to be caught, blamed, shamed, and punished in order for everyone else in the family to feel worthwhile. I only recently learned that this pattern of attitudes had been passed down through both sides of the family for generations.

I was never sure I was valued for being myself. Value seemed to be placed on what I did. In our family we constantly jockeyed for position, trying to earn approval or denigrating someone else in order to look better by comparison. At a very early age I started to make choices based on how I would appear to my parents and any other authority figures who were in a position to judge me.

My parents were not religious. My dad, in particular, was actively hostile to all kinds of religion and rarely passed up a chance to make a disparaging remark about those who loved God. We never went to church (I was sent to Sunday school once, never to be repeated), and the Bible was not part of our family.

When I was a teenager, my grandfather gave me a Bible that his mother had given him. Its almost-new condition indicated that my grandfather couldn't have given me a tour through it after he gave it to me. He seemed to regard it as a kind of talisman to be passed from one generation to the other, but he never discussed its contents or his relationship to God (if any). So it sat on my shelf next to Bertrand Russell's *Why I Am Not a Christian*, and I got as much use out of it as my grandfather apparently had.

My father's career choices meant prolonged absences from home while he tried out new businesses in another country, leaving my mother to contend with raising us the best she could. When he was home, he was capricious and wrathful, and the spankings we got were brutal and inappropriate to the offense. There was no warmth at any time, and I remember being told on more than one occasion, "Get out of my sight! You make me sick!" My mother had her own emotional problems with my father, and she was unable to communicate her emotions to anyone, much less her children. So we were on our own, coping in our unique ways with Dad's anger and rejection of us.

When I was about eleven, I was introduced to masturbation by a classmate. Confused and fascinated, I found that I could feel better and have pleasure, if only for a few moments at a time. Lacking joy in my relationships, I found myself increasingly drawn to self-gratification as a way of getting solace and comfort when I was lonely or frightened or feeling rejected or inadequate.

The isolation bred by my solitary practice would have been bad enough, but along the way I discovered the power of fantasy to enhance the experience and heighten the stimulation. Beginning with the lingerie illustrations in the Sears catalog at my grandmother's house, I soon found out about pornography through a copy of *Playboy* magazine that my grandmother bought for me (thinking, I suppose, that it had something to do with giving young boys suggestions for play activities). When she saw the contents later that day, she quickly confiscated it. But not before my impressionable mind had its contents seared into my brain.

Finding my father's private stash of hard-core pornography on an upper shelf of his study gave further impetus to my lustful fantasies. He apparently had mail-ordered materials that were illegal at that time; similar items can be downloaded from the Internet today. I quickly learned to regard women as objects meant to satisfy my lust and stimulate me. Overwhelmed by the boundless promises of lust, I began attempting to make sexual contact with the girls my own age. I was rebuffed, learning very quickly that sexuality was something shameful. It was to be hidden, to be snickered at in locker rooms, but not to be discussed seriously with anyone.

I was adrift on the sea of lust, with no spiritual input and no sense of God's judgment at all. Each episode brought shame that could not be discussed with any friend, and certainly not with my parents. I felt more and more worthless. Throwing myself into academic pursuits, I became further alienated from my peers.

During all of this, I had the additional misfortune of being seduced by a man in a position of authority. He was a man whom I trusted and liked and whose prominence was such that I feared to tell anyone. Disgusted by the experience, confused by the attention and the sensuality, I felt violated but couldn't admit to my own rage about this until many years later. With my sexuality thoroughly confused, I continued to lust after any sensual experience I could read about or imagine. To satisfy my lust I seduced my younger brother for a period of several years, abusing his natural affections without compassion, pity, or guilt.

Pornography became my escape from the pressure of social relationships and unpleasant responsibilities.

At the same time I continued to seek out other sensual experiences and pornography. I gravitated toward those that were heterosexual, but the more perversely sexuality was depicted, the more stimulated I became. The transient "adrenaline high" was mixed with shame, the fear of getting caught, and the thrill of avoiding detection. The more I was involved with pornography, the easier it became to use it to relieve tension, escape the pressure of social relationships, and avoid unpleasant responsibilities. Pictures on a printed page could promise thrills, ready acceptance, no conflicts—

things that real women and girls my age couldn't offer. Each time I used the pornography I was driven into a depression that followed the exhilaration, and I swore that this was the last time. I reflected on what worthless scum I was. I became more and more isolated from people, rationalizing that if people really knew what I was like they wouldn't want any part of me.

After I began dating, my primary objective was to get the women I dated to meet what I perceived as being my sexual needs. Inflamed with passion by the pornography, I spent hours each day possessed by sexual thoughts and activities, missing assignments because of masturbation, fearful of reaching out socially for fear of rejection, and too stubborn to admit my life was out of control. There were interludes, of course, when my activities were more nearly "normal" because of involvement with organizations, studies, and occasional "friends." Yet even these were kept away from the core of my being because I was afraid of exposure and rejection.

Gradually I overcame my fear of girls enough to make a preoccupation out of seducing them and going as far sexually as I could. As this new outlet for my lust gained proficiency, my abuse of my brother slackened and stopped. I realize now the awful consequences for each of the victims of my lust. They were violated, their boundaries trespassed, their bodies used without care or respect. At the time I could only think of more ways to indulge in evil, each thought more perverse and against society's standards than the last. Masturbation became such a preoccupation that my grades suffered and my social relationships eventually dried up. My constant search for stimulating fantasies and experiences hurt other people, invaded their privacy and drove them away.

When I met my wife-to-be, I was on the rebound from a sexually obsessive relationship that had no solid basis. Although I knew my new love was a Christian, I had only had fleeting contact with "Bible-thumpers," as I called them. She was pretty, intelligent, caring, and needed nurturing; her childhood had been unhappy, too.

I thought she would give up Christianity as soon as she learned the truth. She thought I would convert as soon as I heard the gospel.

Neither of us received wise counsel against the relationship, much less the marriage, although we talked to several pastors before getting married. It was a hodgepodge of a ceremony. My bride read from 1 Corinthians 13 and other Scripture passages, while I said nothing religious in my speaking parts and quoted from secular and mystical sources. Significantly, I didn't vow to be faithful or to honor or cherish my wife. At the time, I was very much "in love," but I hadn't the faintest idea about the commitment my bride was making to love me in the love of Christ.

Initially, my wife, in her eagerness to please her new husband, satisfied my lust. Even in the marriage bed I considered her just another object placed there for my pleasure, to make me feel adequate and loved. I didn't really look very hard for ways to enhance her pleasure, other than to order a copy of a Hindu treatise on sex that included hundreds of acrobatic activities that we weren't athletic enough to accomplish (much to my disappointment). I was still looking for the ultimate sexual high promised by the pornography but never delivered. Such notions as commitment, nurturing, caring, communication, and fidelity were hard for me to understand.

After our first child was born, many bitter arguments ensued about the religious upbringing of our children. I insisted that they would have none. My wife tearfully shared her fear that they would be condemned to hell if they didn't know Jesus as their Lord. She wanted them to learn about Jesus while they were little. I was adamant that our children not be "brainwashed" but somehow learn about religion from someone else when they were adults. Although I took a course on the life of Christ and earned an A, I still rejected the gospel. I was abusive, hostile and blasphemed the living God in my petulance and anger. Meanwhile, my life was in disorder, although I was the last to notice.

Finally, in a time of crisis, having seen many responses to my wife's prayers that I couldn't explain away, I decided to accept the gift of salvation freely offered by the Father through His Son, Jesus Christ. I committed my life to follow Him, having very little idea what that commitment meant. For a time, I was so grateful for having been saved from hell that my lust was put on the back burner. But that didn't last long. I had privately renounced my past sins, but was unwilling to undergo the self-examination and cleansing that are necessary for a child of God to truly express the joy associated with following God in loving obedience.

When preachers or commentators talked about God as a "loving Father," that term seemed an oxymoron; I had not experienced such a father. I was expecting punishment, not praise. At the time, I didn't know what God had said about the matter: "Therefore judge nothing before the appointed time; wait till the Lord comes. He will bring to light what is hidden in darkness and will expose the motives of men's hearts. At that time each will receive his praise from God" (1 Cor. 4:5 NIV).

Shortly after I became a Christian, I engaged in my first act of adultery. I had already had adulterous thoughts, but an opportunity to put my lust into practice presented itself, and I jumped (not fell) into sin. Afterward I was so ashamed that I didn't attempt to continue the relationship. I felt remorse and tried to pray, but I didn't acknowledge to myself or to God my full responsibility in the matter. Three more times over the next several years I took advantage of opportunities to have sexual contact with other women, and my involvement with pornography continued on an episodic basis, adding fuel to the fantasy life that detracted from my relationship with my wife.

I am responsible for my actions regardless of my circumstances.

Some misguided person might offer the "consolation" that perhaps my wife was unattractive physically or emotionally, and that somehow she drove me to these sins. I have two responses: First, my wife was (and is) very lovely, and during those times she was trying to be supportive; second, I am responsible for my actions regardless of the external circumstances. My focus on sex as the means for meeting my emotional needs led to decisions to demand or take that which was not properly mine.

As years passed, my wife began to be troubled by my increasing demands for unusual sex practices, those she considered kinky or perverted. At the same time, my occasional impotence or delay in climax became more frequent. We didn't talk about these things because my wife's occasional ventures into discussing sex were met with hostility, defensiveness, or silence. I was so ashamed of the "rest" of my sex life that I felt it could not be discussed with anyone, including my wife. If anyone knew, my life would be over because I was uniquely sinful and worthy of condemnation or death.

I definitely didn't go to God; He only accepted those who were completely obedient to Him, at least in the "big things." I knew I was going to heaven, but I believed that God was only keeping a bargain. He couldn't really love me with the accretion of sinful things I had done. I felt out of control, powerless to stop my behavior. Even more serious brushes with the authorities didn't stop me from seeking the magical sexual "high" that would make me feel loved.

At the same time I pursued those fantasies, I was rejecting any real friendship or intimacy with my wife, with friends, or within Christ's church. In our local church I was an elder; I led home Bible studies; I even pursued evangelism and saw several people accept the salvation of Christ after I had shared the gospel with them. But inside, I knew no peace.

Some of the pornography I read was "Family Reading," a euphemism for stories about incest. At first the theme seemed repulsive; then it was stimulating like other perverted subjects. I didn't apply it to my own family at first. Then, as my daughter reached fourteen, I began to notice her maturation in an unhealthy way. My language at home became more suggestive, my remarks less appropriate, the jokes I brought home from work more sexual in content. I was less careful about modesty in my dress. When I saw my daughter in swimwear or nightwear, it became more difficult to avert my eyes.

Finally, when telling my daughter good night in her bedroom, I would find one pretext or another to "accidentally" brush a hand against her breast, even while praying with her. This happened over a period of several months. I became afraid of what would happen next, but told myself I couldn't help it, that I really loved my daughter. My ambivalence interfered with my sex life with my wife, and I found myself increasingly impotent with her. Even masturbation failed to satisfy.

One evening I offered to tell my daughter good night. "No, thanks, Daddy, I'm too tired," she said, as she went into her bedroom and firmly closed the door. There were no more good nights after that. She didn't want me to hug her or even touch her, claiming that her muscles were tender from workouts. A gulf grew between us, but in my deception I didn't attribute her rejection of me to the abuse of our relationship, to violating her boundaries as a person, to transgressing God's law. I attributed her coldness to "growing pains," failing to recognize that I had hurt and frightened her and had perverted our relationship.

I didn't confide in anyone what was going on in my secret life.

Several months later, relationships in our family had deteriorated severely. No one was communicating effectively with anyone else, and we were all barely coping with day-to-day existence. After a thoroughly botched vacation trip, with no one talking all the way back home, things became even worse. My wife became severely depressed, entering a psychiatric unit for more than a week. While she was there we were all distraught, yet I did not confide in anyone what was going on in my secret life that corrupted everything in our family.

Although I did not abuse our daughter during that tumultuous period, I failed to take decisive action and she became more depressed than ever. A couple of weeks after my wife returned from the hospital, our daughter ran away. When we finally tracked her down a few days later in a nearby community, she was defiant and didn't want to come back home. One of her acquaintances told us she had narrowly been prevented from committing suicide. So our daughter went into the hospital for a month.

While she was in the hospital, not a hint of the story of her sexual abuse came out until the last week. In spite of repeated questioning by the mental health team and my wife, she denied there was anything between us and so did I. It was as if we believed we could wish away the incidents, that nothing had really happened. But it had and that monstrous sin festered beneath the surface, becoming more foul. There was little progress in our daughter's depression and anger, and daily my wife and I were becoming more distant from one another.

A compulsion to protect myself produced a protracted confession lasting four days.

Finally, I woke up at four o'clock one Thursday morning, sitting bolt upright in bed with a compelling urge to confess everything to my wife. Although my intent was to tell everything, my almost-as-great compulsion to protect and defend myself produced a protracted confession lasting four days. There were falsehoods, half-truths, whole truths, all tumbling together with tears and remorse. She heard about the adultery, the incest with my siblings, seduction by the older man, the confrontations with the authorities. And she kept asking about our daughter while I kept denying there was anything amiss.

Finally, on the fourth evening, I told my wife I had abused our daughter. She sat there in stunned silence and horror. "That explains a lot," she finally said. "I couldn't put things together in my mind, but now events make sense." Just then our son walked in and you know what the rest of that evening was like. A couple of elders from our church came over that night, prayed with my family, encouraged them as much as they could and offered them help. One of them took the guns from our house. My wife contacted the Child

Protection Agency the next day (an essential action, mandated by law when abuse is discovered).

I moved to a less expensive motel for a couple of weeks while my wife decided what to do. I couldn't call the house because my son was there. My days were spent in pain, grieving my losses, berating myself. I found a Bible and began reading verses about those who are in Christ and God's love for us. I cried a lot. I read Psalm 51, King David's confession of sin with Bathsheba, over and over. I prayed aloud to God; I screamed into my pillow and drenched it with tears. I wept over the remains of a wasted life, of broken relationships.

I began to slowly realize how my sins had produced consequences in the lives of others that couldn't be erased. I talked to our friends from church from my motel room, pouring out my anguish to them. I was amazed that they didn't hang up on me. They didn't approve of my behavior, but they were still talking to me.

I couldn't attend the church my wife and daughter were attending, so I looked in the Yellow Pages for a church close to my motel. I was sure my shame was written all over my face, but I knew I had to be with God's people, even if they threw me out on my face. The first service I attended was about sin and God's mercy. I sat there with tears blinding me, the lump in my throat preventing me from singing.

After the service I asked the man who had been sitting next to me to recommend a mature Christian I could talk to. Sensing the urgency in my voice, he introduced me to a man about my age who took me outside to talk. Sobbing, I told him the whole story, sparing nothing. "I don't want your church just to accept me as some kind of super saint, welcoming me with open arms," I said. "I've hurt a lot of people and my sin has hurt me as well."

I'll never forget that man's response: "Friend, this church is a place for healing. You are welcome here." Unmerited grace flooded my heart and I wept uncontrollably at his generosity. I had never considered the church to have a ministry to people wounded by their sin. But I returned the next Sunday and took the risk of meeting some of the elders of the church and the pastor and sharing my story with them. I asked for prayer for my family and for me. The response didn't excuse my sin, but it was clear that they considered me a child of God worthy of respect. I was overwhelmed by gratitude.

My wife was grief-stricken, angry, fearful, and depressed over the revelations of my infidelity. In spite of that, she took time to call me at the motel and check on me. She got me the essentials for living out of the house and smuggled them to me. She spent hours in secluded places with me, talking out her frustrations and encouraging me to deal with reality as I confronted my sins.

We had periods when emotions were so high we didn't talk to one another for days at a time, but God always brought us back to each other.

> *"There are major problems here, but none that God can't handle."*

One of our friends from our old church recommended a Christian counselor he had known for years: "He's a gentle man, full of wisdom, and I've heard that everything he tells you he backs up with scriptural truths so you can check it out." Although I was seeing a secular psychiatrist, we decided to go to this man for help. He listened to the whole sordid story and said, "There are major problems here, but none that God can't handle." He began to teach us to communicate the feelings in our hearts with one another without killing one another's spirits in the process. He taught us the basis for sin and our reaction to it, beginning with Adam and Eve in the Garden of Eden and working from there through the Bible. We began to see hope.

In addition to the counseling sessions, our counselor recommended several books to read as we went along. One book he recommended was *Victory Over the Darkness* by Neil Anderson, a book about Christian maturity. For the first time, I began to understand that because I am in Christ, certain things are true about me that are also true of Christ.

Because of my identity in Christ, I have power over the things in my life that I always assumed were beyond my control. In particular,

I learned that my emotions and my actions are governed by who I believe myself to be. If I believe a lie about my essential nature, whether it is from the world, the flesh, or the devil, then I will act according to that belief. Similarly, if I choose to believe what God has said about me, then I will govern my thoughts and my actions that proceed from those thoughts in accordance with God's will.

I experienced a dramatic sense of joy and freedom in realizing the permanence and solidity of God's love for me that transcends any particulars of sin. It was a profound revelation to see from the Scriptures that I am not just "a sinner saved by grace," but I am a saint who sins, one who is called out and sanctified by God. I learned from our counselor how to appropriate the truth that I have an advocate before the Father who is constantly there to counter the charges made by Satan against God's elect. I began to experience periods of real joy for the first time, interspersed with periods of melancholy and deep, abiding sorrow before God for my sins against Him and against other people, particularly my daughter and my wife.

Times of self-hatred were finally terminated by my wife's reminding me, "You need to remember that if God has forgiven your sins in Christ, you must now forgive yourself." I have had to work toward forgiveness of those who hurt me in the past, not because those hurts are an excuse for sins old or new, but because the unforgiveness kept me bottled up. I have asked for and received forgiveness from those family members I hurt (with the exception of my children, who are still struggling with it), and have been reconciled to them, knowing true intimacy for the first time in my life with my brother and sisters and mother. My father died as an unbeliever a number of years ago, rejecting the gospel till the last. It has been hardest forgiving him for the rage and neglect, but God has called me to that as well.

I had been attending two different twelve-step groups for "sexual addiction," and finally quit when I realized that they were elevating sexual sobriety on a pedestal as the end of their efforts. Although they acknowledged a "Higher Authority," they weren't permitted to identify that Authority as Jesus Christ. When they had a split vote on whether sex was permitted only in marriage or just in a "committed relationship," whether homosexual or heterosexual, I realized I was in the wrong place and left the groups for good.

The only thing those groups did for me was to help me realize a context for my sexual dysfunction in society: There are plenty of people out there involved in sexual sin. But these groups could not offer the spiritual perspective that identified the life-changing power of Jesus Christ inside the hearts of those who trust and obey Him. Because of that, I am hesitant to recommend their "self-help" approach, particularly if it detracts from relationships within the body of Christ. These groups often claim in meetings that the "addicts" are the only ones who can understand one another, that they are the addict's true family. To a Christian, such an attitude misses the point of the body of Christ caring for its members who are hurting.

I learned how we enable Satan and his unholy angels to establish footholds.

The second book I read that shed tremendous light and was a pivotal work in giving hope and direction to my struggle was Neil Anderson's *The Bondage Breaker*. This book deals extensively with spiritual warfare and the demonic side of habitual sin. I learned how we enable Satan and his unholy angels to establish footholds, then strongholds in our spiritual lives as we fail to live in our identity with Christ and appropriate the aspects of His character that are already ours. In reminding me that Satan is a vanquished foe who has no power over me that I do not relinquish to him, the book gave hope for victory in the spiritual and the physical struggle over sin.

I began to read aloud the spiritual truths that Neil had included in both books that show our identity in Christ and the results of that identity. As I affirmed my identity and then struggled with the discrepancy between my attitudes, thought life, and behavior, in contrast to my nature in Christ, I was often overwhelmed with grief and self-condemnation. I renounced the strongholds that Satan had established, experiencing progressive freedom as each trouble area was identified. It is only after months of struggle that I have gotten where God wants me: confident in Him, not in myself, and confident in His love for me that will not fade or fail.

My wife and I have worked for the last year toward re-establishing our relationship, based not on lust and exploitation but on the solid foundation of Jesus Christ. Gradually, we have dealt with issues of sin and forgiveness, and we are friends again. We still have arguments, conflicts, and hurt feelings to deal with, but our tools are better. We are building a track record of success in resolving our past and present conflicts.

The bondage to sin that I allowed to happen has been broken.

I still struggle with my emotions, but I am able to feel the full range from profound sadness to great joy, and God is with me in all of them. Do I still sin? Surely, but I am a saint who sins, and I am able to confess to God, remembering 1 John 1:9: "If we confess our sins, he is faithful and just and will forgive us our sins and purify us from all unrighteousness" (NIV). And very important, I have been freed from the sexual compulsion that grew out of believing Satan's lies about my true nature.

With the help of my therapist I have been learning to recognize and acknowledge emotions. With the help of the Holy Spirit I have the power to do good rather than evil. I have not been magically freed from temptation; the more closely I draw toward God, the more the tempter presents opportunities for sin. Recognizing that my thoughts will bear fruit if they are allowed to, I am constantly making choices for what is right. The bondage to sin that I allowed to happen through my sinful choices has been broken. In the midst of the evil around me, I am learning to flee temptation, resist the devil, and be in the world but not of it. I stand on God's promise:

No temptation has seized you except what is common to man. And
God is faithful; he will not let you be tempted beyond what you can
bear. But when you are tempted, he will also provide a way out so
that you can stand up under it. (1 Cor. 10:13 NIV)

Still, I am confident that God's timing and His methods are perfect, that His plan of redemption has no flaws. I am grateful for His
restoration and I look forward to the time when all wounds are
healed, all tears are wiped away, and reconciliation in Christ is per-
fected. Until then, I am learning how to function as a person who
takes responsibility for his actions, and I am learning to love my wife
the way God intended. Now I am able to pray, to study Scripture
with gratitude, to praise God for His grace, to rest in His provision
for my life. Thanks to understanding my identity in Christ, I am
free! I can live the life God calls me to live!

Five years after the first edition of this book was released, I accidentally met this couple again in a restaurant. They wanted to tell
me about the class on marriage they were teaching in their church.
I hesitated at first, but finally I asked how the children were doing.
"Oh, we are all reconciled, and our son is going into full-time ministry." Talk about the power of God to transform lives.

WHO ARE THE HURTING?

When I was on the faculty at Talbot School of Theology, I taught our
basic ethics class entitled, "Church and Society." The purpose was to
discuss the church's role in society. In the second half of the semes-
ter we invited local experts to address specific moral issues. I enjoyed
the class because every spring it was a learning experience for me as
well. As the guests came to give their presentations, I warned the students not to "pick up everybody's burden" or they would be overwhelmed. However, they should sense their passion, because those

speakers had been called by God to meet the needs of hurting people in our society, and that is also the ministry of the church.

The continuous concern I hear from Christians who work with the abused in parachurch ministries is their frustration with the church. Many think the church is living in denial and even providing a safe haven for wife beaters, child abusers, and alcoholics. Churches fail to defend the victim and provide sanctuary for the abusers, under the guise of avoiding scandal. Consequently, neither the abuser nor the abused gets help. That, of course, is not totally true, but it does happen and all too often.

MALE AND FEMALE SEXUALITY

We are created as sexual beings: Female vaginal lubrication and male erections take place in the first twenty-four hours after birth. Infants need to experience warmth and touch in order for parental bonding to take place, and trust is developed during the first few months of life. Abuse or neglect even during this early time will have lasting detrimental effects, so it shouldn't be hard to see how severely children can be affected if they are abused later in early childhood when there is even greater awareness.

All sexual anatomy is present at birth and becomes developed in early adolescence. Hormones start secreting three years before puberty. In the female, estrogen and progesterone are very irregular until a year after puberty when a regular rhythmic monthly pattern is established. The wall of the vagina thins and vaginal lubrication decreases after menopause, as hormone secretion decreases.

In the male, testosterone increases at puberty, reaches a maximum at twenty, decreases at forty, and becomes almost zero at eighty. Normal aging causes a slower erection and less sexual functioning, but not a complete stopping of those functions. While a man is sleeping he will have an erection every eighty to ninety minutes.

All this is a part of God's wonderful creation, which we are to watch over as good stewards. However, this beautiful plan for procreation and expression of love can be grossly distorted.

Healing a Distorted Sexual Development

God intended sex to be for pleasure and procreation within the boundaries of marriage. But when sex becomes a "god," it is ugly, boring and enslaving. Heaping condemnation on those who are enslaved is ill advised. Increasing shame and guilt will prove counterproductive and will not produce good mental health, Christian character, or self-control. Guilt does not inhibit sexual arousal, and may even contribute to it and keep us from using our sexuality wholesomely as God intends. Instead of condemnation, I would offer the following steps for those who have had a distorted sexual development.

1. *Face up to your present condition before God.* There are no secrets with God. He knows the thoughts and intentions of your heart (Heb. 4:11–13), and you don't ever have to fear rejection by being honest with Him and confessing your sin and expressing your need. Confession is simply being truthful with God and living in continuous agreement with Him. The opposite of confession is not silence but rationalization and self-justification, attempting to excuse or deny your behavior. This will never lead you to freedom. Your journey out of sexual bondage must include God in an honest and intimate way.

2. *Commit yourself to a biblical view of sex.* All sexual expressions were intended by God to be associated with love and trust, which are necessary to ensure good sexual functioning. Recent evidence indicates that trust may be one of the most important factors determining orgasmic capacity in women. To ensure trust means that we never have the right to violate another person's conscience. *If it is wrong for your spouse, it is wrong for you.*

Too many wives have tearfully asked me if they have to submit to their husband's every request. Usually their husbands are asking for some kinky expression hoping to satisfy their lust. Some actually appeal to Hebrews 13:4, saying "the wedding bed is undefiled" and claiming that the Bible permits all expressions of sex in a marriage. No five words are taken out of context more than those. The verse continues: "for fornicators and adulterers God will judge." The idea is to keep the wedding bed undefiled with no adultery or fornication.

A wife can meet the sexual needs of her husband, but she will never be able to satisfy his lust.

A biblical view of sex is always personal. It is an intimate expression of two people who are in love with each other. People who are in bondage to sex or are bored with it have depersonalized it. They become obsessed with sexual thoughts in hope for more excitement, and because obsessional sex is always depersonalized, boredom increases and obsessive thoughts grow stronger. One man actually told me that his practice of masturbation is not sinful because in his fantasies the women have no heads! I told him that is precisely what is wrong with what he is doing. Fantasizing another as a sex object, as opposed to seeing them as a person created in the image of God, is precisely the problem. Even the porno queen is some mother's daughter, not just a piece of meat.

A biblical view of sex is also associated with safety and security. Outside of God's plan, fear and danger can also cause sexual arousal. For instance, sneaking into a porno shop will cause sexual arousal long before an actual sexual stimulant is present. And voyeurism is very resistant to treatment because arousal is not just from the viewing— the excitement comes from violating a forbidden cultural standard. The emotional peak is heightened by the presence of fear and danger.

One man said he was into "exciting sex." He would rent a motel room and commit adultery in the swimming pool where the possibility of being caught heightened the climax. Such people must separate fear and danger from sexual arousal. A biblical view of sex is associated with safety and security so that the maximum fulfillment comes from a complete surrender of oneself to another in trust and love. Some people buy the lie that the forbidden fruit is the sweetest, denying the crucial importance of the relationship between a man and a woman in finding pleasure and fulfillment in sex.

We should also abstain from any use of the sex organs other than that which was intended by the Creator. I was not built upside down, nor intended to walk on my hands. Parts of my body are created to dispose of unusable body fluids and substances. I do not believe oral sex reflects the Creator's design for proper use of body parts, and one does not need to have someone from the opposite sex to participate. Even personal hygiene would suggest that this expression isn't what God intended.

Why are we continually looking for the ultimate sexual experience? Why aren't we looking for the ultimate personal experience with God and each other, and letting sex within marriage be an expression of that? Good sex will not make a good marriage, but a good marriage will have good sex.

3. *Seek forgiveness from all those you have sexually offended.* I encourage every man to go to his wife and ask for forgiveness for any violation of trust. Our wives can sense when something is wrong; don't let them guess. Wives play a critical role in helping their husbands live sexually free in Christ. Men are more vulnerable sexually, and they need the caring support and discernment that a loving wife can provide. Both Doug, from our last chapter, and Charles finally confessed everything to their wives. Humbling? Yes, but that is the path to freedom.

Charles also had to seek forgiveness from his children. In some cases, it may take years before that comes. Sadly, some never come to the point of forgiving their abuser, and so the cycle of abuse continues. Abused children usually become abusive themselves, and their children will suffer the result of yet another parent in bondage. If the victim chooses not to forgive the abuser, he or she is living in the bondage of bitterness. Yet for the restored abuser to live in condemnation because he or she has not been forgiven by the victim is to deny the finished work of Christ. Christ died once for all for the sins of the world. We must believe, live, and teach that in order to stop the cycle of abuse. We all have the right and privilege to throw ourselves on the mercy of God.

4. *Renew your mind.* Abnormal sex is a product of obsessive thoughts. These thoughts become self-perpetuating because of the physical and mental reinforcement that comes from each mental perception and repeated action. The mind can only reflect upon that which is seen, stored, or vividly imagined, and we are responsible for what we think and for our own mental purity.

I remember that when I first became a Christian, I committed myself to clean up my mind. As you can imagine, the problem became worse, not better. If you are giving in to sexual thoughts, temptation doesn't seem that strong, but when you determine not to sin, temptation becomes stronger. I remember singing songs just to keep my mind focused. My life and experiences would be quite innocent compared to most people I have talked to, but it took a long time to renew my mind from the images I had programmed into it earlier.

Imagine your mind to be the coffee in a pot. The fluid is dark and smelly because of the old coffee grounds (pornographic material and sexual experiences) that have been put into it. There is no way to rid the bitter taste and ugly coloring that now permeate it, no way to filter it out. You can, and must, get rid of the "grounds." All pornographic material must go!

Now imagine a bucket of crystal-clear ice alongside the coffeepot representing the Word of God. If you were to take at least one ice cube every day and put it into the coffeepot, the coffee would eventually be watered down to the point where you couldn't smell or see the coffee that was originally in there. That would work as long as you are not putting in one ice cube and one *Playboy.*

Paul writes in Colossians 3:15: "And let the peace of Christ rule in your hearts, to which indeed you were called in one body; and be thankful." How are we going to let Christ rule in our hearts? The next verse says, "Let the word of Christ richly dwell within you, with all wisdom teaching and admonishing one another with psalms and hymns and spiritual songs, singing with thankfulness in your hearts to God."

As Jesus modeled, we must stand against temptation with the truth of God's Word. When that tempting thought first hits, take it captive to the obedience of Christ (2 Cor. 10:5). "How can a young man keep his way pure? By keeping it according to Thy word . . . Thy word I have treasured in my heart, that I may not sin against Thee" (Ps. 119:9, 11). Winning the battle for our minds is often two steps forward and one step back. Eventually, it is three steps forward and one back. Then it's five steps forward and one back, until there are so many positive steps forward that the "one back" is a fading memory. Remember, you may despair in confessing when you fall again and again, but He never despairs in forgiving.

5. *Seek legitimate relationships that meet your needs* of love and acceptance. People with sexual addictions tend to isolate themselves. We need each other; we were never designed to survive alone. Charles sought out Christian help and fellowship. Few do that, however, because of the shame. Consequently, they stay in bondage. When we are satisfied in our relationships, deep legitimate needs are met. Finding fulfillment in sexual expressions instead of relationships will lead to addiction.

6. *Learn to walk by the Spirit.* Galatians 5:16 says, "Walk by the Spirit, and you will not carry out the desire of the flesh."(NASB) A legalistic walk with God will only bring condemnation, but a dependent relationship with Him, with His grace sustaining us, is our real hope. In my book *Walking in the Light* (Thomas Nelson, 1992), I seek to define what it means to have God's guidance and a life that is enabled by His Spirit.

Admittedly, overcoming sexual bondage is difficult, and that is why we need the grace of God. The terrible cost of not fighting for that freedom is too high a price to pay. Your sexual freedom is worth the fight.

PART TWO

Professional Integration

and Current Research

Introduction

The chapters that follow describe the discipleship counseling approach developed by Freedom in Christ Ministries in actual clinical psychotherapy cases. They also include psychological testing data in order to assess the impact of the Steps to Freedom and to investigate the overall efficacy of an overtly Christian therapy approach in general. In short, do the numbers support the assertions that the method and message of Freedom in Christ Ministries bear fruit? Some more dubious readers may have even skipped the testimonies in Part One to find out!

Before we tell you about the research, we thought it would be important for you to know a little more about us (Fernando Garzon and Judith King). How did we even become interested in researching the message and ministry of Freedom in Christ in the first place? We approached Freedom in Christ Ministries from different perspectives. If you're a therapist, perhaps you'll identify with one of us. We've also discovered that many clinicians have stereotypes or misconceptions about Dr. Anderson's work, so we've included a section clarifying some of these common stereotypes. Afterward, we will discuss the advantages to using the Freedom in Christ approach in therapy, and finally the research methodology will be described.

JUDITH'S PERSONAL PERSPECTIVE

At this point in the book, you've read some amazing stories of individuals who have experienced healing and freedom by resolving their personal and spiritual conflicts through genuine repentance and faith in God. They are testimonies of the liberating truth of God's Word and the power of the Holy Spirit. These brave men and women were led through the Steps to Freedom by nonprofessional lay encouragers in a church ministry setting. Now, you might be wondering how this message and methodology can fit into the mental health profession.

That is exactly what I was wondering. As a clinical social worker in the field of mental health, I have worked as an outpatient therapist at a Christian hospital, as well as in private practice for more than fifteen years. I, like many of you, believe in the importance of addressing not only the physical and psychological but also the spiritual components of my clients' problems. I have observed a spiritual hunger in my clients and the world in general as never before, which only makes our understanding of mental health and spiritual well-being more complex. It raises many questions for those of us who have been raised and educated in a Western culture dominated by rationalism and naturalism! With this complexity, should we leave the spiritual component to the pastors and chaplains? More and more we are seeing clients who have been involved in New Age religions or dabbled in the occult. Many describe an awareness of an evil presence and/or struggles with blasphemous and tormenting mental thoughts. They ask for our help in resolving spiritual issues, but as Christian mental health professionals, do we know how? As a case in point, see Chapter 9, which is Joanne's story. Should we refer them to a pastor, or is there a way we can provide spiritual as well as psychological answers in the context of therapy?

For me, striving for a biblical worldview wasn't the main obstacle. Life's experiences have reinforced my belief in the reality of both God and the devil as a spiritual influence. As an eleven-year-old seeker, I had become a Christian at a Billy Graham Crusade. From that time on, I have followed Christ. I have been blessed by His presence, His faithfulness, and His extravagant love. I know as truth that He "is able to do exceedingly abundantly above all that [I] ask or think" (Eph. 3:20 NKJV). Having worked on the mission field for several years, I had seen individuals dramatically set free from demonic influences. As a young adult I had been catapulted into praying for a suffering demonized woman. The only thing I knew how to do was to call on the name of Jesus. He came, and she was set free. I remember experiencing an overwhelming sense of Jesus' love. It was palpable. Not surprisingly, this woman came to a lasting faith in Christ. All of this made an indelible impression on me, but I didn't know how to fit this into my "ordinary" life in an ongoing way.

Through the years of family life, ministry overseas, and then graduate school I had continued to see God's healing love at work, and for that I am grateful, but quite frankly, I had some trepidation of knowing how to address the demonic with my patients with any kind of confidence. Just after I had completed graduate school, I was introduced to Dr. Anderson's material and was challenged by my supervising psychiatrist to read and study his first two books, *Victory Over the Darkness* and *The Bondage Breaker*. Finally, an area of ministry, which for me had many questions, started to come into focus. A group of my colleagues, mental health professionals, psychiatrists, social workers, psychologists, nurses, and chaplains, formed a study group to view, discuss, and evaluate the videos "Resolving Personal and Spiritual Conflicts." We couldn't deny the truths presented from the Word of God and the miraculous interventions that were reported. Dr. Anderson's approach, which has as its core our identity and position in Christ as well as the victory and authority over the enemy, made sense. I was seeing the gospel of Christ at work, "to open eyes that are blind, to free captives from prison and to release from the dungeon those who sit in darkness" (Isaiah 42:7 NIV). We were impressed with the richness and the promise of this entirely solid biblical approach.

The fact was, many of our clients who professed Christianity were still in bondage to sinful habits and were not experiencing any mental peace. They didn't know what it really meant to be a "child of God." I began to use some of Dr. Anderson's material, especially his work on forgiveness, in my seminars with clergy and missionaries overseas. These seasoned Christian leaders also found Dr. Anderson's material and concepts very helpful. I was beginning to wonder if I could use this biblical tool, the "Steps to Freedom," as an adjunct to therapy in my counseling office.

Then my husband and I met Dr. Anderson at a conference for Christian leaders. He recommended that my husband (a psychiatrist) and I attend a Freedom in Christ Conference. There, he said, we could see the process for ourselves, and actually observe as prayer partners led people through individual Freedom Appointments. We did sit in on their counseling sessions and were impressed at the emotional and physical healing that occurred when they recognized, confessed, and renounced sins and lies, and then embraced the truth of who they are in Christ. I received a follow-up letter several months later that testified to the lasting changes a lady had experienced as a result of her Freedom Appointment.

I came home from that conference desiring to integrate the Steps to Freedom into my therapy with people, but quite honestly, I didn't know where to start! I wondered if this material could work in the context of therapy, since most of Dr. Anderson's material at that time had been written for church lay counselors to take people through the Steps in one sitting. After coming back from that conference, my prayer was, "Lord, please teach me. I'm a therapist, You called me to be a therapist, I love being a therapist, but I've no idea how to integrate this into therapy. Please teach me." Little did I know!

Edith

Edith, a new patient, was the first person scheduled to see me in my office when I returned from the FIC Conference. A professional woman in her late fifties, married with grown children, she was an expert in business and computer technology. She had been an active, committed Christian for more than seventeen years but recently had experienced debilitating anxiety with tormenting destructive voices, "strange things" waking her at night, and panic attacks. She was so terrorized by this "evil" she felt that she slept with her Bible and was embarrassed to mention these experiences to anyone. She'd already had fifteen-plus years of traditional therapy. "I know I need spiritual help with this," she said. "Someone told me about Neil Anderson's 'Steps to Freedom' and that I should go through them. Do you know anything about them?" I was amazed at her question since I had not prompted her with my recent musings about the Freedom in Christ approach!

I got out my copy of the Steps to Freedom and was wondering where to start. First, I proceeded with my initial evaluation—addressing the anxiety of the moment, assuring her of confidentiality, taking a short social history, ascertaining her mental status, ego strengths, suicidal potential, support system, and pre-morbid condition. She was ready and even asked to proceed with the Steps to Freedom, so we did. God was gracious and so willing to teach me.

We took two hours that day and covered the first two steps. Out tumbled previously unspoken experiences with the occult, traumas, fears, torments, and false beliefs about herself which she identified, confessed, and renounced. She learned for the first time that as a believer, she could herself submit to God, resist the devil, and command him to flee (James 4:7). And he did! She experienced significant relief from her anxiety. The next day we met for another two hours and completed the Steps. Her tormenting anxiety had disappeared, the accusing voices were gone, and she had slept the night before for the first time in months.

I continued to meet with Edith for the next couple of months, affirming her new spiritual identity and the new truths that she learned, and explored other issues as they surfaced. Edith summed up her experience in the following letter to me:

> During the process of the Freedom in Christ steps I found myself sharing things with a woman I had met just the day before. I shared things with her that I had not shared with anyone else, and things came tumbling out as we prayed and talked through the steps. I felt no need to decide what to share and what not to share. It was as if

each thing had to be said and was then blown away. I realized later that I had experienced no fears of condemnation, no feelings of needing to protect myself, no regrets of *What will she think of me?*

After years of psychotherapy, I know how to play the psychotherapy game, but in this session there were only truth and love and there was finally, finally, finally, no fear. It was as if this session were being directed by an unseen force who knew specifically what I needed and what things had to be brought into the light. Thing after thing seemed to tumble out, and again and again I felt blanketed, covered, and protected by the prayers we prayed together. After I left, I expected the terrible thoughts to return, but my intense fear and anxiety were gone. In its place were actually weapons, which I could use at every attack. I knew I was protected. I knew Satan was defeated. I knew my God reigns. I now understand better than ever before the power of the lies that Satan plants, and the fears that follow and cripple. His greatest deception is that we believe it is something wrong within us instead of taking our stand in Christ with the weapons God has given us.

I'm FREE!

Forever

Redeemed

Eternally

Elevated!

The oppression is gone. The obsession is gone. The fear is gone. The anxiety is gone. I don't think I've hidden it, controlled it, or rationalized it. It's gone, forever, broken by the blood of Jesus. He has given me through the Steps to Freedom the weapons I need to fight the accuser. Our God reigns!

This was my first experience with using the Steps to Freedom in Christ in my office. Certainly, this focused approach brought amazing results for Edith, and for me it was the beginning of another amazing adventure with God. Since then I have led about one hundred clients through the steps in combination with therapy. I thank God for teaching me this tool and I give Him the praise!

While I was learning how to combine the Steps to Freedom in my professional office, I was also involved in training area lay counselors in preparation for the FIC conference that we had organized for the following year. Twelve different churches of varying denominations jointly sponsored this conference. Because of my personal interest in research, I designed an FIC questionnaire (a self-rated symptom checklist consisting of ten questions) to be given to counselees before their Freedom Appointment and three months after their appointment. I wanted to see if the numbers from this survey corroborated the phenomenal results that people reported. Since that conference six years ago, lay counselors from the various churches that participated in the conference have used this survey questionnaire. They have conducted several hundred Freedom Appointments. The data from these collected questionnaires have been summarized in three pilot studies and the results are reported in Chapter 11.

These studies spurred me on to further clinical case studies in cooperation with Dr. George Hurst (formerly the director of the University of Texas Medical Center) and his group from Tyler, Texas, and Dr. Fernando Garzon, who teaches at Regent University. The results of these recent studies utilizing additional psychometrically formed testing instruments are reported in the remainder of this book.

FERNANDO'S PERSONAL PERSPECTIVE

My story is very different from Judy's. Whereas Judy has always been comfortable with the spiritual elements of the case studies you've read in the first part of this book, I would have thought that these people were just mentally ill a few years ago. Indeed, I'm glad Edith hadn't ended up in my office seven years ago! Perhaps hearing my own spiritual journey will help you understand why.

I became a Christian when I was sixteen years old and immediately got involved in various Bible studies and small Christian fellowships. These were very good experiences for me, furnishing much love and support. I continued growing in the Lord and eventually went to college. There I began encountering many friends who clearly needed some emotional healing. These friends went through deliverance, prayer sessions, and studied their Bibles, but they didn't seem to get better. That bothered me, because that was basically all I knew from a spiritual perspective about how they might get help. I became more curious and began asking questions that most of my Christian friends couldn't answer.

After college graduation, I began working at a psychiatric hospital to learn more about helping people. I found I thoroughly enjoyed the work and began considering a career as a psychologist. I eventually went to Fuller Seminary and received my doctorate in clinical psychology. While there, I learned a great deal more about what causes emotional distress and discovered strategies for helping people. Unfortunately, one thing I didn't learn was how to answer my initial questions about why spiritual interventions like deliverance, Bible study, and prayer had been so limited in helpfulness with the people I'd known in college! Without clear answers, I began to de-emphasize the role of the spiritual in the healing process and to focus more on secular techniques. I might pray for my clients occasionally, but that was about the limit of my explicitly Christian interventions after graduate school.

The question of concrete, effective Christian interventions, however, continued to haunt me. I had plenty of excellent secular techniques at my disposal and some very good theology pertaining to integrating Christianity into my work, but the amount of concrete Christian intervention strategies I knew was dismal. Indeed, as I continued my clinical work, I started to ask myself serious questions as a Christian psychologist. If you're a Christian therapist, consider how the following scenario relates to you.

Suppose someone takes a film of your work and that of a secular therapist who happens to be well trained in how to sensitively handle religious issues in treatment. A born-again Christian walks into your office and wants Christianity actively integrated into treatment. Ten sessions are filmed. Let's say that same born-again Christian walks into the religiously-sensitive therapist's office and ten sessions are also filmed. When someone watches both films, will they be able to tell who is the Christian therapist and who is the sensitively-trained secular therapist? Would there be enough concrete differences for an observer to say, "Yes, that's the Christian therapist, and that's the well-trained secular therapist"? As I thought about it, I realized that the only difference between us might be an opening prayer in which I asked God to guide the session or a closing prayer in which I summarized the issues the client brought in that day and asked God to help them. That was unsatisfactory for me. If those were the only overt Christian intervention strategies I used with Christian clients, then I hadn't learned very much that I didn't already know before my graduate school training! In short, if a Christian client wanted Jesus actively integrated into treatment, I had little to offer.

So I began asking the Lord to show me concrete Christian intervention strategies. Eventually, I found Neil's first two books, *Victory Over the Darkness* and *The Bondage Breaker*. Quickly, I saw that these books espoused approaches compatible with a well-researched clinical psychotherapy called cognitive therapy, yet they were much broader in addressing a variety of areas consistent with a biblical worldview. Indeed, these books opened my eyes to an entirely different way of conceptualizing spiritual influences in therapy. They certainly were not the typical deliverance ministries I had been exposed to in my early Christian days. They had something more. Demons were not the major problem; rather, root issues and unresolved conflicts in our lives were the major problem. Based on my previous experiences (and now as a Christian psychologist), I could readily agree with that.

I continued to read other books by Dr. Anderson and cautiously started applying the Steps to Freedom in some of my cases. I found the Steps to be a valuable addition to my work. Since I was also an assistant professor at Regent University, I began wondering whether Dr. Anderson was open to having his approach subjected to scientific scrutiny. Much to my surprise, he was. Chapter 11 describes some of the current Freedom in Christ research.

Judy has already described some of her early work with the Steps to Freedom and how that led her eventually into researching the approach, so I won't go over my own similar experiences in therapy. Rather, we will start by commenting on some stereotypes that many Christian therapists have in regard to Dr. Anderson's work. Let's address these, along with advantages to using the Steps to Freedom, before we go into details about the case study research.

COMMON STEREOTYPES OF DR. ANDERSON'S WORK

Everything Is a Demon Problem

Some therapists who have read or heard of only one of Dr. Anderson's books, *The Bondage Breaker,* may have this stereotype. But even in this book, Dr. Anderson doesn't teach that demons are the primary problem nor the expulsion of demons the only answer. He teaches that the real issue is our relationship with God, and the answer is repentance and faith in Him. He emphasizes that truth sets us free, and a major part of that truth is based on our identity and position in Christ. Dr. Anderson believes that our freedom as believers is more of a truth encounter than a power encounter, and that is consistent with cognitive therapy.

Dr. Anderson has actively collaborated with mental health professionals in several more recent works. His book on depression (*Finding Hope Again*) was written with Dr. Hal Baumchen, a clinical psychologist. He has also written a book with Dr. Terry Zuehlke, a clinical psychologist, and Julie Zuehlke, a psychiatric nurse, entitled *Christ Centered Therapy.* This book on integration addresses the role of a wide variety of factors in spiritual and mental health and discusses numerous Christian interventions that can be included in treatment.

Truly, spiritual and emotional problems arise from a variety of sources, including biological ones. The Bible reflects a broad worldview, addressing a wide range of areas that contribute to emotional distress. Demons can sometimes be involved in emotional distress, but when they are, it is usually because of an underlying issue such as unforgiveness, occult involvement, deception, etc. These issues are the primary problems that need to be addressed rather than the demon itself. Deliverance, if necessary, is a calm, quiet process with the Steps to Freedom. The priority is on resolving root issues much more than an encounter with a demon.

Psychiatric Medications Are Never Needed

Dr. Anderson recognizes the role of biology in many mental disorders and supports the judicious use of psychiatric medications (*See Christ Centered Therapy, Finding Hope Again,* and *Freedom from Fear* for detailed information). He does not believe, however, that medications are the entire answer to a person's emotional distress in most situations. He has said repeatedly, "Taking a pill to cure your body is commendable, but taking a pill to cure your soul is deplorable, and may the good Lord enable us to know the difference."

Psychotherapy Is Never Needed

While Dr. Anderson questions the value of secular psychotherapy because it might promote self-independence from God as the ultimate source of a person's well-being, he strongly supports the role of Christian psychotherapy in the healing process. Again, see *Christ Centered Therapy* for more information. He questions the value of secular psychology as he would question the value of liberal theology. He believes the Bible provides an authoritative basis for a truly Christian psychology.

THERAPEUTIC ADVANTAGES

Let's consider next some possible advantages of using the Freedom in Christ process in clinical treatment. In therapy, the client experiences God's love, in part, through the therapeutic relationship with the counselor as "Christ with skin." The unconditional positive regard of the therapist provides the client, to a limited human extent, with an understanding of the unconditional, unfailing love of our Abba Father. This awareness of the Lord's love deepens further through overt Christian interventions like the Steps to Freedom. It is important to keep in mind that the Steps to Freedom don't set anybody free. Repentance and faith in God are what sets us free. The

Steps to Freedom are only a tool that can be used rightly or wrongly. What is important are the underlying theology and psychology that provide the basis for this approach to conflict resolution.

Used in treatment, the Steps to Freedom must always be put in the context of a caring relationship with the therapist. The Steps themselves are best conceptualized as a flexible framework that has key ingredients of confession, renunciation, forgiveness, and scriptural declarations. Like any intervention, the Steps must not be applied in a formulaic, cookie-cutter manner. The therapist must always be open to the Holy Spirit's guidance in implementing each step. The therapeutic relationship and the Holy Spirit's leading are always key ingredients in making this intervention work. The seven steps are not seven formulas that one mechanically applies. They are seven issues that are critically important in our relationship with God. With these essential ingredients in mind, many positive advantages exist for using the Freedom in Christ process in treatment. The following are some of them.

Clearly Connecting the Client's Faith in Christ with the Healing Process

Therapy is a vehicle for trust, growth, support, and empathy; elements some clients have never experienced before in their lives. It provides a safe, nonthreatening environment for exploration of past hurts with the goal of resolution, healing, and restoration. The Steps clearly connect the therapeutic process with the healing power of Jesus Christ. Their overt, explicitly Christian focus connects the counselee more fully to the role the Holy Spirit wants to play in the healing and recovery process.

Establishing the Client's Identity and Sense of Worth in Christ

Jesus Christ is the only real source of our true identity and sense of worth. If we as therapists try to help people discover their identity and sense of worth without God in their lives, then we are working against the spiritual truth that without God we are incomplete. Indeed, we are ignoring what St. Augustine called a "God-shaped vacuum" in our lives and enabling people to live independent of God. This works against the very purpose of the Gospel and bypasses our deep need for God in our lives.

Helping counselees understand their true identity in Christ promotes a healthy sense of worth, which is founded on an eternal foundation (Matt. 7:24–27). A true identity and healthy sense of worth are only possible as we come to know and understand our relationship with God and who we are in Christ.

Deepening the Client's Faith Commitment

The Steps also provide an opportunity for deepening a client's faith commitment. A key assumption behind the Steps is that the Holy Spirit will lead us into all truth (John 16:13–15), and that the truth will set us free (John 8:32). As many counselees go through the Freedom in Christ process, they report that their faith has been built up. We've even seen some people stop in the middle of the process and say, "I don't know Jesus in this way, but I want to." Truly, in these cases the Steps have deepened their understanding of who Jesus is and how He wants to be more intimately involved in their lives.

Clearly Connecting the Word of God Itself with Healing and Restoration

Many Christians have little or no real understanding of how the Bible relates to their mental and emotional health. The Steps are based entirely on the Word of God. As the client reads the Scriptures from the written prayers and goes through the doctrinal affirmation, it becomes clear how the Word of God is quick and powerful like a two-edged sword, discerning the soul from the spirit, the joints from the marrow. Nothing in all creation is hidden from God's sight. Everything is uncovered and laid bare before the eyes of him to whom we must give account (Heb. 4:12–13).

Increasing Personal Responsibility in the Healing Process

The Freedom in Christ process puts the personal responsibility on the counselee to do the work. Some people have spent years in therapy talking about various problems and getting some relief from the process, yet without really resolving their root issues. The Steps promote taking personal responsibility for problems related to daily functioning as well as their relationship with God. The client must decide and choose to believe the truth and assume their responsibility in partnership with an encouraging and godly helper.

Empowering the Client

Another advantage to using the Steps in therapy is that the client is empowered as he or she learns to discern truth from falsehood. This is similar to secular cognitive therapy. Like this well-researched secular approach, specific tools are taught, which are reproducible outside the office setting. The client learns to connect the discomforting feeling experienced to what is being thought (believed assumption) and to discern whether this thought is the truth or a lie. Unlike secular cognitive therapy, if they recognize that the thought is a lie of the enemy, they have the power through their identity and position in Christ to come against this lie with the truth of God's Word. Such spiritual resources in the battle for the mind are something secular cognitive therapy simply does not have. Clients are transformed by the "renewing of their minds" (Rom. 12:2). Of course, this is a continuing daily process, which is taught and encouraged by the therapist.

Strengthening Object Constancy

Sometimes a counselee is looking outside of himself or herself to relationships for a sense of worth and validation. No internal sense of well-being exists to provide an anchor that stands outside what others might think. This is a layman's description of what many therapists would label "a dysfunction in object constancy." Knowing one's identity in Christ, believing and accessing the truth that He will never, never leave me nor forsake me (Heb. 13:5), strengthens an internal sense of self, thus providing a more solid foundation from which to live life.

The mandate to look up to God for strength and less to others decreases dependency on people to constantly affirm one's sense of worth. "The name of the LORD is a strong tower; the righteous runs into it and is safe" (Prov. 18:10). This strengthening of the core self in a healthy way certainly can help a client with the abandonment issues. Of course, the strengthening of object constancy normally takes time. The Freedom in Christ process can be a valuable tool in promoting that process.

Speeding Up Awareness of Defense Mechanisms

The Steps facilitate the quick identification of defense mechanisms (Step 2). Often, a sort of "aha" experience occurs for counselees when they recognize patterns of thought and behavior for the first time.

One woman we worked with presented with depression and blunted affect. The woman filled out the "defense list" and checked off every one of them! Suddenly, she was able to recognize just how much she was defending against her feelings, along with the depth of her defensive strategies. This increased her motivation to truly deal with these defenses. Going through the Steps was just the beginning of her healing process in regard to her defenses, but the structure of the Steps provided an early indication of where treatment needed to go later.

Shortening the Uncovering Process

Similar to the above, the Steps consist of a thorough spiritual inventory encompassing many different areas of the client's life, areas that are often inadequately investigated in the first few therapy sessions. Because of the comprehensive structure, the process of uncovering issues moves much more quickly than in traditional therapy. People disclose things that normally could take years to get to in traditional therapy.

Before each step, the client asks the Holy Spirit to reveal issues that need to be dealt with. The lists of categories and questions make it easier for the client to "confess" many more issues. For example, in Step 6, covering sexual issues, many times a client will bring out important issues that may not have emerged in traditional secular therapy for months or years.

Confronting the Past

The Freedom in Christ process allows the client to recall past issues and face them squarely. Sometimes resolution comes quickly and sometimes it takes more time to uncover the layers. As therapists, we usually have that time to follow through with the issues, to work with them on an ongoing basis, and to help achieve some resolution. The steps on forgiveness and generational issues are especially powerful in this area.

CASE STUDY RESEARCH DESIGN

So how did we conduct our research? Our methodology would be considered an outcome-based case study design containing both quantitative and qualitative data. Its purpose was to measure Freedom in Christ results in the "real-world environment" of clinical practice. Such research has the advantage of high external validity because it consists of real clinical cases in a real clinical environment. Much psychological research is done in highly controlled university or research clinic settings and thus can appear artificial when compared to the realities experienced by most therapists (Seligman, 1995). There are advantages and disadvantages to both "real-world environment" and well-controlled university studies. Both are needed, and we'll discuss the strengths and weaknesses of each in Chapter 11. For now, our purpose is to tell you what we did.

We worked with ten adult clients in Christian outpatient clinical settings. All were seen by either Judith King or Fernando Garzon. Clients for each often come by referral from another therapist, pastor, or former client. An initial screening for the appropriateness of therapy in each setting is done by a telephone call prior to the first intake and evaluation session. Sometimes people have called to inquire if we do "Inner Healing Prayer," "Steps to Freedom," E.M.D.R., etc. We respond by saying that we are therapists, and as Christian therapists we practice from a biblical perspective. We tell them that we will weave into therapy whatever spiritual intervention seems appropriate for the particular individual.

Most of the clients with whom we work come to our private practice because they are desiring and expecting a Christian approach. We have already spoken with them by telephone. Most are believers, although that is not always the case. We are thankful for the "Wonderful Counselor," whom we call upon to lead the creative orchestration of healing. With our therapeutic skills, we hope to gently probe, explore, and expose the toxic wounds of a client. As believers and therapists, we can encourage the client to have an encounter with God, the ultimate Healer of our pain. The lasting solution is in the healing power and love of Jesus Christ. His truth and light replace the lies and darkness, and the soothing oil of the Holy Spirit comforts the soul and brings hope again. So many times we have felt privileged to stand back and see our loving God touch His precious hurting children. It is at those times that we know we are "standing on holy ground."

Nine female and one male client were seen. Ethnicities varied and the age range was from forty to fifty-six. Five of the clients had a college degree or higher education; five did not answer this question. Five of the clients had read some of Dr. Anderson's works before and five had not.

We were free to vary when we implemented the Steps to Freedom in therapy, depending on the needs of the client. Each client was assessed with several tests prior to receiving the Steps to Freedom, after the Steps, at the end of individual treatment (if given), and three months later. The testing assessed for spiritual well-being, dysfunctional beliefs, and general psychological symptomatology (See "Assessment Instruments Used" below). For five clients, the Steps to Freedom were given near the beginning of therapy. One additional client received only the Steps in one extended session with no further therapy. She was an out-of-area client who specifically requested this intervention, and she was given referrals should she decide to pursue additional treatment. Three clients received the Steps at the end of treatment. One client suffered from a recurrent depression with anxiety due to PTSD and continues in ongoing supportive psychotherapy. The last assessment for this client is actually a six-month follow-up to the Steps instead of a three-month post treatment follow-up. The periodic assessment on all these clients enabled us to see whether the Steps to Freedom and Christian therapy were associated with client reductions in psychological symptom levels and increases in spiritual well-being.

ASSESSMENT INSTRUMENTS USED

As we've written this section, we've tried to strike a balance between what a curious lay counselor wants to know and what a more scientific researcher would want to know about each instrument. In essence, we've tried to report enough details on each instrument to satisfy the serious investigator without putting the rest of you to sleep! Some of the details discussed on each instrument pertain to "psychometric studies." In nonscientific terms, psychometric studies are investigations of how consistent an instrument is in giving scores (reliability) and whether those scores really measure the things the test-makers want them to measure (validity). General summary statements have been made with regard to each instrument's psychometrics. References are also supplied for the more scientific researcher who would like to get further information.

Symptom Checklist-90-Revised (SCL-90-R)

The SCL-90-R screens for a variety of symptoms related to emotional distress and mental health disorders. The test itself contains 90 Likert scale questions that break down into several subscales and three global scales. Of particular importance is the Global Severity Index, an overall measure of psychological distress. The subscales and three global scales are described in the following table.

Table 1: SCL-90-R Scales

Subscales	Brief Description
Somatization	Measures distress arising from concerns about physical health, bodily pains, and physical functioning.

Obsessive-Compulsive	Reflects the occurrence of unwanted thoughts and impulses, as well as the need to perform actions that feel unremitting, irresistible, and unwanted.
Interpersonal Sensitivity	Focuses on feelings of inadequacy and inferiority, especially in comparison with other people. Self-doubt in interpersonal interactions is common.
Depression	Measures symptoms common in clinical depression.
Anxiety	Reflects symptoms common in general anxiety and also panic attacks.
Hostility	Focuses on thoughts, actions, and feelings characteristic of people experiencing anger and resentment.
Phobic Anxiety	Reflects behavioral symptoms consistent with persons suffering from a phobia.
Paranoid Ideation	Assesses for the presence of suspiciousness, paranoia, potential paranoid delusions.
Psychoticism	Focuses on a graduated continuum from mild interpersonal alienation to full-blown psychosis. Symptoms of withdrawal, isolation, and psychosis are included in this subscale.

Global Scales

Global Severity Index (GSI) The best single measure in the SCL-90-R of overall perception of emotional distress. Derogatis (1994) suggests that this scale be utilized in cases where one summary measure is needed.

Positive Symptom Distress Index Calculates the average level of distress the subject endorses for each symptom experienced.

Positive Symptom Total The number of symptoms endorsed regardless of distress level reported.

The SCL-90-R requires a sixth-grade reading level and takes about fifteen minutes to administer. This instrument has been subjected to psychometric studies to investigate the reliability and validity of each scale. Acceptable reliability and validity data have been obtained (Derogatis, 1994). The measure has also been normed for adults and adolescents.

Scale scores are reported in T scores, and the reporting of raw score equivalents is also common in research studies. Area T scores permit the comparison of an individual's personal score on each scale with a reference group. In this case the reference group is adults used in the SCL-90-R psychometric research. A client's T score of 50 is at the fiftieth percentile of the adult reference group, while a score of 60 is at the eighty-fourth percentile of this same group. The higher the T score, the higher the percentile rank of the individual's score in comparison to the adult outpatient client reference sample.

The Dysfunctional Attitude Scale (DAS)

The Dysfunctional Attitude Scale is a forty-item Likert scale instrument intended to identify maladaptive beliefs that may predispose people to emotional disturbance, particularly depression (Weissman and Beck, 1978). Each item contains a statement that is rated by the test-taker on a 7 point scale, with 1 indicating total agreement; 2 agree very much; 3 agree slightly; 4 neutral; 5 disagree slightly; 6 disagree very much; and 7 totally disagree. The total score for the forty items is then summed up, with lower scores reflecting more adaptive responses. Scores range from 40 to 280. Two parallel forms of the test exist and version A was used in this study. Psychometric reliability and validity data have been obtained (Oliver and Baumgart, 1985; Dobson and Breiter, 1983; Beck, Brown, Steer, and Weissman, 1991).

Freedom in Christ Ministries (FICM) Survey

This brief questionnaire has a few demographic items and twelve Likert scale questions (J. King, G. Hurst, H. Parks, 1999). The first six items focus on psychological symptoms and are rated on a scale from 1, equaling no problem, to 10, equaling a severe problem. The second six items focus on different areas of spiritual, physical, and emotional functioning. Currently, no psychometric research has been done on this instrument. Table 2 contains a copy of the Steps to Freedom in Christ Pre-Appointment Questionnaire.

Table 2: Freedom in Christ Ministries Survey

STEPS TO FREEDOM IN CHRIST – PRE-APPOINTMENT QUESTIONAIRE

The purpose of this Questionaire is to gain information for the purpose of making a study of the results of the Steps To Freedom appointments in the lives of the people who participate. This study will culminate in the publishing of a paper presenting the results to the Medical, Psychological, and Christian communities. Your personal information will be kept in the strictest confidence. You will be given another questionaire following your appointment and again in a few months. Thank you for your participation.

(PLEASE PRINT)

Identification Number:_____   Date:_____

Name (Optional):_____

Male___ Female___   Single___ Married___ Divorced___ Widowed___   Birth Date:_____

Education ____Years   Ethnicity _____

Have you read *"Victory Over the Darkness" and/or "Bondage Breaker"*?   Yes___ No___

Have you gone through the Steps To Freedom before?   Yes___ No___

Are you a Christian? Yes__No__	How many years?____ years	Do you attend church regularly? Yes__No__

On a scale of 1 to 10, how would you rate yourself in the following areas? (1 is no problem; 10 is severe problem)	1	2	3	4	5	6	7	8	9	10
1. Depression (Hopelessness)										
2. Anxiety										
3. Fear (irrational)										
4. Anger (unhealthy)										
5. Tormenting thoughts and voices										
6. Habits and/or behavior over which You have little control										

On a scale of 1 to 10 how would you rate your function in the following areas? (1 is very good; 10 is very poor)	1	2	3	4	5	6	7	8	9	10
7. Self Esteem										
8. Ability to function in daily activities										
9. Satisfaction in relationships										
10. Physical Health										
11. Bible study and prayer										
12. Reality of God in your life										

The Spiritual Well-Being Scale

As the name implies, the Spiritual Well-being Scale (SWBS, Paloutzian and Ellison, 1982) is a measure of a person's self-perceptions of spiritual contentment. The measure contains 20 seven-point Likert items with the following range: 1 (Strongly Agree), 2

(Moderately Agree), 3 (Agree), 4 (Neutral), 5 (Disagree), 6 (Moderately Disagree), to 7 (Strongly Disagree). To control for response set problems, half of the items are worded in a positive direction and half in a negative direction.

The SWBS contains three scaled scores: an overall Spiritual Well-Being Score (SWBS), a subscale score for religious well-being (RWB), and a subscale score for existential well-being (EWB) (Paloutzian and Ellison, 1982). Ten items measure religious well-being and ten of the items measure existential well-being (Ellis and Smith, 1991). Religious well-being focuses on how a person feels about the quality of his or her spiritual life in relation to God. The existential well-being scale pertains to how well the person feels adjusted to self, community, and surroundings. Notions of life purpose and satisfaction are included in this subscale. Scores range from 20 to 140 for the overall spiritual well-being scale and 10 to 60 for the religious well-being and existential well-being scores. Higher scores indicate higher levels of well-being for each scale. The overall spiritual well-being scale score will be the primary focus in this study.

Psychometric research has been done on the SWBS with mixed results. Reliability data has been relatively sound (Paloutzian and Ellison, 1982). However, some investigators have expressed concerns about possible ceiling effects with certain religious populations (Scott, Agresti, and Fitchett, 1998) and variable factor structures have been found (Ledbetter, Smith, Fischer, Vosler-Hunter, and Chew, 1991; Miller, Fleming, and Brown-Anderson, 1998). Despite the mixed psychometric results, the SWBS continues to be one of the most widely used measures of spirituality in research today (Boivin, Kirby, Underwood, and Silva, 1999). Indeed, currently, there appears to be no better spiritual well-being instrument with superior psychometrics to use in its place.

A final caveat should also be mentioned in interpreting SWBS results with the clients used in this study. The SWBS has only been researched with nonclinical "normal" subjects. No psychometric studies on this instrument have occurred with adult psychotherapy clients. This is a problem with all currently available psychology of religion instruments (Richards and Bergin, 1997). Again, while an imperfect instrument, the SWBS is the best spiritual well-being measure currently available.

The Steps to Freedom in Christ Qualitative Client Satisfaction Inventory

The Steps to Freedom in Christ Client Qualitative Satisfaction Inventory is an eight-item Likert scale instrument intended to measure the client's perception of the Steps to Freedom's benefit and the overall care of the therapist/lay counselor. Scores can range from 8 to 40, with higher scores indicating greater levels of satisfaction. Two items, 3 and 5, are reverse-scored. Currently, no psychometric data are available for this instrument. Table 3 contains a copy of this questionnaire.

Table 3: The Steps to Freedom in Christ Qualitative Client Satisfaction Inventory

This questionnaire is designed to measure the way you feel about the Steps to Freedom ministry that you have received. It is not a test, so there are no right or wrong answers. Answer each question as carefully and as accurately as you can by placing a number beside each one as follows.

1 = Not at all
2 = Very little, rarely
3 = Somewhat, average
4 = Often, more than anticipated
5 = Very much, above what was anticipated
X = Does not apply

1. _____ My therapist really seemed to care about me.

2. _____ I would recommend the Steps to Freedom to people I care about.

3. _____ I was disappointed in my experience of the Steps to Freedom.

4. _____ I felt my therapist really knew what s/he was doing.

5. _____ My therapist put me down when I expressed reservations or concerns.

6. _____ Compared to other types of therapy or ministry I've received, I found the Steps to Freedom to be a valuable addition.

7. _____ The help I got from the Steps to Freedom was better than I expected.

8. _____ I feel much better now than when I first came here.

The Client Satisfaction Questionnaire-8 (CSQ-8)

The CSQ-8 is a psychometrically researched client satisfaction questionnaire commonly used in clinical research (Attkisson and Zwick, 1982; Larsen, Attkisson, Hargreaves, and Nguyen, 1979). Eight questions are rated on a four-point Likert scale, with four questions reverse-scored. Scores range from 8 to 32, with higher scores reflecting greater client satisfaction. Items query the following general areas: the quality of the treatment, whether the client would recommend others to go through a similar treatment program, the level of satisfaction with the amount of help received, and whether the client would come back for similar services if help were needed again.

Qualitative Client Satisfaction Questions

Open-ended client satisfaction questions were also asked. These included the following:

1. Have you had therapy before without the Steps to Freedom as a component? If so, how did it differ?

2. On a scale of 1–10, one being not helpful at all and 10 being the best (most useful) part of therapy, where would you rate the Steps to Freedom in your therapy?

3. What did the Steps to Freedom add to your therapeutic experience? Please describe.

4. Was there a particular section or part of the Steps to Freedom that you remember as being especially helpful?

5. Were the Steps to Freedom in therapy discouraging or not helpful? Please describe.

6. Would you recommend that Christian therapists learn the Steps to Freedom? Why?

7. What would you say to new Christian therapists learning the Steps to Freedom?

SUMMARY

So now you have an idea of how we became interested in research-ing Freedom in Christ, some common stereotypes many therapists have about the Steps, and some of the advantages to utilizing the Steps to Freedom in therapy. The case study research model has also been described. The section that follows details the treatment of Gregory, Joanne, and Mary, three of our clients.

A THANK YOU TO ALL OUR CLIENTS

We want to thank each of the ten clients who agreed to be a part of this research project. Confidentiality is the foundation stone of a thera-peutic relationship. As therapists, of course, this is of utmost impor-tance to us. We assure clients in the initial session, and affirm it throughout therapy, that what they say in our offices will go no farther than the office walls without their full knowledge and consent. We value what they share with us in their vulnerable disclosures and will not betray their confidences. So we are ambivalent about writing the stories of some of these brave clients who have consented to be a part of this clinical study, even though these same clients have encouraged us to write about the value of using Dr. Anderson's Steps to Freedom as a part of therapy. We owe them a debt of gratitude. We have been the ones blessed in working with them.

All the identifying information of the clients has been disguised.

Each person who graces these pages has read every line of his or her story and offered input. These stories are true, although we have changed some of the circumstances and details to protect the identity of the individuals. In some cases, the disguise has included a fitting similar life experience while still maintaining the integrity of the personal story. The disguise is complex and will prevent any recognition by the reader, except by the client him/herself. We hope that if you are a Christian mental health professional reading these client stories, you will be encouraged to at least consider using Dr. Anderson's Steps to Freedom as an adjunct to therapy.

CHAPTER 8

Case Study I: *Gregory*

IDENTIFYING INFORMATION

Gregory is a forty-five-year-old, college-educated, third-generation Hispanic male who is well acculturated. During the first fifteen years of his marriage to Susan, his wife, the couple spent time as overseas missionaries with an Evangelical Fundamentalist denomination. Gregory and Susan left full-time ministry for several reasons, one of which was the unhappiness of Susan. "When I married him, he wasn't a minister, and I didn't bargain for all the religious ministry stuff," Susan reported. After returning to the U.S., Gregory had begun working at a secular job, just "trying to pay the bills and survive." Recently, he has gotten a better job in human resources with an up-and-coming chemical company.

Gregory is bright, articulate, handsome, and somewhat defensive, but openly searching for answers for his severely troubled marriage. He and his wife have been married for twenty-seven years and are parents of four children who are all married.

PRESENTING COMPLAINTS

Gregory came seeking help with his difficult marriage, which was becoming more and more intolerable for him. With the "constant barrages and outbursts of anger" from his wife, he was now feeling helpless and hopeless. Unable to cope anymore, he'd given up but felt trapped because of his Christian value system, which did not include the option of divorce. You would have never guessed he was having these problems if you knew him at work. There he appeared to be thriving, all the while becoming more passive and avoidant at home. Gregory was seeking help, but his wife was not willing to come to therapy. "It's your turn," she said. "I've already done all that anger stuff!" He admitted that he felt depressed and was very angry. While sleep and appetite were normal, he had decreased energy, a sense of hopelessness, and a decreased enjoyment of life.

HISTORY

Gregory described his childhood family life as being "good days, happy days, as I look back. We had no television so we spent a lot of time reading and also memorizing Scripture." The Christian family lived in the country in a run-down, but clean, rambling clapboard house when he was young. "There were a lot of us, nine brothers and sisters, so we protected and looked out for each other." Gregory's parents were "loving and affirming." Of the two, his father appeared more unstable, and his mother was the one "who held things together." It was a family rule to guard their social image, because they believed it was very important that the family "look good" to outsiders. The family also moved frequently, since his father often changed jobs. The lack of money was often an issue, and the children were raised in a somewhat legalistic manner.

The family history of Gregory's parents revealed a few more clues about his internal dilemma. His mother was raised in a missionary family. "My grandfather was very intelligent," Gregory noted. But his grandfather was also obsessively committed to his missionary calling to the point of neglecting his own family. Thus, Gregory's mother suffered as a missionary child of an emotionally and physically abusive father. Most of the extended family knew about this gentleman's "bizarre behavior," his instability, and the emotional trauma this imposed on the family system, but the family felt helpless to change any of the circumstances.

Gregory became a Christian through the influence of some high school friends when he was sixteen. He developed into a very zealous evangelizer. He often felt depressed if he didn't think he was "witnessing" enough. He readily admitted that he was (and is) very hard on himself, especially as it relates to his Christian faith.

Gregory met his wife in high school. Her family was different from his family in socioeconomic status, values, and religious experience. He was attracted to her beauty, intelligence, and character.

Assessment

Gregory presented with some mild depression, which seemed directly related to the unhappiness in his marriage. His symptoms did not indicate an endogenous (predominantly biologically based) depression but appeared more related to his sense of helplessness, repressed anger, and disappointment with his marriage. He worried about becoming more emotionally detached from his marriage, although he remained committed to it. He was disappointed with himself for leaving "full-time ministry" and he was searching for direction in that area. Should he stay with his present job? Should he consider full-time mission work again? He was eager and looking for help. Gregory's testing supported my initial impressions, which were depression and a low sense of spiritual well-being.

Case Conceptualization

Gregory had reached a point in his life where he was exhausted from trying to take care of everyone else, especially his wife and children. He felt responsible for their happiness, and was experiencing a deep sense of failure in not meeting that goal. He had grown up as a "people pleaser," and he never really learned how to process his own emotions. He was afraid of his anger and didn't know how to deal with it in a healthy way. His boundaries were blurred and he lived with guilt and self-condemnation. He was looking for help with "self assertion, codependency," and the passive-avoidant style of dealing with conflict, which he used when he felt hopeless and powerless.

COURSE OF TREATMENT

I had seen Gregory's wife, Susan, a number of years earlier. At that time, we had worked on her anger management. She had benefited from going through the Steps to Freedom and encouraged her husband to go for therapy and "do the same thing." Gregory had finally followed through on her request and was open to looking at his own issues.

For many clients, I start with the Steps to Freedom or utilize the intervention somewhere near the middle of therapy. Gregory was different. I worked with him for eleven sessions, his full course of individual therapy, before going through the steps. During those individual sessions, we worked on his recognizing his own emotions, giving himself permission to look deeper and feel the pain of past disappointments, traumas, and unfulfilled dreams. We explored family-of-origin issues, which contributed to his denial and insulation of emotions, and explored some past childhood traumas for which Gregory experienced some healing. The Holy Spirit revealed many lies he was believing as a result of past traumas and experiences. I encouraged him to start keeping a journal about his feelings, and he began to face the fear of disappointing people and the fear of not being liked.

His expectations became more realistic and he began to set boundaries in his marriage. Slowly, he began to change his step in "the dance of anger" with his wife. Obviously, Gregory had made some good gains through his work in therapy. He was clearly more in touch with his own emotions. With this new openness, the Steps to Freedom were implemented as part of his treatment.

Steps to Freedom

Initially, Gregory was reluctant to embrace the truth of his identity in Christ, and he "kind of" believed in the devil. He thought the enemy had been at work in his family when one of his sisters attempted suicide, but he wasn't sure about James 4:7: "Submit therefore to God. Resist the devil and he will flee from you." Could it be taken literally, that he himself could confess and renounce the work of the devil? He agreed to take the Steps booklet home and look up the Scriptures for himself, which he did. He was somewhat open to the process, because a close friend had experienced radical change and healing after going through the Steps. Finally, Gregory agreed to go through the Steps to Freedom and complete the questionnaires. I will describe this process by sessions. In combination with therapy, it took four sessions of varying length (2 one-hour, 1 ninety-minute, and 1 two-hour appointment).

Discussion Questions for Therapists

You might be thinking, *How could this person benefit from the "Steps to Freedom"? Why even consider this intervention if therapy is progressing?* As Christian therapists, we know the value of helping people deal with past traumas, and we have been taught to recognize mental and emotional disorders. However, most of our training has been on the horizontal plane between therapist and client. The vertical relationship that exists between the client and God, the relationship that ultimately will bring lasting healing, often goes unattended. I had a fairly good understanding of Gregory, but God knows him perfectly. We had established a good therapist-client relationship, but the most important relationship was between Gregory and his heavenly Father. I was leading him in biblical truth as I understood it, but the Spirit of Truth could do so much more if we allowed Him. How do we overtly encourage this personal encounter with God for our clients in the context of Christian therapy? The Steps is one option.

I have found countless times that healing comes from God's Word. Sometimes we, who are familiar with God's Word, tend to minimize or overlook its inherent power. The Steps to Freedom are mostly scriptural prayers that the client prays. In the process of going through the Steps, clients begin internalizing God's words. The Steps themselves have no magical qualities. They are just a tool that can be used rightly or wrongly. *Who* sets people free is Christ; *what* sets people free is their response to God in repentance and faith. Hebrews 4:12 says: "The word of God is living and active. Sharper than any double-edged sword, it penetrates even to dividing soul and spirit, joints and marrow; it judges the thoughts and attitudes of the heart"(NIV). Using the Steps to Freedom in therapy provides an opportunity for the client to experience an encounter with the living God, who is the only source for their life, freedom, and wholeness.

SESSION ONE

Introductory Prayers

I always start our Step sessions with the opening prayer, which affirms the presence of our God: "You are the only omniscient (all-knowing), omnipotent (all-powerful) and omnipresent (always present) God." I pray that prayer aloud with the client. It's good for me to hear it! It's a wonderful truthful reminder to me, the therapist, about who God is, as we together commit our session to God and invite the presence of the Holy Spirit as the Wonderful Counselor to orchestrate this process

The client and I then read aloud together the declaration from Steps to Freedom, which affirms the authority we have in Christ. Gregory prayed aloud, "In the name and authority of the Lord Jesus Christ, I command Satan and all evil spirits to release me in order that I can be free to know and to choose to do the will of God." Gregory found it very comforting that we would not be taken on some kind of a power encounter with demons, which is often feared by clients and counselors alike. He continued the prayer, "As children of God seated with Christ in the heavenlies, we agree that every enemy of the Lord Jesus Christ be bound to *silence*. We say to Satan and all your evil workers that you cannot inflict any pain or in any way prevent God's will from being accomplished in my life."

Step 1: Counterfeit Versus Real

We began the first step, which renounces previous or current involvement with occult practices and false religions. Gregory prayed the prayer that asks the Heavenly Father to search his heart and reveal to him any involvement unknowingly or knowingly with cultic or occult practices, false religions, or false teachers. I was amazed that Gregory had very few activities to renounce. Most clients have numerous past "non-Christian" activities to renounce. His particular family had been very strict and therefore he had been very careful to avoid anything non-Christian. He said he'd had some nagging thoughts that had become a bit of an obsession about the need to witness, but he had gotten through those times by reading the Word and praying. He remembered as a ten-year-old finding some pornography and was worried that a "spirit of lust" had attached itself to him in some way. He renounced that and sensed some relief especially when he announced, "I am the bride of Christ." He felt a sense of "purification." I explored this with him further and made a note to readdress the issue again in Step 6.

Gregory needed time to talk about his obsessive fear of being deceived. We discussed the fact that when you know Jesus as a Shepherd, in an intimate way, then you can discern His voice as He leads you. "Gregory, if you're worried about that," I said, "just be obedient to James 4:7 by submitting to God and resisting the lies of the enemy. You *can* be assured that the devil will flee, based on God's Word! In fact, let's do that right now. I'll agree as you verbally submit to God and exercise your authority in Christ by commanding Satan to leave your presence." I explained that when we submit to God in the name of Jesus, the Holy Spirit will lead us into all truth. It is our responsibility to test the spirit and to take every thought captive to the obedience of Christ (2 Cor. 10:5). If you find yourself thinking thoughts that aren't true according to God's Word, then don't believe them. If you aren't sure about whether the Spirit of God or an evil spirit is leading you, then submit it to God. "Lord, would you show me the true nature of this spirit?" For more instruction on discernment and the leading of the Holy Spirit, see Neil's book, *Walking in the Light* (Thomas Nelson, 1992).

Step 2: Deception Versus Truth

Next, we looked at the problem of self-deception and self-defenses. We know that this process of overcoming the lies that we have believed and the defenses that we have used over the years to protect ourselves is not an instantaneous experience. It will take us the rest of our lives to renew our minds. What I've found, as I've worked with clients in this step, is that it's a place to begin. It's a way to identify self-deception and defense mechanisms. Often for the first time, clients recognize that their underlying assumptions and defensive patterns don't fit with the truth of God's Word. Gregory was able to see this. He said, "Maybe I don't have the handle on truth that I thought."

As Gregory prayed and looked at the ways we can defend ourselves, a light seemed to go on for him. He could see himself in all the defenses except displacement. By identifying his use of denial, fantasy, emotional insulation, regression, projection, and rationalization, Gregory became much more aware of them in the future. At least they were red flagged. We had already been working on some of these defenses in therapy, but this further clarification seemed helpful to him. He could see the variety of ways he deceived himself.

For Gregory, it was important to normalize the reality of defenses in his life, as it is for everyone. I explained that we all develop defense mechanisms before we come to Christ as a means of coping with life in this fallen world. As we mature and our vertical relationship with our Creator is strengthened, there is no need to hold on to self-centered defense mechanisms since Christ is our defense. Trust, internal security, and identity grow as we open ourselves up to the love and affirmation of God, who accepts and loves us unconditionally. The Holy Spirit reveals to the client the defense mechanisms (which are essentially the same as flesh patterns or mental strongholds) that need to be replaced by a genuine faith in God.

Statement of Truth

Most clients find reading the doctrinal affirmations in the Statement of Truth aloud is strengthening, comforting, and sometimes convicting. It is important to observe the clients as they are reading the affirmations and to invite them to pause if they are having difficulty reading, understanding, or internalizing the words. These affirmations are like a road map.

One client (not Gregory) who was an "active church member" stopped mid-sentence in the following affirmation: "I believe that He delivered me from the domain of darkness and transferred me to His kingdom."

"I'm still in that domain of darkness!" she exclaimed. As we paused to discuss this, she said that she had never invited Christ into her heart. She had wondered what was missing. I led her in prayer, and she received Christ as her Lord and Savior. What a joy to witness the soft tears of gratitude trickle down her cheeks. She had encountered the life-changing God, and the angels in heaven rejoiced! When Gregory went through the affirmations, he felt "comforted and strengthened on the inside."

We finished the session with Gregory praying the Daily Prayer, one of the prayers noted in the Steps section on Maintaining Your Freedom. It is intended, as the name indicates, as an ongoing prayer after the Steps are completed. For all my clients, I have found this to be a good way to put some closure to the sessions while the process of the Steps to Freedom is still continuing.

SESSION TWO

This was a planned ninety-minute session, which I prefer. Being in private practice, I sometimes have the option to schedule longer appointments. Ninety minutes gives me time to process the previous session and assess particular situations during the client's week that were impacted by the previous work. Gregory was promoted at work, and he had successfully negotiated a family situation that was "very emotional." That week he was able to recognize one of his defense mechanisms and was able to pull back, regroup, and try approaching the conflict in a different way. In this second session we were planning to complete the third step on forgiveness.

Step 3: Bitterness Versus Forgiveness

Having been to seminary and having been in full-time ministry, forgiveness was not a new issue for Gregory. He preached on this subject and counseled others to forgive. He'd already done lots of forgiving himself. In this step we ask the Holy Spirit to reveal names of people that we have not already forgiven from our hearts, and we find that people even like Gregory usually have many people they need to forgive. Forgiveness is key to experiencing freedom from our past. The need to forgive others is also essential for our spiritual victory. The apostle Paul says in 2 Corinthians 2:10–11, "If you forgive anyone, I also forgive him. And what I have forgiven—if there was anything to forgive—I have forgiven in the sight of Christ for your sake, in order that Satan might not outwit us. For we are not unaware of his *schemes*"(NIV, emphasis added). The word, *schemes*, is translated elsewhere in 2 Corinthians as "minds" (4:4; 11:3), and "thought" (10:5), which reveals that the spiritual battle is primarily fought in our minds.

Gregory didn't need much teaching on what forgiveness was and what forgiveness wasn't. Some clients have very distorted views on this subject. If that is the case, I do some teaching and provide them with some handouts I have prepared so they fully understand what forgiveness is and how to do it. As a Christian therapist, I deal with forgiveness issues in therapy, person by person, as incidents come up over time. Having the client pray and ask the Lord to reveal whom they need to forgive helps significantly in this process. More comprehensive spiritual work seems to happen in a much shorter time. I've seen this over and over again. Even when clients think they don't have unforgiveness issues, like Gregory, names will come to their minds in response to their prayer. I write these names down as they share them with me.

This step usually takes the longest amount of time for most people. Processing this step in therapy allows me to take my time. I can explore and go deeper with the issues raised in the process of forgiving. I make notes regarding additional issues to be explored at a later time in treatment. It is not uncommon for the Holy Spirit to bring up issues that have been forgotten in the conscious mind. Deeply embedded lies often surface as they face past traumas. We have discovered that people are not necessarily bound to past traumas; they are bound to the lies they believe as a result of past traumas.

Gregory, much to his surprise, had issues of unforgiveness toward his father and his mother (most of us do!). Then Gregory recognized and listed the individual offenses that he currently had against his wife. "I thought I had already forgiven Susan, but I hadn't thought of that incident before," Gregory exclaimed. I explained to him that forgiveness is often like an onion; it is often peeled layer by layer. "We choose to get on the road of forgiveness and off the road of unforgiveness," I said while holding my arms up in a Y, trying to demonstrate the changing of direction from darkness to light. "When we're on the road to forgiveness and another layer gets peeled off, we deal with it. Forgiveness is a choice, but complete forgiveness for some is a process." The current research that is being done on this process is interesting and will be noted in the end comments. We don't heal in order to forgive; we forgive in order to heal. Healing may take time, but forgiveness is a crisis of our will. It is a choice that we all have to make.

After forgiving others, Gregory had to forgive himself. He had more trouble with this than forgiving other people. This is a very common occurrence in therapy, especially for perfectionists and those who are raised in legalism. Gregory felt guilty about his struggle with lust. Even though the sexual fantasies that accompanied his occasional viewing of an R-rated movie seemed minimal given the whole spectrum of sexual addiction. He also seemed to be carrying a significant level of self-hatred regarding this part of his life. I explained that stress makes us more vulnerable to sexual temptations that arise out of our own carnal nature and mental attacks from the evil one (*The Way of Escape* by Neil Anderson, 1994; and Mark R. Laaser's *The Secret Sin*, Zondervan, 1992).

Forgiving ourselves is, in reality, acknowledging and accepting the forgiveness of God. We discussed how his inability to accept God's forgiveness contributed to his self-hatred. He was unconsciously trying to gain God's approval through his behavior, not recognizing that he was already loved, accepted, and approved through the work of Christ. He was concerned that if he forgave himself it might make it easier for him to perpetuate his driven lifestyle because he would then know that he could forgive himself again. This line of thinking is deceptive because he is using his self-hatred to punish himself, which in turn keeps him in bondage to his drivenness. Not accepting the forgiveness of God is more a matter of pride than humility. This often comes as a surprise to people. I had him repeat 1 John 1:9: "If we confess our sins, He is faithful and just to forgive us our sins and to cleanse us from all unrighteousness"(NKJV). He responded affirmatively when I asked him if he believed that. I looked him in the eyes and said, "Gregory, based on what God's Word says, you are forgiven. Do you believe that?" "Yes," he said. "Then receive His forgiveness," I gently repeated. "Now, Gregory," I continued, "if God forgives you and then you don't forgive yourself, where does that put you in relation to God?" Gregory saw his own elevated position above God. As specific activities and thoughts were confessed, he was able to receive God's forgiveness and let himself off his own hook.

It was at this point that we deviated from the typical order of the Steps and jumped to Step 6, Bondage Versus Freedom. This step focuses on habitual sins and especially sexually immoral uses of our bodies. Gregory worked through the prayers of confession and cleansing in this step, experiencing great relief. Gregory experienced a whole new level of freedom!

SESSION THREE

I had thought in this session that I would proceed with Steps 4, 5, and possibly 7 depending on the time, since we had now covered Steps 1, 2, 3, and 6. Gregory arrived for the appointment happily reporting what was happening at work. There were new responsibilities and opportunities in doing the type of work that he believed he could "put his heart into."

Unfortunately, Gregory was in the middle of a recent marital crisis and needed to talk about it. He was not emotionally prepared to continue the Steps. He was very angry; he and his wife had had a major argument during which he felt she had been abusive, irrational, and very hurtful to him. He had put up some boundaries and was keeping his distance. He said he was not willing to talk to Susan because whenever he speaks, she interrupts and takes over. "It's hopeless," he said. "I'm so mad I can hardly stand it!"

We spent the session processing this rage. He had written his wife an angry letter, stating his boundaries. He was able to vent and process his anger, which resulted in a better understanding of himself and his marriage. He was learning to recognize his anger and break his avoidant relational style, a presenting problem before therapy. We came up with some practical ways that he could break the silence without compromising himself. We discussed some healthy realistic boundaries, and explored what for him might be a core emotion underneath the anger. Like most clients, Gregory didn't realize that anger can be a secondary emotion, and that unresolved issues underneath the anger often fuel its intensity when conflict arises.

Gregory was able to see that a deep sense of fear was his main unrecognized emotion, and behind every irrational fear is a lie. "I'm afraid that my marriage will break up, that my whole life will be ruined. I'm also afraid," he said, quietly struggling to hold back the tears, "that Susan might get sick, die, or even leave me!" As he softened, he was able to see that Susan was probably dealing with some of her own grief issues, because of their youngest daughter getting married, and perhaps also her own fear as they faced the empty nest for the first time. At the end of the session, Gregory had processed some of his anger in a healthy way and realized that his fears were based on assumptions not facts. He also had some new tools and strategy in place. He also was becoming more aware of the spiritual battle that was going on for his mind. He said, "I think that the enemy influences my mind more than I've realized in the past."

SESSION FOUR

Several weeks had lapsed since the last appointment due to summer vacation schedules and Gregory's increased traveling for work. He had done well with Susan since the last appointment. They had negotiated and decided that instead of avoidance and passivity, his usual ways of dealing with anger, that he would leave for a time but promise to come back and discuss the issues when they had both cooled down. This worked! Consequently, Gregory felt more successful in his marriage. We proceeded with Steps.

Fear Exercise

It seemed appropriate to deal with the many fears that seemed to have surfaced for Gregory in the last session. I had given him the "Steps to Overcoming Fear" from Steps to Freedom. He had taken them home to study and to think about it them. This process of overcoming fear is based on the book *Freedom from Fear*, by Neil Anderson and Rich Miller (Gospel Light, 1999).

As we processed the exercise on fear, Gregory felt that this was the most help to him so far in the Steps. Indeed, his comment made sense to me based on our last session. Gregory was able to recognize and let go of his fears—fears of not measuring up, losing his reputation, making mistakes, and his kids not becoming Christians. He also let go of his fears that life will be overwhelming and he'll lose his vibrant ministry and focus. He was able to see how fearful he was of Susan's anger. He also confessed his fear of failure and his fear of people, which contributed to his being such a people-pleaser.

Many people who adopt people-pleasing behaviors suffer from a deep fear of rejection. Gregory confessed this. As the root of rejection was exposed in this exercise, Gregory recalled a painful experience that he experienced as a child on the playground at school, where he had been beaten and mocked by some older boys. We prayed together asking the Lord to reveal His healing presence in this memory while Gregory felt the pain again. The Lord revealed the lie that he had believed from that experience, which was, "It's not safe to trust people." He renounced that lie and others that accompanied this traumatic experience. Then he accepted and announced the truth about being in the safety of God's care according to Psalm 18:2: "The LORD is my rock, and my fortress, and my deliverer; my God, my strength, in whom I will trust; my buckler, and the horn of my salvation, and my high tower"(KJV). Jesus set him free from this painful memory with the truth and His powerful presence.

Steps 4: Rebellion Versus Submission; Step 5: Pride Versus Humility

We then processed Step 4, which deals with submission. Gregory needed some clarification as to what it means to submit to one another in marriage. We discussed Ephesians 5:18–25, and I diagrammed three stages of submission:

1. First, we submit to God and are filled with the Spirit (v. 18). This is vertical.

2. Second, we submit to one another's needs as brothers and sisters in the body of Christ (v. 21). This is horizontal.

3. Third, we assume our responsibilities, which for Gregory meant that he was to love his wife as Christ loved the church (v. 25).

I asked Gregory, "Wouldn't you say that to die for someone is pretty submissive?" Paul continues in the passage by instructing wives to submit to their husbands. "This is not difficult for a wife if fulfilling the above," I said to Gregory. It becomes more of a mutual submission to the lordship of Christ. On that point, Gregory agreed that often God speaks to Susan and that he needs to "hear" more what God is saying to him through his wife.

Gregory was able to see just how much this perspective could help him in maintaining his communication with Susan. We then proceeded to Step 5 (Pride Versus Humility). In this step, Gregory really came to terms with being a people-pleaser rather than a God-pleaser. Since we had already done Step 6 after the forgiveness section, we proceeded to the final step.

Step 7: Acquiescence Versus Renunciation

This step addresses the sins of the parents, which have been passed on from one generation to the next. By this time, these had become fairly obvious to Gregory. When a client wonders whether to include a certain issue or pattern, I usually say, "Well, why don't you include it since it came to your mind after you prayed. It can't do any harm." Some of Gregory's family patterns included the following: fear of failure, not living up to your potential, not finishing well, people-pleasing, denial in the form of viewing life through rose-colored glasses, lust, passivity, and laziness.

During this step, I also encourage the client to think about the family blessings that have been passed on and we also make a list of those. Clients then give thanks for the traits and family blessings that they have picked up from their physical heritage. For Gregory, these included intelligence, social skills, a sense of humor, attractiveness, passion, creativity, loyalty, and Christian commitment.

ASSESSMENT OF PROGRESS AND FOLLOW-UP

We had now finished both individual therapy and the Steps. I gave Gregory the assessment instruments to fill out for the next week. Here are my notes for that session:

Gregory looked lighter. He said that things are going better than ever before—work, marriage—it's like they are having a new start—Susan seems more tolerant—he is listening more to her while she talks without trying to solve the problems—he is expanding in his work—he is also more aware of the presence of the Holy Spirit in his life. We talked about this for awhile . . . He does seem more open . . . He feels now that he and Susan can come in together to kind of sum things up and come up with a game plan. We've planned another appointment . . . in which he and Susan will come in together.

When Gregory and Susan came for their follow-up session, there was a visible improvement compared to the initial couples session when they were distraught, hopeless, and very angry with one another. In fact, at that time I had wondered if this couple could make it together! They reported that now they were communicating much better, they had a better sense of their own identities, roles, and boundaries. Susan reported that Gregory was more honest and forthright, and that he had assumed more leadership in the family. This she respected. Their sex life had improved as well as their cooperation and partnership in the relationship.

Both reported that they had experienced God in a new way as a result of their experiences with the Steps. For example, they indicated that they had become more acquainted with the Holy Spirit as a person of the Trinity. I often find the Steps to Freedom do encourage a new awareness in most people of the daily reality of the Holy Spirit. Clients are encouraged to practice listening to what God is saying to them. For many, this is a new life-giving experience and encounter with God. To help maintain the gains that had been made, I met with Gregory and his wife once a month for three months to do some supportive marital work.

Testing Results

SCL-90-R Gregory's testing supported his and his wife's assessments of his progress. The following tables show Gregory's overall decline in his symptom levels as noted by the SCL-90-R. Scores are reported in raw score equivalents and T scores (in parentheses).

Tables 1–3

When Given	Interpesonal Sensitivity	Depression	Anxiety	Hostility
Pre-Steps	.56 (61)	.85 (65)	.4 (60)	.33 (55)
Post-Steps/Tx	.33 (56)	.46 (59)	.4 (60)	.17 (49)
3 Mth marital	.22 (53)	.69 (63)	.3 (56)	.17 (49)

When Given	Somatic	Obsessive-Compulsive	Phobia	Paranoia	Psychoticism
Pre-Steps	.08 (43)	.70 (60)	0 (44)	.17 (49)	.1 (53)
Post-Steps/Tx	.25 (53)	.60 (59)	0 (44)	0 (41)	.1 (53)
3 Mth marital	.08 (43)	.80 (61)	0 (44)	.17 (49)	0 (44)

When Given	GSI	PSDI	PST
Pre-Steps	.4 (59)	1.29 (53)	28 (59)
Post-Steps/Tx	.3 (55)	1.08 (46)	25 (58)
3 Mth marital	.32 (56)	1.04 (45)	28 (59)

GSI=Global Severity Index
PSDI=Positive Symptom Distress Index
PST=Positive Symptom Total

Clearly, the individual therapy prior to the Steps to Freedom had had a beneficial effect on Gregory. Few of the scales on the pre-Steps testing, therefore, began at high levels. Given this circumstance, caution is warranted in interpreting his results.

Depression, Gregory's working diagnosis, did begin at levels that might attract clinical attention and then decreased to normal levels following the Steps. Other scales related to Gregory's marital concerns, such as Interpersonal Sensitivity and Hostility, also decreased in score after the Steps. The decrease in several scale scores, combined with the fact that no scale scores were at levels of clinical concern after the Steps, support the Steps' contribution as a component in Gregory's care.

As noted, the three-month follow-up included monthly marital consultations. Gregory's anxiety level went down from borderline normal to normal levels following these sessions. The depression subscale appeared to increase slightly to the borderline-normal range, suggesting that regular monitoring of Gregory's depression level would be wise in the future. All other scale scores were within normal levels. Thus, each component of treatment—individual therapy, the Steps to Freedom, and the monthly marital consultations—were associated with symptom level reductions on the SCL-90-R.

FICM Survey Several of Gregory's FICM survey responses also yielded an interesting pattern. Below are two tables of his results.

Tables 4 and 5

	Depression	Anxiety	Fear	Anger	Thoughts	Habits
Pre-Steps	2	4	3	3	2	3
Post-Steps/Tx	2	3	3	2	1	2
3 Mth marital	2	2	3	3	2	2

	Esteem	Functioning	Relationships	Health	Bible/ Prayer	Reality of Life in God
Pre-Steps	3	2	5	2	3	2
Post-Steps/Tx	2	2	4	2	2	2
3 Mth marital	2	2	3	2	2	2

Like the SCL-90-R, the previous eleven sessions of therapy led to low starting points for this 10-point scale (higher scores indicating more distress). Thus, caution is merited in interpreting the findings. Despite the low starting points, some changes were still observable. After the Steps, Gregory reported a decrease in several areas related to his problems—anxiety, anger, disturbing thoughts, uncontrollable habits, relationship dissatisfaction, and difficulties with Bible study and prayer. Only disturbing thoughts and anger went back up in the three-month follow-up, and this was only from 1 to 2 and 2 to 3 respectively, again indicating low original distress. Additional decreases in anxiety and relationship dissatisfaction were reported after the marital sessions. No changes were observed in depression, daily functioning, physical health, or reality of God in Gregory's life, all of these starting at a level of 2 and having very little room for improvement.

DAS On the Dysfunctional Attitude Scale (DAS), Gregory's scores also started at low levels of maladaptive beliefs prior to the Steps (106). This level dropped following the Steps (97) and was at 104 after the three monthly marital-support sessions were over. Again, these fluctuations all suggested low levels for maladaptive, depressogenic beliefs.

Summarizing the SCL-90-R, DAS, and the FICM survey, despite the low scale elevations at the beginning of Gregory's experience with the Steps to Freedom, observable decreases in several SCL-90-R scales and various FICM survey items were noted. Again, one must be careful in interpreting testing beginning at these levels; however, the three instruments, taken together, do support an association between the Steps to Freedom and improvements in Gregory's emotional condition. The Steps appeared to be beneficial; in this case, even at the end of a productive individual therapy.

SWBS What about Gregory's spiritual condition? The table below describes Gregory's Spiritual Well-Being Total Score. Higher scores indicate increased spiritual well-being.

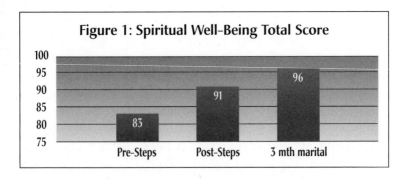

Figure 1: Spiritual Well-Being Total Score

Gregory's overall spiritual well-being is observed to increase after the Steps to Freedom and also following the marital sessions. This is an encouraging sign since the Steps to Freedom focus specifically on the client's spiritual condition as well as the emotional condition.

Client Satisfaction Data The client satisfaction data supported the role of each portion of treatment. Greg scored a 31 out of 32 on the Client Satisfaction Questionnaire 8, indicating a very high level of satisfaction with his treatment. His qualitative data on the open-ended questionnaire given at the end of treatment also provided enlightening information.

Gregory indicated that it was the "Steps in tandem with wise therapy" that was helpful for him. He had needed to work in therapy on issues such as codependency, anger management, and conflict resolution. "I'm slower to get the deeper things of the heart," he noted. Gregory felt particular help from the Steps in several areas. Specifically, the sections on forgiveness and fear provided "specific prayers for areas of struggle in my life" and were of great benefit. Dealing with the guilt from past sexual issues and experiencing God's forgiveness were "very freeing." Gregory concluded his comments with some words for therapists learning about the Steps: "Therapy needs to be holistic and that includes the arena of spiritual warfare. The Steps to Freedom will equip you as a therapist with a comprehensive, well-thought-out approach."

Treatment Implications

Gregory's experience provides a good example of how therapy and the Steps can interweave to create a unified, holistic treatment for the client. Without prior therapy to address Gregory's defenses against feeling his emotions, the Steps might have become a cognitive exercise of limited value. Gregory had to be in touch with his heart for the Steps to maximally benefit him.

The Steps themselves helped Gregory deal with issues of lustful thoughts and his need to forgive others and to accept God's forgiveness of himself. They further highlighted his defenses and set the stage for a deeper releasing of these defenses while adopting Christ as his true defense. My previous experience using the Steps in therapy also was helpful. I knew that deviating from the typical order of the Steps was important when Gregory brought up material in Step 3 (the forgiveness step) that also was closely related to Step 6 material (Bondage Versus Freedom). Instead of proceeding to Step 4, I went directly to Step 6. I also processed an important marital conflict in the next session rather than continuing directly with the Steps. These adjustments emphasize the principle of using the Steps as a flexible framework under the guidance of the Holy Spirit. I still believe it is very important to process Step 1 first with clients who have been involved in cults or the occult, since you want to eliminate that kind of spiritual interference at the very beginning.

Gregory's forgiveness work itself was enlightening as well. Many Christians think they've done all the forgiving they need to do when they begin this step, but the opening prayer shows them differently. Gregory was therefore surprised when God brought up several people and incidents that he needed to address. This is common and is consistent with the idea that forgiveness is a crisis of the will, but a lifetime process. I've found that the onion analogy explained by Neil in Chapter 2 can help many clients understand the forgiveness process better. Dr. Everet Worthington and Dr. Robert Enright are researching the forgiveness process and have developed process-oriented forgiveness interventions that can go nicely with the principles outlined in this part of the Steps to Freedom (Worthington, 2001; Enright, 2001).

SUMMARY OF FINDINGS

Gregory's case differs from the other cases noted in this section because the Steps to Freedom were given at the end of individual treatment instead of at the beginning or in the middle. This was due partly to his emotional insulation and partly because he was not experiencing noticeable spiritual manifestations. Psychological and spiritual assessment measures, along with Gregory's own client satisfaction information, suggest that the Steps to Freedom can be a beneficial ending therapy intervention as well as a beginning or intermediate treatment phase strategy. While the relatively low pre-Steps testing scores suggest caution in interpreting his results, a clear trend in the additive effect of using the Steps to Freedom is noted. Further research utilizing the Steps as an ending intervention with more empirical designs is recommended.

CHAPTER 9

Case Study II: *Joanne*

As I begin to tell Joanne's story, I am struck again with what a privilege it is to work with the clients who come to us for help. We have the opportunity to be used by God to set captives free and bind up the brokenhearted. People trust us with their hearts, their wounds, and their pain. I do not hold that trust lightly but rather lift these precious children of God to our Lord for His continued healing, intervention, and maturing in their lives. For I know that the transformation by the renewing of our minds is a lifelong process.

IDENTIFYING INFORMATION

"I don't know how to make intimate relationships work," Joanne sadly declared as she slumped in her chair. A highly competent marketing consultant who enjoyed much professional success, she felt like "mush" when it came to intimate relationships. She reported that she was depressed and lonely. From what I learned about Joanne in that first session, her opening remarks made sense.

Joanne is a thirty-seven-year-old well-acculturated third-generation Asian-American woman with no children. She is a very attractive woman of slight build who lives alone. She appeared pale and somewhat physically frail. Joanne had suffered numerous physical ailments such as an autoimmune disorder, which made her more susceptible to infections, anemia, and fibromyalgia. She had been seeing medical doctors on a regular basis.

Joanne had had years of therapy with numerous therapists, so many she "couldn't count." Yet, she continued to feel depressed and frustrated. From all this previous experience, Joanne was now very sophisticated and savvy about the process.

Her relationship history truly was "mushy." Joanne had been married briefly, but now had been divorced for more than fifteen years. Her former husband, whom Joanne described as a creative and intelligent man, verbally and physically abused her. Joanne left this marriage, although the divorce was traumatic for her. Later, she had several other relationships with men who emotionally abused her, including a long-term relationship with a man whom she expected to marry but didn't. "It felt just like a divorce," she said. At a business conference, she met a friend who suggested that she look at the Freedom in Christ material.

Joanne came to see me looking for answers from a Christian perspective. "I think I need spiritual help with some of my problems along with the therapy," she commented. "I'm pretty good at understanding my psychological issues, but I feel that only God can really heal me. I've tried everything else." Indeed, as I heard her story, I believed she had tried everything else! In addition to several traditional counseling experiences, she had experimented with numerous alternative healing methods and many self-help methods. Nothing gave her the peace or emotional and physical healing she was seeking.

Since Joanne was looking for therapy to include distinctively spiritual interventions, I felt comfortable discussing some options with her. She listened and expressed interest in exploring the Steps to Freedom so I gave her the books *Victory over Darkness*, *The Bondage Breaker*, and a copy of the Steps to Freedom to take home and read. Normally, as a part of the informed consent process for the Steps to Freedom, I encourage these preliminary readings.

PRESENTING COMPLAINTS

Joanne presented with symptoms of depression. She had been to see her doctor three days previously and he had started her on an anti-depressant medication. She now reported feeling "pretty sleepy and washed out" since beginning the medication. On a symptom checklist, Joanne endorsed the following: loss of meaning in life, poor physical health, crying spells, feeling easily hurt, depressed mood, loneliness, unresolved grief, feeling inferior, "no one understands me," health concerns, dislike for being alone, chronic worry, inability to relax, fearfulness, hypersensitivity, anxiety, and feeling like smashing things. She was not suicidal, although she said that she sometimes thought it would be easier if she just didn't wake up one morning.

History

Joanne's father was a retired military person and her mother a retired restaurant owner. Joanne's parents are both alive but have been divorced for many years. Home was not a happy place. They had waited until the children were in college to make the final break, even though there was an emotional divorce for as long as Joanne could remember.

Family life growing up for Joanne was lonely and sterile. Her mother was not home much, and when she was, there was a lot of fighting. It seemed that Joanne could do nothing right, though she tried again and again. She kept hoping for just a little bit of affirmation, but was continually disappointed.

Both of Joanne's parents were demanding and critical. "My mother was always mad at my father, and she [also] took it out on us kids." The privacy of Joanne's bedroom seemed to be her only peaceful place. When her father was at home, which was infrequent, everyone "walked on eggshells." Joanne has two other siblings, a younger brother and an older sister. There was some family history of depression on her father's side.

Currently, the family remains quite distant and detached from one another, living in different states. "They take very little interest in my life and have not been very supportive, even through some very difficult times. When I do see or talk with them, they are [still] very critical of me."

Joanne was raised in a strict Catholic environment. She shared that she had believed in God most of her life, and became a born-again Christian at a young age. Sadly, she was very wounded by some evangelical Christian friends when they harshly judged her for an instance of sexual immorality that became known to them. Forgiveness and restoration didn't seem to be a part of their repertoire. They never let her forget her sin, and even though Joanne had repented, these friends virtually shunned her. The church further wounded her during her painful divorce. More misunderstanding, legalistic criticism, and unrelenting correction were showered upon her, again devoid of much support or love. Joanne vowed thereafter to stay away from evangelical Christians and began exploring more liberal religions and alternative healing methods. This journey now seemed to be coming full circle, as she reported returning back to faith in Christ alone when she started seeing me. She had also just started attending an evangelical Bible-believing church.

ASSESSMENT

Joanne's interview suggested the presence of depression, anxiety, and numerous somatic complaints. Her testing results prior to the Steps supported these findings. In previous treatments, Joanne stated that she'd had much difficulty taking antidepressant medications. Given these experiences, she thought that she would discontinue her present antidepressant medication.

I encouraged Joanne to give the medication a reasonable trial (a couple of months) and explained to her what an endogenous depression was. She hadn't understood how sometimes a depression could be the result of a chemical imbalance. With her numerous physical complaints, her family history, and her interview findings, I thought it was quite possible that she could be experiencing an endogenous depression. Obviously, her medical doctor agreed, so I was supportive of his medical judgment. I also explained to her that if there was no change in her mood or improvement in her health in the next couple of months she should consult with her doctor about discontinuing the medication. We would monitor her symptoms in therapy and she would keep checking in with her medical doctor.

CASE CONCEPTUALIZATION

Joanne was clear in the initial evaluation that she was looking for some spiritual help as a component to her therapy. She'd had some frightening spiritual experiences that she wasn't sure about (Step 1 description below). In her past courses of therapy, she had explored early family-of-origin issues ad nauseam. "I've talked about all of that on and on and on . . ." she said. Cognitive therapy had also been unhelpful. Thus, conceptualizing her case from these perspectives seemed of limited value.

Given her extensive history of treatment, I decided to start with the Steps to Freedom and see where that would lead us. Perhaps biological and spiritual influences were the key elements in her long-term depression. In essence, I chose a fluid case conceptualization, electing to utilize the Steps to Freedom both as an intervention and an assessment tool. My hope was that it would help me discover the high-valence issues that had been missed in the previous therapies while simultaneously serving as a treatment intervention for these issues. Subsequently, a truly accurate case conceptualization might emerge with further therapy interventions becoming more obvious.

COURSE OF TREATMENT

I saw Joanne for ten sessions. The first appointment was the evaluation session, the next four sessions contained the Steps to Freedom work, and the last five sessions were follow-up and therapy-focused. Most of the sessions were for one hour; two Steps sessions were ninety minutes each; and one session, her second appointment (when we first began the Steps), was two and one-half hours. This was unusual, but I felt it was necessary.

STEPS TO FREEDOM

Joanne had read all the material I sent home with her the week before. She said she had some more information to tell me before we got started on the Steps.

She hesitantly said, "I feel as if I have an evil presence. Do you think this is possible?" She reported that most people think she's crazy talking about this. I assured her of my sincere attention and openness to this and began to explore with her when she first was aware of this evil presence. She began to tell me that her symptoms had started when she was in a therapy appointment with a New Age–type counselor who hypnotized her. However, according to her report, he also consulted a channeler as part of his therapy for all his patients. He would consult with a certain "spirit guide" of this channeler for information to help him in the treatment. Then he would use this information in various ways, in the talk therapy as well as in the hypnotism. Joanne shared with him that she did not feel safe in his office; however, he dismissed her comment and blamed her fear on her father issues.

Shortly after she started these counseling sessions with the New Age therapist, she had a poignant nightmare. She dreamed that she was lost in the woods when a black cat sprang out of nowhere and viciously bit her finger. When she reported this to her therapist the next week, he told her that an evil presence had come into her. From that time on, she reported feeling a foreboding darkness enfolding her and defeating her. "In the dream, this dark presence of the cat uttered what felt like a curse over me," she said. Sometimes it would lessen, depending on what she was doing, but it was always there and she knew it. She wondered if the therapist's involvement with the channeler on her behalf had opened a door to the enemy. I knew then that we should proceed with the Steps.

DISCUSSION QUESTION FOR THERAPISTS

At this point I might ask other counselors, "How would you handle this spiritual problem in your office?" Some might refer her to a pastor. Others might lament, "We didn't learn this in graduate school!" Some, based on your worldview, might have even dismissed Joanne's concerns offhand as a product of her unconscious mind.

In the past, this problem would have felt overwhelming to me. I could pray, but then where would I start? And how could I cover it all? With the Steps to Freedom, I had a reliable tool to use and I was thankful! I knew from a number of past experiences like this that I could help Joanne find freedom from this spiritual bondage. She would do the work and have a tool that could be used by herself in the future. I have seen so many people come to freedom in Christ that I was actually excited to proceed. That may surprise you, but I knew that in the name of Jesus she would experience freedom from this demonic force. The work had already been done on the cross. As children of God "seated with Christ in the heavenlies," the enemy was already "under our feet." When Joanne understood her position in Christ and made choices to confess and renounce various practices, she would be set free from any demonic influences.

SESSION ONE

Step 1: Counterfeit Versus Real

I had already shown Joanne the following diagrams, which I usually draw for clients as I am explaining our position in Christ. I find it very important for Christians to understand their true position, especially when there is a history of occult involvement and the person feels oppressed.

Diagram 1

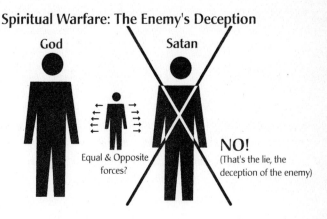

Spiritual Warfare: The Enemy's Deception

God Satan

Equal & Opposite forces?

NO!
(That's the lie, the deception of the enemy)

Diagram 2

Spiritual Warfare: The Reality
HEAVEN

Right hand of the Father God the Father

Jesus

Body of Christ, the church, connecting head to feet

Christian attached to Head but ignorant of worldview

Moves into position under Christ's headship (authority)

Feet (Satan) under Christ's feet

Earth's atmosphere

demons / angels

EARTH

Initial Prayer and Declaration

We started at 4:30 P.M. and finished at 7:00 P.M. This is much longer than I usually spend, but once we started the step, I felt it was important to complete it. I was struggling with some of my own life and family issues that day, so I wasn't feeling "full of faith" when we started. But as I silently confessed my own inadequacy and dependency on God and prayed with Joanne the initial prayer and declaration, I knew afresh that it was God's work; that God Himself was present, powerful, and all-knowing. He knew about her and He knew about me.

Joanne prayed: *Dear Heavenly Father, I ask You to guard my heart and my mind and reveal to me any and all involvement I have had, either knowingly or unknowingly, with cultic or occult practices, false religions, or false teachers. In Jesus' name, I pray. Amen.*

Joanne had been on a quest for knowledge and healing. She was desperately looking for help, but she had been deceived and was going to the wrong sources. Because several Christians had wounded her in the past, she had become protective, bitter, and unforgiving. She had unknowingly opened the door to the enemy by her participation in occult activities and had suffered immeasurably.

In the Non-Christian Spiritual Checklist she checked the following: consulting psychics, medical intuitives, channelers, and fortune-tellers. She had experimented with Reiki, Avatar, Silva Mind Control, numerology, tarot cards, and psychic dreams. In a previous dream, she experienced a voice speaking to her and felt it had come from God. In responding to this voice, she had apparently been empowered with counterfeit power from the evil one. This experience seemed to give her added strength at times, and increased her knowledge about people and circumstances. She had also been a member of a liberal "Christian" church, which incorporated a lot of New Age thinking.

During all these non-Christian practices, she had continued to suffer physical symptoms; her anemia did not seem to respond to treatment and she still had pain in her skeletal musculature. I realized that much of her involvement in these practices had come about as she sincerely searched for truth and relief from her emotional and physical pain. The enemy had taken advantage of her quest. She was surprised that so many of the activities she had participated in, even as a child, were considered occult. She thought that term was given only to satanic rituals.

Joanne confessed and renounced in the name of Jesus all of these activities. She also renounced the spirit of infirmity that she felt had attached itself to her long ago, and lying spirits to whom she had been listening and calling on for help. In addition she confessed and renounced the Ouija board, body lifting, the magic eight ball, séances, clairvoyance, spirit guides, fortune-telling, palm reading, astrology, hypnosis, New Age medicine, blood pacts, crystals, reincarnation, "Course of Miracles" Forum (insight), TM, yoga, martial arts, tai chi, and involvement with psychics.

As she confessed and renounced these activities, she was visibly changed. She looked different and seemed lighter and more energized. There was obviously some closure happening. I knew she had a sensitive spirit and was now trying to follow God with all her heart. She had joined a Bible study at church, but did not know how to get rid of these evil influences from her past life. Despair had characterized her life. Many times she said there was a voice inside that would hound her: *Why don't you just die? You can't be happy. You'll never be loved, even by God. You don't deserve to exist.* It should be noted that Joanne did not exhibit typical symptoms suggestive of a psychosis or dissociative identity disorder, so I felt confident we were dealing with a spiritual issue. This persistent nagging voice was gone after completing this step. She would continue, however, to fight her more egosyntonic self-condemning thoughts in the coming weeks by learning to recognize them and learned to take "every thought captive to the obedience of Christ" (2 Cor. 10: 5).

I asked her to do the satanic ritual involvement renunciations because of her extensive involvement in the occult. The announcement that was meaningful and pivotal for her was: "I announce and accept only the leading of the Holy Spirit." It is important as we seek wisdom and direction that we check our source. It must line up with the Word of God. God is faithful when we ask to be filled by the Holy Spirit, who is the Spirit of Truth. Psalm 139:23–24 reads,

"Search me, O God, and know my heart; try me and know my anxious thoughts; and see if there be any hurtful way in me, and lead me in the way everlasting." This verse was comforting to Joanne as she made a commitment to be led by the Holy Spirit. She also felt great sadness, since she realized that although she had truly wanted to hear God's voice and leading in her life, she had been deceived by some of the New Age teachings on how she could achieve this. This became an issue later for ongoing exploration in therapy when it led to some self-condemnation.

We prayed for healing throughout the process. I asked her to hold a wooden cross on her finger that was hurt in the dream by the cat bite in her nightmare. Since she is a visual person, this symbolic act was comforting to her. It symbolized what Jesus, her Savior, had accomplished for her on the cross. It also spoke to her of a new start. Tearfully, Joanne confessed to God and received His forgiveness. I reminded her of the promise from God's Word: "If we confess our sins, He is faithful and righteous to forgive us our sins and to cleanse us from all unrighteousness" (1 John 1:9 NASB). Scripture also tells us in James 5:16, "Therefore confess your sins to each other and pray for each other so that you may be healed. The prayer of a righteous man is powerful and effective"(NIV).

Being able to make these confessions to another person, even if that other person is a therapist, can be healing! Sometimes we just need to hear the words from another person: "I have heard your confession and, based on God's Word, you are forgiven." At the end of this session, Joanne asked if she could pray her own prayer. It was beautiful and moving. She confessed to the Lord that she had been looking for answers in the wrong places, and for not seeking Jesus. Her ending was dramatic and deeply heartfelt: *Jesus, I'm coming home. Just like the prodigal, I'm coming home to You, Lord Jesus.*

I knew I was "standing on holy ground," and was thankful for God's extravagant love, which I had seen demonstrated to His cherished child. Joanne's courage and honesty with God blessed me. What an honor it is to participate in God's healing work! I gave her the affirmations to repeat daily and asked her to read aloud the daily prayer each morning. We talked about discernment and counterfeit guidance, and the necessity of believing only that which is true. I prayed for her protection and healing before she left. These words ended the notes I made after this session: "Jesus, You're the answer. Hallelujah!"

SESSION TWO

This appointment was a regular one-hour session. I had asked Joanne to continue working through the Steps on her own and she had been diligently doing this. She was committed; in fact, she had decided to devote her entire week to studying the material.

Many clients do benefit from working through the material on their own. I recommend stopping if the process becomes too difficult, with the understanding that you'll address these difficulties in the next therapy session. Some clients need the support of another person to do this work. However, Joanne did well with it on her own. When I asked her for feedback from the last session she said, "I felt cleaner . . . It felt good to cleanse me and to cleanse my house." She told me then that she had thrown out many items, like books, crystals, and other symbols related to the occult activities in which she had participated and subsequently renounced.

She wanted to talk more about therapy-related issues—about her loneliness, her disappointments in relationships, her ambivalent relationship with her mother, her sadness about not really having a family of close connections, and her longing to belong somewhere. She had already done work on her issues of codependency with past therapists, but now was beginning to see things "in a new light." She discussed some specific relationships in which she continued to give and give because she said, "I wanted to get something back, a family." Usually this resulted in frustration and more loneliness.

I explored with Joanne further how she deals with her emotions, explaining that emotions are E-motion (energy in motion) and gave her my handout on processing anger. When I asked her about the emotion of anger and how she deals with anger, she said, "Anger is what I feel the most." She was open to considering that she used her anger to cover up more painful and sad feelings. In therapy, I sensed that she needed to do some grieving and experience some healing on a deeper level so that her anger would be used less defensively. She explained that with her ethnic background, anger was difficult for her; she didn't know how to process this emotion in a way that would give her satisfying results. "My anger has not gotten me where I want to be," she said.

Step 2: Deception Versus Truth;
Step 3: Bitterness Versus Forgiveness

We continued with these steps. As Joanne worked through Step 2 on deception versus truth, she checked almost all of the items in self-deception and self-defense. The prayers affirming her desire for truth were helpful and "solidifying." The Statement of Truth was an encouragement to her, and I suggested that she read those words of Scripture regularly. She wanted to process Step 3 on forgiveness in the time that was left because she said she'd spent considerable time on this at home. "I have a list of about forty-five names of people that I need to forgive," she said. At the top of the list was her mother.

Joanne had read many books on the subject of forgiveness. She seemed to have a good understanding of the concept of forgiveness and didn't have any questions. I was questioning whether we had enough time (about fifteen minutes) but proceeded at her insistence and apparent readiness. For some people, just making the choice to forgive and speaking this forgiveness out loud to God is extremely helpful. It puts them on the right road and reminds them of the decision that they have made as the layers of the onion peel away and the healing comes with the passage of time. The advantage, then, of doing this in therapy is that the therapist can pick up on issues and relationships that need deeper exploration and resolution. This indeed did happen in the next session, especially in regard to Joanne's relationship with her mother and some of those wounding Christian friends. I asked Joanne, "How many times did Jesus say that we are to forgive our brother, when Peter asked him?" She knew that passage of Scripture from Matthew 18:21–22, and replied, "Seven times seventy. That's a lot of layers."

Sometimes people think that if anger surfaces again after they have made the choice to forgive someone, the forgiveness didn't work. That's a common misunderstanding. In fact, it's a relief for clients to learn that once they are on the road to forgiveness, after they have made the choice to forgive, that God's grace and light are available to them to continue the process of forgiveness as another layer becomes exposed. The clue often is the experience of more anger when they think about it. They have to tell themselves: "I choose to stay on this road of forgiveness and deal with any new layer. The decision has been made. I am not going to go over again in my mind what I have already dealt with."

I had another client who had been deeply wounded by a Christian leader. She made the choice to forgive. In fact, when she finished therapy with me, she created a beautiful poster collage with probably a hundred presentations of the word choice cut from magazines. *Choice* is an important word for me when I am doing therapy. That is another reason I appreciate the Steps to Freedom as a therapeutic tool, because the working principle of the Steps is that the client is empowered to make their own responsible choices. We make a choice to forgive someone. This is the beginning of the healing process, and we choose to forgive, since we ourselves have been forgiven by a merciful God, through Jesus Christ (Matt. 6:14). This same client called me a year or so later and said, "I think I'm on the last layer of the onion in my forgiveness toward 'so and so.'"

SESSION THREE

Joanne had struggled through the week before this planned ninety-minute session. She had begun second-guessing herself, wondering why God hadn't stopped her when she started looking for help in the occult and New Age religions. "I was just trying to find the truth!" she said. "I guess I'm angry at God too. After all the Christians that have hurt me deeply, why wouldn't I go in the other direction?" she asked. As we explored this further, she mentioned some specific people and talked about the incidents. More pain surfaced and was processed. After a while, she said, "I guess I want to forgive them too." This hadn't come up in the last session. One advantage of doing the Steps in an ongoing therapeutic relationship is that you can keep doing the spiritual work as it comes up. So Joanne chose to forgive the individuals she had talked about, and with that, let go of some of the related pain. She again confessed her anger toward God. When a sense of closure was apparent, we proceeded to the next step.

Step 4: Rebellion Versus Submission

This was a big one for Joanne. As she prayed, "Dear Heavenly Father, You have said that rebellion is as the sin of witchcraft and insubordination is as iniquity and idolatry (1 Sam. 15:23)," she stopped. "Yes, I have been rebellious toward authority and toward God. With the abuse I suffered, it's been difficult for me to trust and submit." This led to a discussion about the very nature of Satan and rebellion. He was kicked out of heaven for this reason and he now perpetuates rebellion in God's children here on earth. I suggested Joanne read aloud Revelation 12:9: "The great dragon was hurled down—that ancient serpent called the devil, or Satan, who leads the whole world astray. He was hurled to the earth, and his angels with him"(NIV). This was new information for Joanne. As she continued to read the Scripture, I could see that it was impacting and empowering her. "Then I heard a loud voice in heaven say: 'Now have come the salvation and the power and the kingdom of our God, and the authority of his Christ. For the accuser of our brothers, who accuses them before our God day and night, has been hurled down. They overcame him by the blood of the Lamb and by the word of their testimony'" (v. 10–11 NIV). "Yes," she said, "I have heard a lot of those accusations." Joanne confessed her rebellion toward God and prayed: "I choose to be submissive and obedient to Your Word. In Jesus' name, amen."

Discussion Questions for Therapists

In our own practice, how should we handle clients who have problems with authority? Clearly, exploring client wounds inflicted by past authority figures (like parents, for example) is an important part of treatment. The anger from these incidents must be processed and the connection made to current rebellious behaviors, but is that sufficient? What spiritual resources can be brought to bear on this problem? I must confess that I didn't know of many Christian therapy interventions specifically designed for this issue before I began using the Steps to Freedom. I have found the Steps a valuable tool that helps bring closure and motivates clients to change their behavior in this area of their lives.

Step 5: Pride Versus Humility

Joanne looked over the pride categories and said, "Well, I guess I have to check most of these areas. I thought I could do it all myself, but it hasn't worked." In a previous session, she had talked about the martyr role she had adopted for herself, the belief that she would always have to suffer and be punished. She was able to see, as we talked about this, that underneath that role were pride and rebellion. "I was sort of a self-righteous victim," she commented. We also discussed how her inability to receive God's forgiveness of herself was a form of pride. In essence, Joanne was thinking that she should be held to a different, higher standard than other people. These themes fit into the driving, self-defeating habit of perfectionism. "I should be better than this!" Joanne readily grasped these ideas. For many clients, the most difficult forgiveness work is toward oneself. I have heard many clients say, "I can forgive others, but I won't forgive myself." Joanne now recognized the seed of pride behind that statement.

Step 6: Bondage Versus Freedom

In this step Joanne was able to deal with all her past sexual experiences, which had defiled her. The value of this step as I have seen over and over again is that a person can take care of this in one fell swoop. It is done and over with. As clients renounce the unrighteous use of their bodies and ask God to break the ties to those with whom they have been sexually active, they are set free and cleansed. In my previous therapeutic experience, this would not happen as comprehensively. Clients might disclose some of their sexual history bit by bit, but when Joanne prayed, "Lord, I ask You to reveal to my mind every sexual use of my body as an instrument of unrighteousness. In Jesus' precious name, I pray. Amen," God did just that! She confessed the sexual relationships with men specifically by name, the covert sexual innuendoes from her sexually-addictive, immoral, alcoholic father, the impact of the pornography left around the house by him, and she broke the spiritual ties with all of the people involved. This process is based on Romans 6:11–13 and 1 Corinthians 6:15–20.

DISCUSSION QUESTIONS FOR THERAPISTS

While many Christian therapists acknowledge the spiritual aspects of sexual unions, they essentially ignore the implications of this reality in their work with clients. The Bible makes it very clear that "the two shall become one." Does this matter, or is it just a flowery metaphor? How should we as Christian therapists handle this reality in therapy?

I have found that for many of my clients breaking spiritual ties formed in nonmarital sexual unions has been of great benefit. Two other clients who were significantly helped by this step come to my mind. One was an elderly retired minister's wife who had been suffering physically and emotionally for many years. I was treating her for depression. We also had gone through the Steps to Freedom. In Step 6, she broke down and confessed an immoral affair forty years previously that she had never been able to talk about to anyone. She had lived with guilt and suffering, even though she had confessed it to God over and over again. When she went through this step and talked about it, she was incredibly set free. As she prayed the following prayer aloud, I could see and hear the relief, the release, and the healing that were happening to this precious older saint.

Lord, I renounce all these uses of my body as an instrument of unright-eousness and by so doing ask You to break all bondages Satan has brought into my life through that involvement. I confess my participation. I now present my body to You as a living sacrifice, holy and acceptable unto You, and I reserve the sexual use of my body only for marriage. I renounce the lie of Satan that my body is not clean, that it is dirty or in any way unacceptable as a result of my past sexual experience. Lord, I thank You that You have totally cleansed and forgiven me, that You love and accept me unconditionally. Therefore, I can accept myself. And I choose to do so, to accept myself and my body as cleansed. In Jesus' name. Amen.

After a client prays the above prayer, I suggest that they symbolically "put a stake down," a visual reminder that they have done some serious work. When the enemy then tries to torment with the words "you're not really clean, you're not forgiven," the client more easily recognizes that as a lie and can look at something concrete such as a date written in their Bible by the Scripture: "If we confess our sins, He is faithful and righteous to forgive us our sins and to cleanse us from all unrighteousness" (1 John 1:9 NASB). They make their stand against the accuser by saying, "No, I am forgiven and cleansed. I made the choice on (date). I am a child of God and dearly loved."

I sometimes have clients tear up the piece of paper with the list of people they have forgiven or names of people with whom they have had unholy sex. At the conclusion of therapy with the above older lady, she mentioned that this "stake" was a very important reminder to her and her newfound freedom from the guilt of this ancient affair. This step was liberating and crucial to her newfound freedom and health.

Another client, an eighteen-year-old, who was experiencing depression after breaking up with a boyfriend, benefited from Step 6. This committed Christian woman, who thought of herself as one who had high moral values, had been sexually involved with her boyfriend. She believed that she was maimed for life and would never be forgiven by God. Of course, this would be depressing! Step 6 provided her the opportunity to confess, renounce and to receive God's forgiveness. She could now "put a stake down," get a new start, and not continue the sexual behavior in which she no longer wished to engage.

Perhaps our worldview as therapists has limited us in considering the spiritual aspects of this part of our clients' lives. Our worldview may also have limited us in developing effective spiritual interventions in this area. If you are not currently addressing the spiritual aspects of nonmarital sexual unions in your practice, we encourage you to do so by utilizing this approach in Step 6.

Physical Abuse and Trauma Bonds

After Joanne had prayed the prayers related to the sexual bondage, she asked me about physical abuse. She wanted to pray about that because she felt that the physical abuse at the hands of her parents, and later her husband, had wounded her deeply and also affected her spiritually. While there isn't a specific prayer for this in the Steps, Joanne spontaneously prayed, "Lord, I renounce the physical abuse and any effects it had on my body, soul, or spirit, and I break those ties." She did this specifically for each person.

As Joanne prayed, I couldn't help but think about current psychological trauma bond theories that are used to explain why people remain stuck reenacting past traumatic events in their current lives. Briefly, the traumatic experiences become deeply engrained at both an emotional and physiological level for trauma victims, resulting in a deep connection to the events, despite a current rational abhorrence for the events. The Holy Spirit may have been inspiring Joanne with a way to begin breaking the connection.

After her renunciations, the session naturally flowed into a time of asking the Lord to lead her through a process of recalling painful memories. I reminded Joanne that Jesus is the same yesterday, today and forever (Heb. 13:8), and that He is able to heal the traumatic emotions of past hurtful memories in the photo albums of our lives. After I explained the process, she eagerly consented to pray for the presence of Jesus through the Holy Spirit, to shine His Spirit of truth. I am careful here not to suggest any images. I just wait for the client to share with me what they are experiencing. When she prayed, she saw what looked like a filter, which allowed only negatives about herself. These were the lies she believed while receiving the verbal and physical abuse. When she forgave those individuals and pictured putting them at the foot of the cross, this image separated from her and she said, "I'm at the cross. Jesus' blood is flowing over me and cleansing me." This was very significant for Joanne, and she said she felt very comforted as she experienced the presence of Jesus and heard Him speak the words: *You are My child and I love you.*

Step 7: Acquiescence Versus Renunciation

Joanne prayed the prayers "rejecting and disowning all the sins and iniquities of my ancestors." Some of the sins of her ancestors included sexual infidelity, lust, illegitimate births, abandonment, self-pity, and loneliness. By this time in the process, Joanne had experienced more fully her true identity in Christ. She had been set free from many oppressive influences of the evil one. She had also done some good therapy regarding her family of origin issues, although this was not finished. She had continued to do the forgiveness work that she had begun in Step 3. Step 6 relating to the sexual and physical bondage was important. So when she came to Step 7, it became more a summary of the issues with which she had already dealt. She simply read through this step and, finishing, said, "I agree. That felt good. It's covered!"

SESSION FOUR

This fourth session was three weeks later. Joanne reported that she was doing very well. In fact, she had decided to make a major career change and was already in the process that included a move. She had more physical energy although she knew that she had to pace herself. Most of this one-hour session was spent in processing a new relationship in which she had been tempted to behave in her codependent style. She was able to catch herself and see that this dating relationship would not be healthy for her. She was able to get in touch with her anger indicating that something was wrong. She wanted to confront this man but decided this would take her to a place of intimacy that she didn't want. Joanne's processing of the event told me she was learning to set clearer boundaries for herself. While she wanted to blame herself for even going on the date, I thought she was fairly successful. She had at least recognized what was going on and made a decision not to get involved. This was growth, especially in light of her history of relationships with men who used and abused her.

We worked through the "fear" sheet from the Steps and also another sheet that I use regarding family curses. This was helpful for Joanne. We had completed the Steps to Freedom. I gave her a copy of the list "Truth Versus Lies" for her continuing study, and also gave her a copy of the "Surrender Prayer," which many people find helpful. We finished by her praying the "Daily Prayer." When she left this session she said, "Actually, I am doing a lot better."

Summarizing Joanne's treatment with the Steps, Joanne wanted to forgive herself for the past and her present situation in life. Being a melancholic, introspective, self-contained person, she tended to obsess about her lack of "family success." We had processed this and how this habit of self-condemnation was defeating to her. With her newfound identity in Christ, she was ready to renounce her identity as a victim and a martyr. When she did this she appeared to experience much relief. She wanted to make a new clean start with God and move toward a future free from her "old baggage."

As I had hoped, the Steps also helped me identify further areas for work in therapy. Joanne's strong perfectionism and performance orientation were key influences in her life that needed more work.

Strengthening her identity as a child of God was also critical, versus the familiar position of being a martyr or victim. Finally, the continuing powerful influence of Joanne's poor relationship with her mother needed more addressing. This disappointing relationship had been a theme from the beginning of therapy. She had addressed this in the "forgiveness" step and also in Step 2 where she had believed lies about herself related to the continuing degrading criticisms from her mother.

ASSESSMENT OF PROGRESS, CONTINUED THERAPY, AND FOLLOW-UP

I had four more sessions with Joanne. During these sessions, we continued looking at her perfectionism and strong performance orientation. Cognitive restructuring around these issues was helpful. This element of therapy focused on the transforming and renewing of the mind that must continue to take place in the ongoing process of conforming to God's image (Rom. 12:2). Joanne was free from many of the evil influences of her past, and this made a significant difference! However, transformation continues for all of us.

During a couple of these sessions, we also worked on Joanne's present relationship with her mother. She continued to learn to recognize the lack of bonding with her mother, something that had been pointed out by other therapists. One particularly difficult interaction during the months of therapy triggered some painful childhood memories. The interaction reinforced Joanne's thoughts that she had believed from childhood that she was not wanted or valued. Because of going through the Steps she was able this time to see that these were lies, not the truth. Healing prayer was useful in making that truth a heartfelt reality. As Joanne reached back in her memory and experienced the pain of the childhood images again, we asked Jesus to heal the emotional wounds. In the memory picture, she felt the Lord's touch, His tender comfort, and His words of love to her. Her identity as a child of God was further strengthened and expanded as she asked the Holy Spirit to fill this part of her heart. She noted a "sense of deep peace" as she left that day.

Given Joanne's relationship with her mother, I was not surprised when she experienced some anger with me in a therapy session. She was able to express this anger, testing it out with me in the therapeutic setting and still experiencing acceptance.

At the close of therapy, Joanne seemed to be in a safer emotional space where she could begin to grieve the loss involved in her lack of relationship with her mother. She also appeared capable of coming to a measure of acceptance about this sad reality. She was blaming herself less, and exhibiting less black-and-white behavior regarding the management of her anger. She was being more honest and setting clearer boundaries for herself.

Regarding the medication, Joanne had discontinued that in consultation with her doctor by our second session. She didn't want to handle the side effects. While her symptoms of depression had decreased significantly in treatment, medication in the future would still need to be a consideration should a relapse of depression occur.

Joanne had benefited from both therapy and the Steps to Freedom. She had a tool that she could use herself in the future. She knew how to protect herself spiritually and how to resolve her own spiritual conflicts. She was discovering the value of having Christian fellowship and accountability relationships in the body of Christ. She was empowered by her identity as a child of God and her position in Christ. She was now aware of the practical power of the Word of God to overcome evil influences.

Joanne thanked me, saying that she had appreciated my directness, my confrontations, my compassion, and the Steps to Freedom. She said that all aspects of her treatment had been very helpful to her, and she was functioning much better. She finished by saying, "It's pretty exciting. God is doing some amazing things!"

Testing Results

SCL-90-R Joanne's testing results showed a pattern suggestive of a positive response to her treatment. Figures 1–3 highlight some of her SCL-90-R findings in raw score equivalents.

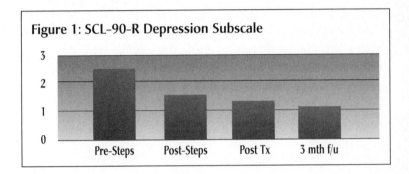

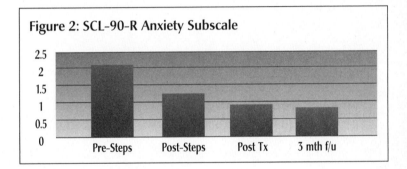

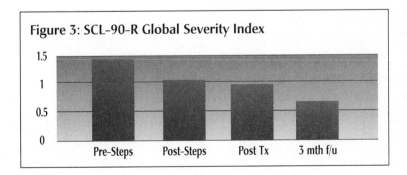

Table 1 below describes Joanne's SCL-90-R results in more detail. Scores are reported in raw score equivalents and T scores.

Table 1

	Pre-Steps	Post-Steps	Post-Tx	3 Mth f/u
Somatic	1.17 (65T)	1.25 (66T)	0.42 (53T)	0.25 (49T)
Obsessive-Compulsive	1.10 (64T)	0.80 (60T)	0.70 (58T)	0.70 (58T)
Interpersonal Sensitivity	1.11 (66T)	1.00 (64T)	1.67 (71T)	1.00 (64T)
Depression	2.46 (72T)	154 (67T)	1.31 (65T)	1.15 (63T)
Anxiety	2.10 (72T)	1.20 (67T)	0.90 (63T)	0.80 (61T)
Hostility	0.83 (63T)	0.50 (57T)	0.67 (60T)	0.33 (54T)
Phobias	0.43 (61T)	0.43 (61T)	0.29 (58T)	0.14 (54T)
Paranoia	1.17 (66T)	1.00 (63T)	0.83 (62T)	0.83 (62T)
Psychoticism	1.20 (73T)	1.00 (71T)	0.90 (69T)	0.70 (66T)
Global Severity Index	1.41 (69T)	1.07 (66T)	0.89 (64T)	0.70 (61T)
Positive Sx Distress Index	2.05 (66T)	1.52 (56T)	1.45 (55T)	1.26 (50T)
Positive Symptom Total	62 (69T)	63 (70T)	55 (66T)	50 (65T)

Following the Steps to Freedom, ten out of twelve scales on the SCL-90-R exhibited a decrease in score, including the key overall indicator of emotional distress, the Global Severity Index. Likewise, ten out of twelve scales further decreased with therapy. Each component of treatment appeared to positively impact Joanne's treatment. The three-month follow-up data suggests these gains were maintained or improved upon as Joanne continued her growth process. While she likely needs to continue monitoring her progress, she appears headed in the right direction.

Similar to the other cases reported, one has to consider whether random measurement error could account for these SCL-90-R results. That is possible. While an identifiable trend in symptom reduction is noted, large decreases did not occur. One could argue that the steady improvement could be an artifact of instrument psychometrics.

However, if this were the case, the testing would show a more random pattern of small increases and decreases in the scale scores. Thus, while measurement error cannot be totally discounted, the number of scales decreasing in symptom levels and the congruence of this instrument's findings with the FICM Survey Items (see below) support an association of both the Steps and therapy with improvements in Joanne's condition.

FICM Survey Items FICM Survey Items also suggested lower levels of distress with Joanne's treatment. Figures 4 through 8 describe these changes. Lower scores on this 1–10 scale reflect less distress.

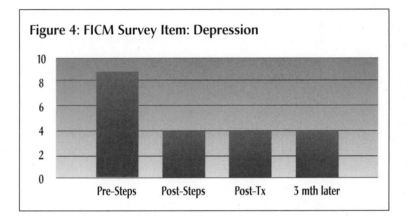

Figure 4: FICM Survey Item: Depression

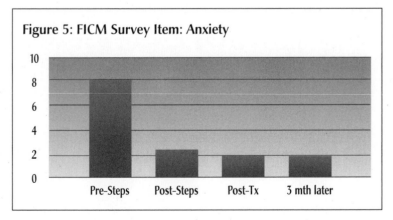

Figure 5: FICM Survey Item: Anxiety

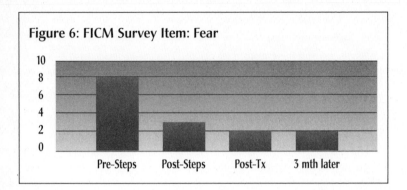

Figure 6: FICM Survey Item: Fear

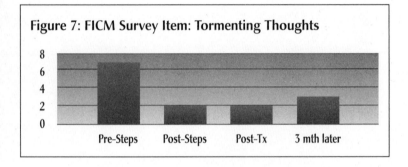

Figure 7: FICM Survey Item: Tormenting Thoughts

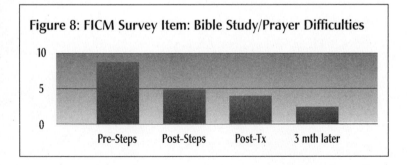

Figure 8: FICM Survey Item: Bible Study/Prayer Difficulties

Table 2 Summarizes FICM Survey results for each item.

	Pre-Steps	Post-Steps	Post-Tx	3 Mth f/u
Depression	8	4	4	4
Anxiety	8	3	2	3
Fear	8	3	2	2
Anger	5	2	4	3
Tormenting Thoughts	7	2	2	3
Habits	4	2	2	2
Self-Esteem	4	3	7	3
Daily Functioning	5	3	3	3
Relationship Satisfaction	8	5	8	6
Physical Health	9	6	5	5
Bible/Prayer Difficulties	8	5	4	3
Reality of God In Your Life	8	6	7	3

DAS Concerning dysfunctional beliefs that might predispose Joanne to depression, she received the following scores on the Dysfunctional Attitude Scale. Lower scores indicate more adaptive beliefs.

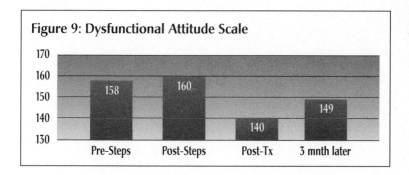

Figure 9: Dysfunctional Attitude Scale

Joanne started with a mild level of dysfunctional beliefs. While the Steps did not appear to significantly effect these beliefs, the therapy process itself was associated with a decrease in maladaptive cognitions. This gain was diminished somewhat at the three-month follow-up, but her status remained in the same mild range.

SWBS As her initial presentation suggested, Joanne started treatment with a relatively low level of spiritual well-being. Figure 10 describes Joanne's total Spiritual Well-Being Scale scores.

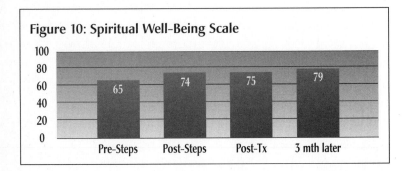

Figure 10: Spiritual Well-Being Scale

Joanne's scores indicate some improvement, with room for more growth. When considered in conjunction with FICM Survey items on Bible Study/Prayer, Reality of God in Your Life, and Joanne's satisfaction questionnaire responses (see below), this hypothesis of moderately improved spiritual well-being is strengthened. The Steps appear correlated with Joanne's overall improvement in this area. My prayer is that this trend of improvement continues as Joanne persists in the ongoing process of renewing her mind.

Client Satisfaction Joanne scored a 27 on the Client Satisfaction Questionnaire-8, suggesting a high level of satisfaction with her treatment. Some of her responses to the FICM satisfaction survey items included the following:

> I am grateful that God led me to my therapist and to the Freedom in Christ process. I can see now that even though I felt anger at God for not saving me from my bad choices, He never gave up on trying to lead me back home . . . For most of my life, I had felt that God's love

was tied to how good I was. This made it difficult for me after going through the process, not to see God as standing there with His hands on His hips and a stern look on His face, saying, "I can't believe you've made this many mistakes! What's WRONG with you!" This is the ongoing process of bringing thoughts captive to the obedience of Christ. It is difficult for my family to show mercy because of their own woundedness, so I need to ask God frequently to help me accept His love and mercy and give it to others. I still struggle at times believing God could love me when I fail to live according to His Word and His will so often. What I need now is a steady diet of prayer and of God's Word reminding me that I *am* His precious child. I think this is a critical follow-up to this process, otherwise guilt and condemnation can come into our house, like the demons who were cast out and came back and found the house empty [Luke 11:24–26].

While I was exercising the other day, I was praying out loud and started to play the role of the prodigal daughter speaking to God. "I want to come home, God," I said, "but I feel so unworthy. I've made so many mistakes!" I then heard another voice come through my prayer. It was God's voice and He said, "I don't care what you've done in the past, I only care that you've come home; I have blessings waiting for you!" I saw God's arms outstretched, and I felt His love and mercy and the need to accept God's forgiveness. I don't feel that every day, but it's getting easier. God is transforming me, glory to glory. Praise God.

TREATMENT IMPLICATIONS OF THE CASE

In going through the Steps to Freedom, Joanne had benefited most from Step 1, which addresses occult, Step 3, which addresses forgiveness, and Step 6, which addresses sexual bondage. Each person is different, and it's usually quite evident which of the particular steps have deeper impact on the person. Going through the Steps also enabled me to identify more clearly areas to address in therapy—Joanne's perfectionism, her performance orientation, and her relationship with her mother.

Some of my discussion questions previously posed have emphasized issues relating to a client's non-Christian spiritual activities. Does this really matter in treatment? It's interesting to note that Joanne, a nonpsychotic, nondissociative client, felt that there was a voice always condemning her. After going through the Steps to Freedom, she felt that voice was gone. She still had to struggle with self-condemning thoughts that were part of her old nature (flesh). We can resist the devil and he will flee, but we cannot tell our flesh to leave. That is overcome as we renew our minds to the truth of God's words. Understanding her authority in Christ over the kingdom of darkness really did matter for Joanne. Given Joanne's rather extensive involvement with New Age experiences, it makes sense that when she renounced these activities, something happened. She still had some self-critical tendencies to deal with at the end of treatment, but that sense of an oppressive critical presence was no longer there. Her response to the FICM Survey item on tormenting thoughts appears to highlight this sense of relief.

We raised the question earlier of the spiritual impact of sexual acting out. Is it just a physical act, with no spiritual bonding? If we as therapists truly believe something spiritual does happen in the sexual act, then it's time for us to develop ways of addressing this element in treatment. Step 6 in Dr. Anderson's approach is a good place to start. Having a biblical worldview greatly impacts our therapeutic practice.

Going through the Steps to Freedom also set the stage for Joanne's lifelong process of transformation and renewing of the mind. Her issues of perfectionism and performance orientation would continue to need her personal attention, but now she knew better how to apply God's Word to counteract these works-oriented tendencies.

Joanne also learned some new forms of prayer to help her in her relationship with God and challenging maladaptive beliefs. Some of her responses to client satisfaction survey questions indicate the usage of healing prayer as an ongoing coping strategy outside the therapeutic context. Part of therapy always involves helping the client develop better coping strategies to live their life. Enhancing the client's ability to access their spiritual resources in Christ as a part of their regular daily coping may decrease the likelihood of relapse. As more long-term outcome studies are done on Christian interventions such as Freedom in Christ, this observation may become more than just a hypothesis.

CHAPTER 10

Case Study III: *Mary*

IDENTIFYING INFORMATION

"My friend Sharon sent me here. I've been meaning to come for a long time. Yesterday I saw her and she seemed to be her joyful, bubbly self again. She gave me your name again, so here I am." Mary, a neat and attractive woman, sat down and began to tell me her story. As she talked, I began sketching out a family genogram and taking her history. She began to relax and answered my questions regarding the details of her personal, marital, and family histories.

Mary is a thirty-eight-year-old white married female of Italian and German descent. She has been married to John (the first marriage for each) for sixteen years. They have four children (three girls and a boy ages 14, 9, 7, and 2). Her husband is a family physician in a rural private practice.

PRESENTING COMPLAINTS

"My life is out of control," Mary complained. "I can't make my husband happy, my kids talk back all the time and I just scream at them, [and] my house is a mess!" Mary maintained that she didn't know what to do with her anger, although she felt it a lot! When I asked Mary to describe how she usually was, she said, "Usually, I'm a happy, caring, and helpful person. Lately, I've been disorganized,

really crabby, and kind of depressed . . . I can't seem to get motivated to do anything around the house, the laundry doesn't get
done, the dishes stay in the sink for days, and there's clutter everywhere." The more her husband complained, the less she wanted to
do. Although she attended church with her family, she said that it
was not helping her much. She struggled with guilt and "heavy baggage" in her spiritual life. Her self-esteem was low and she felt discouraged and lethargic. "I just don't like myself," she said.

HISTORY

During her teen years and early twenties, Mary had been into the
party scene, with its alcohol, sex, and frenetic activity. Sadly, her
sexual promiscuity led to an unexpected pregnancy and subsequent
abortion. Socially, she reported having had lots of friends and met
her husband, John, at a party. He, too, was into this lifestyle.

John was in medical school while she worked full-time as a travel
agent. They had a long courtship and enjoyed partying together.
Mary became a Christian through a work associate. "It changed my
life," she said. Because of her changed life, John, a backslidden
Christian, began reevaluating his own faith, and, shortly thereafter,
recommitted his life to Christ. Soon, the couple became engaged
and got married.

After the birth of their third child, Mary experienced postpartum
depression for which she was treated medically. Nine years later, she
was diagnosed with cervical cancer, which led to a hysterectomy.
She responded well to the surgery and stated, "I've put that behind
me now." Since then, the couple have been raising their children,
working long hours, and finding life at home to be an increasing
struggle. Discipline problems with the children and her husband's
perfectionism about the house being tidy were especially challenging. She complained, "He seems to be more critical and demanding
. . . and I have less and less energy . . . I try to keep the peace, or he
just gets very quiet for days."

Despite her growing sense of depression, John was very resistant to her coming for therapy and he made it very clear to her that he would never go to a therapist himself. I wondered if this would change over time. I thought that marital therapy could be a potentially worthwhile treatment component for both of them.

Mary is the middle child of five siblings. Her father, a car salesman, was a man of both strengths and a significant weakness. He had been disabled by polio as a child. In spite of this disability, he had managed to function quite well on many levels. He became a gifted musician and even produced his own recordings, but his alcoholism dramatically impacted the family.

"We just ignored it and stayed out of his way," Mary said. The drinking, however, produced constant parental arguments and a dysfunctional family lifestyle. "My mother was always working, money was tight, and we seemed to fight a lot." The family was nominally Catholic and attended church on Christmas and Easter, if that. On Thanksgiving Day, when Mary was twenty-one years old, her father suddenly died of a massive stroke. There had been no warning signs. After her father's death, Mary's mother remained a widow for ten years. Subsequently, she remarried and moved out of the state.

Assessment

When Mary completed a symptom checklist, she marked the following: lack of energy, frequent sweating, shaky hands, feeling tense, cold feet and hands, headaches, feeling easily hurt, lacking in confidence, feeling grouchy, depressed, feelings of guilt, loss of sexual interest, can't "get going," feeling angry, overly sensitive, quick-tempered, and impatient with people. Mary was experiencing symptoms of depression with marked irritability.

She has been on 40 mg Prozac for two years, which, she stated, is helping. She has been on a regulated estrogen patch since the hysterectomy. Her doctor the previous year also started her on a medication for attention deficit disorder.

CASE CONCEPTUALIZATION

Since Mary was receiving medical help for her depression with some positive results, I felt that resolving some of her emotional and spiritual conflicts, along with anger management, would be most beneficial. Mary usually tried to please people outside the home, often at the expense of her own needs and those of her family. She was also codependent with her husband. These characteristics contributed to her own unresolved anger, which she acted out passively toward her husband. For example, she would go on a shopping spree "to take care of myself" and tell her husband that she was going to a church meeting. She would then tell her husband that food was costing more these days.

COURSE OF TREATMENT

I saw Mary for fifteen sessions over the course of eight months. The first two sessions of treatment were evaluative. Mary was interested in starting the anger management and was also interested in going through the Steps to Freedom, which she had heard about from her friend. I gave her an anger inventory and some reading to do on the subject for the second session. I also asked her to monitor the times when she experienced the anger and the circumstances, to determine some of her triggers. Then we would discuss more productive ways to deal with her anger, which she could practice as homework. I also explained to her the Steps to Freedom process, and she consented to have this as part of her treatment. Her friend, who had recommended the therapy, told her how much the Steps had helped. Treatment goals were to decrease the symptoms of depression and to increase her satisfaction in her relationships with family and God. We did the Steps to Freedom in eight sessions. Sessions Six and Seven consisted predominantly of dealing with therapeutic issues, while Session Eight completed the intervention.

THE STEPS TO FREEDOM
SESSION ONE

Opening Prayer and Declaration

I asked Mary to read through the prayer and declaration silently in order to give her some time to take in the meaning of the words. Then we prayed these prayers together. She said it felt good. It was good to declare out loud our dependence on God. "It's like you're inviting God into the session and that He's in control," she said. She didn't have any problems with any of the concepts or the words, and seemed eager to proceed.

Step 1: Counterfeit Versus Real

"I'm kind of superstitious," Mary said. I asked her what she meant by that. "Oh, if the light turns before I get there, then the evening will go well and he won't be mad at me." We talked about this snippet of magical thinking, but it didn't appear to be a major influence in Mary's life. We went through the columns of the Non-Christian Spiritual Checklist. She checked the usual things that many children experiment with: Oujia board, magic eight ball, and reading horoscopes. "But these were just silly games we played as children," she said. I assured her that it wouldn't hurt to renounce activities just in case they had impacted her in some way. "This way, we'll know they're taken care of for good," I said. She mentioned some movies that had left "spooky" feelings and a television program entitled *Dark Shadows*, which had left continuing foreboding feelings.

Usually, I pause at the conclusion of the lists of these non-Christian experiences. We prayed and asked the Holy Spirit to speak to her if there was anything further to deal with. This is a good time to model listening to God. Often, the client thinks of something else and then takes care of it. They begin to learn that listening to God is not so difficult! Mary didn't "hear" anything else, i.e. nothing came to mind, so we continued. I encouraged her then to read the announcements of her identity as a child of the light. "I am the bride of Christ." She smiled as she read this one. "That means He really must have forgiven me," she sighed. I could see that this truth was going deeper and that the Holy Spirit was ministering to her.

Step 2: Deception Versus Truth

It's important to observe the clients when they are praying in order to pick up on any resistance or blocks. If facial expression portrays some consternation, you can stop and ask if anything is bothering them. Mary was worried about using written prayers and wanted to talk about her concerns. They reminded her of her childhood religious experience when she had to recite Catholic liturgies. I explained that there is nothing magical about these steps. They are just biblical prayers asking for the Lord's guidance for the purpose of resolving personal and spiritual conflicts, which we all have. God's Word does have the power to change us. By reading the prayers aloud, she was making an announcement to the spiritual realm of her intention to be right with God. Speaking aloud would also help to reinforce these truths in her mind.

After hearing Mary's concerns, I explained further the rationale for this step. I explained that the brain was like the hard drive on the computer, and our old flesh patterns and messages were the software with which it was programmed. Our spirit could be born again, but we still had to renew our minds, which had these flesh-based software problems (Pity we all couldn't just delete the program and install a new one!). This, I explained to Mary, was part of our spiritual transformation, which is a continuing process for every believer. Once these issues were addressed, Mary was able to pray without any difficulty. I made it clear that she could stop or pause at any time to talk further.

Mary identified some of her self-defeating defenses, in particular, denial, projection, insulation, and fantasy. We talked about how she had developed these defenses as a child in order to survive. Now, with a surrendering heart, she was asking God for help with them. Mary had already been working on the deceptions that she used to protect herself and to please her husband. She told me that the week before she had chosen to be truthful by disclosing some things to her husband. His initial reaction "wasn't good," but he did listen. They had a good talk and the next day they got up early and started a devotional time together. This was very helpful, she said, and she was encouraged. Her homework was to begin to recognize these defenses in her daily life and also to repeat the doctrinal affirmation every day.

I was working with another client for six weeks and I didn't feel that we were getting very far in therapy. We had started to go through the Steps to Freedom and had come to the second step, which deals with deception versus truth. She prayed the following prayer: "I acknowledge that I have been deceived by the father of lies [John 8:44], and that I have deceived myself [1 John 1:8] . . . I now ask the Holy Spirit to guide me into all truth [John 16:13]." She abruptly stopped mid-paragraph and said, "I've been lying to you. I've been taking someone else's prescription medication and I'm addicted to it." I was flabbergasted. Since I have a specialty in substance abuse, I "thought" I was tuned in to these kind of problems! This step provided a break in the case and with that honesty, healing work began. Some Christian clients may lie to us, but lying to God is another issue and they seem to know the difference. God is good and His Word sets captives free.

SESSION TWO

When Mary arrived at this appointment, she said she had a "terrible headache." John was at home sick and she had called to cancel the appointment. When she got off the phone, her husband asked her why she had canceled. "You should look after yourself and not be so concerned about everyone else," he said. "These last weeks have been the best of our lives!" With John's encouragement, she changed her mind and came for the appointment. I was surprised by his assessment and asked her if she thought it was true. "Yes," she responded. She reported that she'd felt more in control of her life. She'd been less anxious, more honest, and she'd been keeping her house up because she wanted to, not because John told her she had to. There also seemed to be less fighting, and the children were helping more with the chores. I asked her to rate her main problem, which she believed was "her low sense of worth," on a scale of 1–10, with 10 being no problem at all. When she started therapy, she said it was a 5. This day she rated it as an 8 or a 9. She said, "I'm more tuned in to God's Spirit in me. I can feel God's love and help." She told me that she had been reading the doctrinal affirmation every day and she was finding this *very* helpful. "It made me realize where I get my strength from."

Mary had been trying to get her affirmation from others by doing good things for people. Grasping for external affirmation had actually anesthetized her to her true internal self. She had been out of touch with her internal identity and her relationship to God through Christ. As she opened up to God and began the process of clearing out the static, she was able to realize her identity in Christ and to feel more nourished and strengthened as she experienced the reality of God. She also made a point of taking her medications more regularly. Both of these factors contributed to her improvement.

Step 3: Bitterness Versus Forgiveness

I wondered if we had enough time to proceed with Step 3 on forgiveness. Mary had already worked through it at home and had made a list of the people she wanted to forgive. She was going away the following week with her own family. If she began the process of forgiving these people, I thought that would positively impact her time with them.

Mary began the process, starting with her abortion. She wanted to forgive the doctor who had performed the procedure. She had already done significant work with a Christian post-abortion support group and had experienced some major healing and forgiveness. Mary also had significant episodes to forgive regarding her parents, especially their lack of spiritual influence and direction in her life. I made notes to follow up on this and other new information. I knew that there would be ongoing issues to process with her family of origin. I also planned to continue with this step in the next session.

SESSION THREE

Acknowledging the Lord to be the Wonderful Counselor and inviting the Spirit of Truth to orchestrate the session is the most important part of this process. This means that I, as a counselor, need to tune in to the Spirit, to continually clear out the static in my relationship with God and to learn with God's help to refine my own "listening ear." At the start of this session, there was a major disruption outside that was a distraction to me. It seemed that Mary also was "stirred up." As we prayed again the opening prayer and declaration, which I pray at the beginning of every "step session," I sensed a physical relief myself in the atmosphere and a realization of God's presence. The client settled in as well.

Mary wanted to talk about the abortion again. Perhaps her forgiveness of the abortionist in the previous session had allowed her to go deeper with this traumatic experience. She felt that there was still some lingering depression related to this post-abortion experience. I agreed. She still had some pain and traumatic emotions related to the memories. We took this to the Lord in healing prayer. Mary saw herself again placing her baby in Jesus' arms. Even though she had experienced this many years before in prayer with her support group, Jesus again consoled her and assured her of her child's safety with Him. She would see the child again when she got to heaven. Mary appeared to experience much healing and relief from this prayer time.

As we continued with the forgiveness process, I was mindful of Mary's identification of projection as one of her defenses in Step 2. She now had forgiven the doctor, but what about herself? Could some of her concerns have been a projection? Mary wasn't sure she had forgiven herself, so we focused on this. It seemed important that she have an opportunity to confess to another person, choose to forgive herself, and in so doing open herself up to receive more emotional healing from the Father's hand.

There was more to the self-forgiveness work than just the abortion. The exploration revealed another area of present temptation for

Mary. She had occasionally logged onto pornography on the Internet and was feeling guilty about this. Fortunately, her usage of pornography was very sporadic and rare. As mentioned in Joanne's case, it was so helpful for me as a therapist to have a tool of confession and renunciation to be able to lead the client to some closure in these areas.

Like Gregory's case, we skipped to Step 6 instead of proceeding through the normal sequence of steps. There, with the structure and guidance of the written prayers, Mary renounced all sexual liaisons previous to her marriage and also all pornographic experiences. I explained that sexual intimacy between husband and wife is part of what it means to be one—body, soul, and spirit. Past sexual intimacy or experience outside of marriage impacts the soul and spirit of a person, causing difficulty in present sexual functioning. I have found it helpful for the client to symbolically "cut" those invisible "unholy strings" and thus sever any influence from these past experiences. I have encouraged some to hold up their Bible, "the Sword of the Spirit," and in Jesus, name, symbolically cut through, in the air, any unholy spiritual bonds. This symbolic act of breaking these bonds can help them to remember in the future. This is just another way of putting down a stake at a specific time and a place in the presence of another person who has heard their confession and renunciation of these behaviors. Mary was successful in cutting the spiritual ties that had developed because of her experiences. If Mary had had a pornographic or sexual addiction, further treatment interventions would have been needed as an ongoing part of therapy. As a precaution, I decided to periodically assess her in this area.

As noted, we skipped from Step 3 to Step 6 in order to appropriately deal with the issues that the client had surfaced. This often happens. The order is usually not as important as following the Spirit in the context of a caring relationship. However, Step 1 should always be done first, since it can eliminate spiritual interference that could hinder the process. I've already noted that some therapists may not address this area at all. A spiritual conflict requires a spiritual solution, but you probably won't find such an answer in psychology textbooks.

SESSION FOUR

This was a one-hour session that was mostly therapy. Mary said she was feeling "in a funk," as if she was slipping back into her old patterns. She had found herself getting more and more angry at her husband due to his criticisms and complaints. When he would criticize her, she would feel hurt, turn her anger against herself with self-denigrating messages, and then withdraw and avoid him. I explained to her that therapy is a process, not an instant cure. At least now she was recognizing these patterns, which was progress. I noted that she was becoming more aware of her codependency and, in doing so, was beginning to recognize and feel the pain of her loneliness, along with her disappointment in people for whom she had expectations. We spent some time exploring this sadness, and she was willing to let the tears flow.

After this time of processing, we started to look at Steps 4 and 5 (Rebellion Versus Submission, and Pride Versus Humility), especially as to how they related to her codependency. "I've always been taught that I shouldn't be selfish," she said. We looked at the Scripture about loving God with all your heart, soul, and mind, and loving your neighbor as yourself (Matt 22: 37, 39). She hadn't thought about the "as yourself" before. "You mean, it's okay to take care of me?" she asked. I explained that as we open ourselves vertically to love God and experience His love for us, it becomes possible for us to appropriately "love ourselves." It's often difficult for the client to go deeper with this message. I have used the following meditative exercise to help clients process this truth:

I started by saying, "Mary, God loves you today, just as you are, and He knows you more than anyone else." Then I had her do an exercise that helped her internalize the truth that she is a child of God.

"Mary, repeat out loud, 'I am a child of God.'" She did this.

"Now, repeat it again but this time emphasize the first word, 'I,' and pause to think about what that means."

She said, "I . . . am a child of God."

"What do you think that means, Mary?"

"Well, 'I' means everything about me, who I am on the inside and outside, all my weaknesses, my secrets, my problems, who I am today including my failures."

"Now emphasize the second word, 'am,'" I said.

"I *am* . . . a child of God."

"What does that say to you?"

"That I am, right now, in the present tense, sitting here in your office, with all my pain, right now, this very moment, His child." Was I seeing some relief in her face?

"Now, repeat the third word, 'a.'"

"I am *a* child of God. Well, I am one of many. I'm not alone, there must be other children, I belong to a group, maybe a family," she said.

"Now emphasize 'child.'"

"I am a *child* of God."

"What are the characteristics of a child, Mary?"

She hesitated. "Hmm . . . they're dependent, they don't know everything, they make mistakes, they need someone to take care of them." I sensed that the reality of this truth was going deeper; she was experiencing it more on an affective level. She was feeling some relief. It was wonderful. God's Word was getting through.

"Now, emphasize the last phrase, Mary."

"I am a child *of God*."

"Mary, what's coming to your mind now about God?"

"Oh, He's the Creator of the sun, moon, and the stars. He is so big! He is also the Creator of intricate little wildflowers and everything in between, my children, this whole universe! Wow!" I could "see" her heart expanding with the experience of God's love by the expression on her face, the gentle tears, and her relaxed body.

"Now, say it all again and let your heart be nourished and encouraged with this new sense of what that means."

"*I am a child of God.*"

For her homework, I asked her to repeat that affirmation every day. We finished the session with the daily prayer.

DISCUSSION QUESTION FOR THERAPISTS

The Bible talks about meditating on Scripture much more than reading it (consider Joshua 1 and Psalm 119, for example). Likewise, clinical psychology emphasizes the value of relaxation and meditation for dealing with stress and anxiety. Do most Christians meditate on Scripture? Notice that I'm not talking about memorizing Scripture. Sadly, it appears scriptural meditation is rarely practiced. The New Age has pilfered this biblical mandate and made it into something many Christians shun. Have you found ways to integrate distinctively Christian meditation into your practice? Many of my therapist friends haven't, though they agree with its value. Perhaps the above example will stimulate your thoughts about how to use scriptural meditation in therapy. At the end of the Steps, Dr. Anderson has a list of who we are in Christ taken from his book *Who I Am In Christ* (Regal Books, 2001). This has been extremely valuable for many clients.

SESSION FIVE

It had been three weeks since the last appointment because of my traveling and Mary's vacation. She reported to me that she was surprised at her reaction when she went to a video store. She had selected videos for herself, and the old R-rated movies just didn't have the same appeal. Also, she observed, she had not been tempted with the Internet pornography. Both these occurrences pleased her, and reinforced my initial impression that this wasn't a full-blown addiction.

Step 4: Rebellion Versus Submission

Like most clients, Mary had questions about "submission." I did some teaching on this, explaining that submission is not about being controlled by some other human being. This misperception, of course, was an area of conflict for her in her marriage. It didn't help that John, because of his own insecurities, was controlling and dominating of Mary. He kept telling her that if she would just be a "submissive" wife, the marriage would be fine. She would stand up for herself initially but would eventually get worn down by his manipulations. He was so persistent with his harassing debates and arguments that eventually she would begin to doubt herself and give in. Then, of course, she would be resentful on all fronts, toward him and also toward herself. These were the times when she would act out this anger by deceiving him with lies about where she was going and what she was spending. When she resorted to deception, her inner talk became even more self-critical and self-defeating. Thus, Mary's nonassertiveness and belief that she could not be her own person fueled this cycle. She wanted to follow God and to submit to Him, but she realized that she hadn't been doing that. She hadn't realized that Satan's native language is lying (John 8:44) and that the behavior he seduces us to is "rebellion [which] is as the sin of witchcraft" (1 Sam. 15:23 NKJV). "This is a new concept for me," she said. I assured her that I've found that to be true for most people. The Steps to Freedom are instructive to people as well as freeing.

Step 5: Pride Versus Humility

Having a tendency to be more a people-pleaser than a God-pleaser was significant for her. "I thought that was being humble, not proud," she said. We explored that for a while, looking at the roots of her people-pleasing behaviors and her fear of being rejected. We had talked before about these issues. Self-neglect can be an issue of pride and manipulation. "I will look after you so that you will give me what I need."

Step 6: Bondage Versus Freedom

We had covered the second part of this step regarding the sexual acting out and abortion earlier. Mary reported that she continued to experience more freedom and relief in this area, and her behaviors had changed significantly. So the important part of this step had already been done. We looked at the first part, "the deeds of the flesh" taken from Galatians 5:19–21. She prayed the prayers regarding the substance abuse and the abortion from her past. We identified that there was work to be done regarding the plaguing fears that she experienced. I gave her the separate "phobia worksheet" to take with her as homework for the next session.

Session Six

This one-hour session again was mostly therapy. Mary had had some disciplining issues with one of her younger children and she wanted to talk about this. We explored the specifics and she came up with a plan for some structure and positive reinforcement. We looked at the collusion that sometimes happens in the family system and talked about some boundary issues. This led to talking further about her own family-of-origin issues, like the dysfunctional parenting styles of her mother and father, and what it meant to be in a family system with an alcoholic parent. At the end of the session, we went over the "phobia sheet," which she had spent time on at home. This was "helpful" she said.

Session Seven

In this one-hour session, we discussed Mary's day-to-day experiences of parenting with her children. She thought the disciplining had been going better. She and her husband were talking about situations and blending their complementary strengths in the parenting process. They were also praying together for their children.

Session Eight

Mary said that she'd been reading through Step 7 about the sins and iniquities being passed on from one generation to the next, and she wanted to take care of "that stuff."

Step 7: Acquiescence Versus Renunciation

We started again by praying the initial prayers and declarations. We then talked about the specific problems in her family background that she had identified. These included alcoholism, adultery, deception, fornication, violence, and bad temper outbursts. She renounced all of these when she prayed: "I here and now reject and disown all the sins and iniquities of my ancestors including (she specifically mentioned all the above)." She continued, "As one who has been delivered from the power of darkness and translated into the kingdom of God's dear Son, I cancel out all demonic working that has been passed on to me from my ancestors." In doing this, she had symbolically put the power of the cross between herself and her parents and grandparents and then, on the other side, a cross between herself and her own children in case she had passed any of these same unholy spiritual influences on to them.

Peter talks about the "futile way of life inherited from your fore-fathers" (1 Peter 1:18 NASB). Is this inheritance physical, psychological, or spiritual? The correct answer would seem to be all three. Is the influence of our families limited to nurture and nature, or is there also a spiritual link between ourselves and our ancestors? The spiritual link is more obvious for clients who have had parents or grandparents who participated in the cults or the occult. It is also significant for those who have picked up their family traits through the nurturing (or lack of nurturing) process. Jesus said, "A pupil is not above his teacher; but everyone, after he has been fully trained, will be like his teacher" (Luke 6:40 NASB). For the first five years of our lives, our parents have been our predominant teachers. We are all too familiar with the well-known cycle of abuse, but it doesn't have to continue if we are new creations in Christ. We are never guilty of our parents' sins, but because they sinned we are exposed to their influence and have to live with their results. The Cross dealt with the sin, and we experience our freedom through repentance.

This completed the Steps to Freedom. The next five appointments were therapy sessions.

APPOINTMENT ELEVEN

Mary had some general comments to make about the value of the Steps from her perspective. "It's made me more aware of God and how I need Him in my life, I've been challenged to not watch pornography or to go on the Internet." She indeed had stopped this behavior since she had prayed about it and renounced it. A side benefit of this changed behavior was an improved sexual intimacy with her husband. She was more honest and assertive and they were both happier. We spent some time during this session exploring some of the sexual issues in the marital relationship with suggestions for enhancement. She reported that she had more of a desire for a consistent devotional life, since she was more aware of the reality of God's presence in her life. We talked about different ways that she could be more accountable with Christian friends in a Bible study as well as ways that she could organize her private devotional time.

We also began to talk about termination issues. When the client arrived for the last session, she mentioned that while driving to the appointment she was wondering what she would talk about. I told her that this usually was a good signal that we were about to conclude therapy. "Yes," she said. "I remember at the beginning of therapy that a week seemed too long and I couldn't wait to get here." The plan we agreed upon was appointments every two to three weeks, then once a month, concluding therapy in three months.

APPOINTMENTS TWELVE, THIRTEEN, AND FOURTEEN

These appointments included more work on Mary's anger management, with specific journaling assignments to do over the week. She believed that she was becoming more assertive and that sometimes this caused problems in the marriage. "I think I'm being more honest. That feels better to me," she noted. She recognized that she definitely felt happier when she had consistent devotions. "When I am aware of God's presence I have a lot more strength from the inside," she said. She is practicing what she has learned about boundaries. "I'm trying not to take as gospel truth what John says about me. I don't have to be perfect." We also worked on her behavior of overextending herself and then feeling stressed afterward. This was a challenge for her. "It's hard for me to say no." I agreed with her assessment. We explored some of the roots that hinder her in this area.

At one of the appointments, Mary realized that she had forgotten to take her medication some of the days. This seemed to make a difference in her mood state, so I encouraged her with some ways that might help her to be more consistent with the medication.

Appointment Fifteen—Assessment

In this appointment, we summarized the gains that had been made. Mary felt on a scale of 1–10 (10 being high depression) that during treatment she had gone from a 7 to a 2. She was learning to deal with her anger in more healthy ways by being more assertive, honest, and much less deceptive. Overall, she noted, "I'm not as angry as I used to be . . . Sometimes I'm still a grouch, but at least I recognize it now and have some tools to deal with it."

Mary wasn't experiencing guilt from the past, which she did before. She was more realistic in recognizing her strengths and weaknesses, especially in disciplining the children, and was collaborating more with her husband rather than fighting him. "I'm letting John do what he does well and I'm not feeling threatened. I'm able to accept our differences without putting myself down." Concerning organizing the house, Mary stated she felt that she was making progress in this area as well. When I asked about her other initial presenting problem, her sense of worth, she said that it had improved probably from a 3 to a 7. When I asked for her feedback regarding the Steps to Freedom in her therapy, she said, "It was good. It helped me to realize that Satan can have a hold on you even when you're a Christian. Now I know that Jesus breaks those bonds."

Testing Results

SCL-90-R Figures 1–4 describe some of Mary's SCL-90-R results. Scores are reported in raw score equivalents.

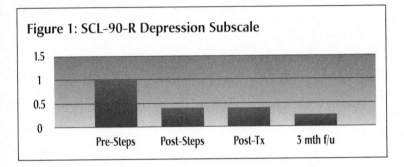

Figure 1: SCL-90-R Depression Subscale

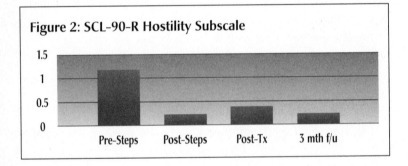

Figure 2: SCL-90-R Hostility Subscale

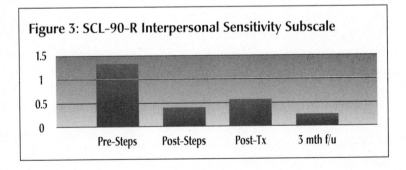

Figure 3: SCL-90-R Interpersonal Sensitivity Subscale

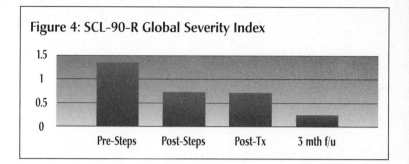

Figure 4: SCL-90-R Global Severity Index

Table 1 describes each SCL-90-R Scale score. Scores are reported in raw score equivalents and T Scores. Results indicate a clear reduction in symptom levels following the Steps. Symptom levels remained at normal levels at the end of treatment and in the three-month follow-up.

Table 1

	Pre-Steps	Post-Steps	Post-Tx	3 Mth f/u
Somatic	0.50 (55T)	0.58 (57T)	0.67 (58T)	0.08 (41T)
Obsessive-Compulsive	0.70 (58T)	0.70 (58T)	0.60 (57T)	0.5 (54T)
Interpersonal Sensitivity	1.33 (68T)	0.33 (50T)	0.56 (59T)	0.22 (50T)
Depression	1.00 (62T)	0.31 (50T)	0.31 (50T)	0.15 (46T)
Anxiety	0.30 (52T)	0.10 (44T)	0.10 (44T)	0.0 (37T)
Hostility	1.17 (68T)	0.17 (48T)	0.33 (54T)	0.17 (48T)
Phobias	0.00 (44T)	0.00 (44T)	0.00 (44T)	0.00 (44T)
Paranoia	1.00 (63T)	0.50 (57T)	0.00 (41T)	0.00 (41T)
Psychoticism	0.60 (65T)	0.00 (44T)	0.00 (44T)	0.00 (44T)
Global Severity Index	0.73 (62T)	0.30 (52T)	0.31 (52T)	0.12 (43T)
Positive Sx Distress Index	1.35 (53T)	1.08 (45T)	1.08 (45T)	1.10 (46T)
Positive Symptom Total	49 (64T)	25 (54T)	26 (55T)	10 (44T)

FICM *Survey Items* Figures 5–10 describe some of Mary's FICM Survey items. Lower scores indicate less distress.

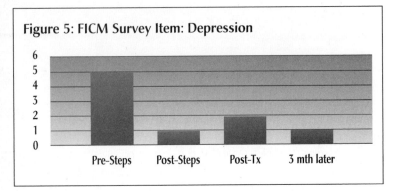

Figure 5: FICM Survey Item: Depression

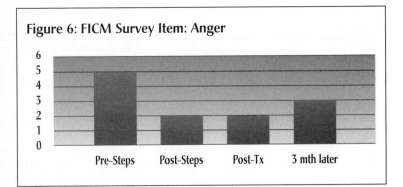

Figure 6: FICM Survey Item: Anger

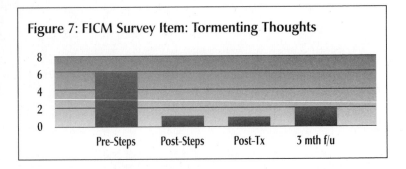

Figure 7: FICM Survey Item: Tormenting Thoughts

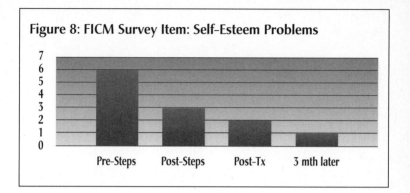

Figure 8: FICM Survey Item: Self-Esteem Problems

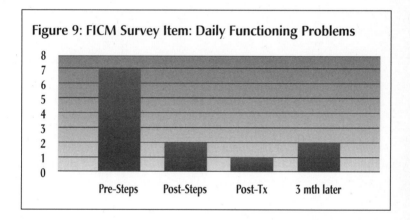

Figure 9: FICM Survey Item: Daily Functioning Problems

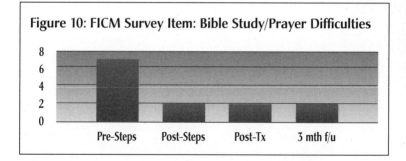

Figure 10: FICM Survey Item: Bible Study/Prayer Difficulties

Table 2

	Pre-Steps	Post-Steps	Post-Tx	3 Mth f/u
Depression	5	1	2	1
Anxiety	5	1	1	1
Fear	2	1	1	1
Anger	5	2	2	3
Tormenting Thoughts	6	1	1	2
Habits	3	1	2	2
Self-Esteem	6	3	2	1
Daily Functioning	7	2	1	2
Relationship Satisfaction	7	2	2	2
Physical Health	6	2	2	2
Bible/Prayer Difficulties	7	2	2	2
Reality of God in Your Life	3	1	1	1

Table 2 depicts all of Mary's survey item responses. Results suggest a clear decrease in perceived distress levels after the Steps. These results were maintained at the end of treatment and in the three-month follow-up.

DAS Figure 11 describes Mary's Dysfunctional Attitude Scale scores. Lower scores suggest more adaptive, less depressogenic beliefs. Mary started with a mild level of dysfunctional beliefs, which decreased even farther with the Steps and treatment. The lower levels of dysfunctional beliefs were maintained at the three-month follow-up.

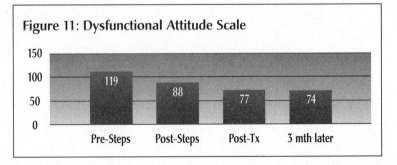

Figure 11: Dysfunctional Attitude Scale

	Pre-Steps	Post-Steps	Post-Tx	3 mth later
	119	88	77	74

SWBS Figure 12 depicts Mary's overall spiritual well-being scores. Higher scores indicate higher degrees of spiritual well-being. A clear pattern of improved spiritual well-being is observed. Taken together with Mary's spirituality items in the FICM Survey data above, one can surmise that Mary has grown spiritually during treatment with the Steps and other interventions.

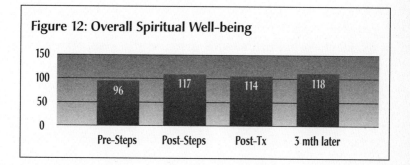

Figure 12: Overall Spiritual Well-being

Client Satisfaction Information Mary scored a 35 on the FICM Client Satisfaction Inventory, indicating a high degree of satisfaction with her treatment. Some of Mary's comments in the additional open-ended satisfaction survey questions included the following:

- "The Steps focused on the spiritual battle in conjunction with my other struggles rather than on just the struggles."

- "I would rate the usefulness of the Steps in therapy as a 10."

- "The Steps showed me the 'cure' for my problems, not just relieving the symptoms."

TREATMENT IMPLICATIONS

Mary's testing results suggest a clear correlation between receiving the Steps to Freedom in the context of therapy and symptom reductions. These results were kept or improved upon with continuing therapy, and three months after treatment Mary still maintained her gains.

While marital work was never a part of treatment, Mary's personal growth also impacted her marriage for the better.

Yet, there's another part of Mary's outcome that is most meaningful for me as a therapist. Mary's increased spirituality was clearly correlated with all these results. She grew in her sense of spiritual well-being, her pursuit of intimacy with her heavenly Father, and in having personal devotional times. Her enhanced connection with God appeared to influence John, as the couple began praying together on a regular basis. Being a Christian therapist, I believe this is the ideal outcome that most of us want as therapists. Mary had a deeper relationship with God, improved emotional health, and an improved marriage. Praise the Lord! The important question now is, How do we as therapists increase the number of cases we see that have this outcome? I believe that the Steps to Freedom provided a structured way of addressing both the spiritual and emotional issues in Mary's life. As she grew in one area, she naturally grew in the other. A similar pattern can be noted in the other cases in this book. True, therapists cannot generalize from a few case studies, but they can evaluate results in their own private practices themselves and see what they find. We must do further scientific studies to investigate the Steps to Freedom, but hopefully these case studies have spurred you on in your own thinking about how to apply distinctively Christian interventions in psychotherapy. I believe you'll find the Steps to Freedom a useful tool in your therapeutic approach. The chapter that follows summarizes the findings of all ten case studies.

CHAPTER 11

Summary of Research Results and Conclusions

So now you've had a chance to read some nonclinical and clinical case studies utilizing the message and method of Freedom in Christ Ministries. While the testing results of the last three cases are encouraging, you may have some remaining questions. What implications does this have for me as a therapist or potential client? What conclusions can we draw from these research results?

To answer these questions, we will first summarize the data of the other cases and briefly give a report of additional research that is being conducted on Freedom in Christ Ministries. Then we will comment on what prominent academic researchers in the area of religious interventions recommend in regard to an appropriate research strategy to scientifically investigate these types of interventions. That will tell us where Freedom in Christ is in the process of scientific exploration and also alert us to current limitations in what can be said. Finally, we'll take off our researchers' caps and put on our clinicians' caps to make some final comments.

SUMMARY OF CLINICAL CASE STUDY RESEARCH

As noted in the introduction to Part Two of this book, ten cases were researched. Five adults received the Steps early in treatment, three late in treatment, one received only the Steps, and one case involved a chronic condition. We've described two cases of the Steps early in treatment, Joanne and Mary, already in detail. To give you a better idea of how this group as a whole fared, we've combined data on the five "early Steps" cases. Figure 1 shows the Global Severity Scale of the SCL-90-R in raw score equivalents. One client did not receive this instrument so data is presented on four clients. Lower scores indicate less distress. The Pre-Steps, Post-Steps, Post Treatment, and 3 month follow-up standard deviations for each reported average were .49, .38, .33, and .32 respectively.

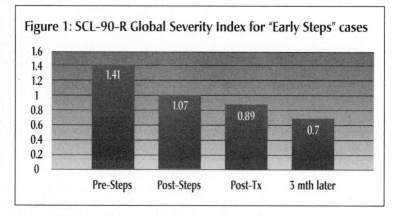

Figure 1: SCL-90-R Global Severity Index for "Early Steps" cases

Figure 2 illustrates the Dysfunctional Attitude Scale results. Lower scores indicate fewer dysfunctional beliefs endorsed. The Pre-Steps, Post-Steps, Post Treatment, and 3 month follow-up standard deviations for each reported average were 18, 30, 23, and 40 respectively.

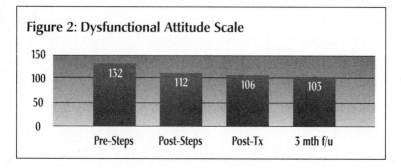

Figure 2: Dysfunctional Attitude Scale

Figure 3 indicates the total Spiritual Well-Being scale scores. Higher scores suggest greater spiritual well-being. The Pre-Steps, Post-Steps, Post Treatment, and 3 month follow-up standard deviations for each reported average were 16, 16, 15, and 21 respectively.

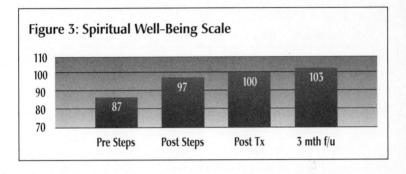

Figure 3: Spiritual Well-Being Scale

The low number of cases prevents statistical analysis of the findings; thus, caution is advised in interpreting the results. One must rely on a visual inspection of the data to note any potential trends. Again, cautiously, one can observe a trend in the direction anticipated for beneficial treatment with the Steps and Christian therapy. This improvement appears maintained at the three-month follow-up. Further case studies of a similar format are needed to permit statistical confirmation of this preliminary finding.

We've already reported on one case, Gregory, that examined the influence of the Steps when administered at the end of treatment. Here is a brief summary of the other two "late Steps" cases, Sarah and Gail. Sarah was a depressed, middle-aged, African-American professional counselor and seminary professor who went through the Steps at the end of therapy. The Steps were done partly because she wanted to learn the process. In the first step, when she came to the list of non-Christian activities she noted that her father had been very active in Free Masonry. This had never been dealt with previously, nor had it been uncovered in twenty-two sessions of therapy. This was very noteworthy. Below is a table describing her Global Severity Index, Dysfunctional Attitude Scale, and Spiritual Well-Being Scale results.

Table 1

	Pre-Steps	Post-Steps/Tx	3 months later
Global Severity Index (SCL-90-R)	.4 (55T)	1.29 (57T)	.28 (52T)
Dysfunctional Attitude Scale	77	96	78
Spiritual Well-Being Scale	96	107	116

Like Gregory's case, one must be cautious in interpreting results at the end of therapy. Sarah's scores are mixed. On the Global Severity Index and the Dysfunctional Attitude Scale, she started with normal range scores and increased (but remained in this range) after the Steps. There was some improvement in spiritual well-being noted, and her three-month follow-up suggested that she had maintained or improved her condition further.

Gail was struggling with symptoms of depression and a very conflicted marriage. She was in both marital and individual therapy. I had already seen her for twenty-nine individual sessions prior to the Steps. She and her husband were being seen conjointly by another colleague. Gail was looking for closure to a trauma that had some spiritual implications regarding an abuse some fifteen years earlier of her young child. The family had already benefited from several individual and family therapists over the years, but since the physical and sexual abuse of the child had occurred at the hand of a perpetrator who was reportedly active in the occult, there still seemed to be some unresolved spiritual issues. Gail wrestled with her image of herself as a responsible, caring mother. The Steps helped her resolve the guilt she felt over not catching the abuse earlier, helped her solidify the forgiveness issues, and gave her a needed closure tool for these unresolved historical issues. She said it best in some of her responses to the qualitative questionnaire:

> The Steps were a tool to help bring closure to much of the other work I'd done, and put everything into perspective—a biblical framework. They are also a tool that can be used again and again in life.

Gail went on to say how the step on forgiveness had been very meaningful.

> My goal after my child was abused was to be able to release the perpetrators to God and let Him deal with them. I had done that for the most part by the time I got into therapy. However, the Steps helped me to continue that release, to reaffirm it and to choose to forgive several other people who had hurt me deeply. Although necessary, it is not enough to just talk about the hurt and the feelings surrounding trauma events. Without something like the Steps, you can get mired down in feelings and don't go beyond them to effectively release the person and their actions to God and choose to forgive. Being hurt, betrayed, etc., is a hazard of life. So I view the Steps as invaluable, not only in therapy, but as a tool for life—to release the offenses to God, to choose forgiveness, and to rise above the sludge and be able to live life abundantly.

This is another example of the Steps to Freedom being an extremely helpful adjunct to therapy. Gail's results noted below suggest a small reduction in psychological symptoms and improved spiritual well-being. The same precautions noted for Gregory and Sarah apply to Gail's findings.

Table 2

	Pre-Steps	Post-Steps/Tx	3 months later
Global Severity Index (SCL-90-R)	.46 (56T)	.20 (48T)	.16 (46T)
Dysfunctional Attitude Scale	76	77	66
Spiritual Well-Being Scale	94	102	105

Marilyn was a middle-aged Latina client who had been suffering from a recurrent long-term depression that included major symptoms of anxiety. The onset of these symptoms occurred as the result of physical abuse by a family member four years previously.

She had been diagnosed with post-traumatic stress syndrome. She was on a variety of medications, which had been only marginally helpful due to her hypersensitivity to medications because of a previous bout with viral meningitis. She had had one previous psychiatric hospitalization, and had experienced electroconvulsive therapy twice. Shortly after I began seeing Marilyn (an intake evaluation and one session), the Steps were administered over an eight-session period. Her follow-up data was six months after the Steps, with ongoing psychotherapy and medication management. She is continuing ongoing monthly supportive psychotherapy.

Table 3

	Pre-Steps	Post-Steps/Tx	6 months later w/ ongoing Tx
Global Severity Index (SCL-90-R)	1.23 (68T)	.78 (63T)	.89 (64T)
Dysfunctional Attitude Scale	99	96	93
Spiritual Well-Being Scale	96	100	107

While Marilyn's test scores indicate only mild improvements, her clinical functioning actually has improved. Before I began seeing her, she would have one to two days per week of incapacitation during which time she stayed in bed, sometimes unable to function. In nine months of treatment, including the Steps and further excellent medication management, she has only had two such days total. While her multidisciplinary treatment prevents strong statements about what elements are associated with her improvement, Marilyn rates the Steps as very high in helping her. She is more aware of spiritual warfare and now actively prays and brings thoughts captive to Christ. In the qualitative questionnaire regarding the helpfulness of the Steps in therapy, on a scale of 1 to 10 (10 being most useful), she said the following: "Probably an 8 or 9. It has helped me see more clearly where Satan had strongholds in my life and showed me how to stand more securely against him because of my position in Christ." She continues to become discouraged at times because she is still experiencing anxiety and depression, but her improved functionality is noteworthy. Again, the complexity of her case suggests caution in giving too much credit specifically to any particular element for her improvement, but it is encouraging that Marilyn has felt helped by the Steps. The client wrote: "The Steps to Freedom added to my therapy experience because there is so much concise biblical teaching in the material, along with the prayers that have been helpful to me in dealing with specific emotional problems I have dealt with." Marilyn was familiar with the Freedom in Christ message, and had even gone through the Steps in a group setting at a conference. She felt that the one-on-one process was more helpful in the therapeutic setting. "Going through them one on one with a therapist over a period of several weeks was most helpful."

The last case I'm reporting involved working with a depressed, Caucasian, middle-aged professional woman, Jennifer, who was having significant marital difficulties. She was from another town and specifically requested the Steps, so I took her through them in one sitting with no therapy. Of course, I would have liked to have conducted some individual as well as marital work if that had been possible. I gave her referrals to follow up with some counseling in her area, but she decided not to seek further treatment. Thus, Jennifer's results indicate treatment with only the Steps by a well-trained mental health professional.

Table 4

	Pre-Steps	Post-Steps/Tx	3 months later
Global Severity Index (SCL-90-R)	1.28 (69T)	1.09 (67T)	0.63 (60T)
Spiritual Well-Being Scale	69	83	97

The Dysfunctional Attitude Scale was not given in Jennifer's treatment. Jennifer's test scores suggest improved spiritual well-being and an improvement over time in terms of her psychological symptoms. She claims that the Steps changed her life. She was about to divorce her husband but decided against it. For the first time she stated she felt free from the baggage of her past life. In the qualitative questionnaire she responded: "I can honestly say, I feel different; God showed up. He is faithful. The area of freedom I sense the most is with past guilt. I'd rate the Steps to Freedom at a 10 for me. It was like getting past sins all on the table once and for all. I now know that I am forgiven once and for all. What a relief." She was very enthusiastic and appreciative.

OTHER RESEARCH ON FREEDOM IN CHRIST MINISTRIES

Other research on the Steps to Freedom has been done. In Dr. Anderson's seminars, individuals are led through the Steps to Freedom in the group seminar setting during the conference. In addition, seminar participants may sign up for individual "Freedom Appointments" that are given at the conclusion of the seminar, mostly by FIC staff members. After the seminar leaves town, lay encouragers who have been trained in the various hosting churches conduct the Freedom Appointments. One of the goals of the Freedom in Christ Conferences is to train laypeople who will continue the ministry in the churches. This has happened in our area. Over the years, we estimate that hundreds of these Freedom Appointments have been conducted. Faithful lay encouragers, servants of the Lord, continue to labor week by week. They have stories to tell similar to the ones that you have read in Part One of this book. Judith King, MSW, ACSW, studied these two groups of people in the following way:

I (Judith) have conducted three pilot studies on Dr. Anderson's Steps to Freedom in the Michigan area. The first study was conducted following Dr. Anderson's seminar with counselees who were led through appointments by Freedom in Christ staff, in 1996. Following the seminar, a brief prequestionnaire was given persons who were scheduled for

Freedom Appointments with FIC staff. The ten-item initial questionnaire that we developed was the forerunner to the twelve-item FICM Survey questionnaire described in these clinical case studies. The self-rated scale had one item each to rate depression, anxiety, tormenting thoughts or voices, and addictive habits over which the person felt little control, on a scale from 1 to 10. The person was also asked to rate their levels of inner conflict or distress, daily functioning, tools of spiritual warfare, reality of God in their life, devotional life, and Christian fellowship. Three months after their initial appointment participants were sent the same questionnaire and asked to again rate themselves in the above ten categories. The average group percent improvement in symptoms of depression, anxiety, inner conflict and especially tormenting thoughts, and addictive habits are noted in the table below.

Pilot studies Number 2 and Number 3 in Michigan involved lay counselors in the west Michigan area, leading counselees through Freedom Appointments in many different churches of various denominations. Usually, these participants have read some of Dr. Anderson's materials, but not always. Most have not had the opportunity to attend a seminar. Under the auspices of "The Ministry of Healing" (Dr. George Hurst, University of Texas-Tyler), in cooperation with FIC, the original questionnaire was refined and changed to include two additional questions, as described in the introduction. This improved FIC questionnaire was given to the participants before their Freedom Appointment and then three months afterward as described above. The average group percent improvement in symptoms is also noted in the table below. I owe a debt of gratitude to the many committed lay encouragers who helped with these pilot projects.

Table 5: Percent Improvement

	Depression	Anxiety	Inner Conflict	Tormenting Thoughts	Addictive Habits
Michigan Pilot 1	64	58	63	82	52
Michigan Pilot 2	47	44	51	58	43
Michigan Pilot 3	52	47	48	57	39

Pilot Study 1 had 30 participants, Pilot Study 2 had 55 participants, and Pilot Study 3 had 21 participants. All One Way ANOVAs
performed on the three pilot studies were significant at the .05 or
lower level. Caution is advised because no measurement took place
shortly after the Steps, and many things could have happened in participants' lives other than going through the Steps to improve their
scores. The fact, however, that each group experienced sizable
changes on these rating scales is encouraging for further research
with better designs, and this is happening. These initial pilot studies
got the ball rolling and provided some preliminary encouragement
especially to pastors, who are usually overloaded with counseling
responsibilities. In fact, many pastors in the Michigan area have
become enthusiastic and supportive of the FIC material due to the
hundreds of people, their own parishioners, who have been positively
impacted through Freedom Appointments with lay encouragers.

In the first introduction, Dr. Anderson mentioned the research
project done by Dr. Garzon and his research team on a divinity class
that experienced Dr. Anderson's seminar and the Steps to Freedom.
In this project, 24 divinity students completed several psychometrically normed testing measures prior to the weeklong seminar, after
the seminar, and three weeks later. The instruments given included
the SCL-90-R (previously described), the Beck Anxiety Inventory,
and the Rosenberg Self-Esteem Inventory. Statistical analyses of
preclass seminar, postclass seminar, and three-week follow-up data
occurred. The following table describes the average and standard
deviation (SD) of several scale scores. Global Severity Index scores
are in raw score equivalents.

Table 6

	Pre-Class Seminar Avg	SD	Post-Class Seminar Avg	SD	3 Week Follow-Up Avg	SD
Global Severity Index (SCL-90-R)	0.81	0.54	0.38	0.44	0.29	0.27
Beck Anxiety Inventory	8.87	6.56	2.67	3.01	3.63	3.79
Rosenberg Self-Esteem Inventory	30.00	4.80	33.79	3.40	33.46	4.91

The following table describes the statistical analyses of the above results to see if there were statistically significant differences present. Repeated measured ANOVAs were performed.

Table 7

Measure	df	F	p
Global Severity Index (SCL-90-R)	2, 22	12.45	< .01
Beck Anxiety Inventory	2, 22	19.12	< .01
Rosenberg Self-Esteem Inventory	2, 22	16.99	< .01

The analysis did suggest statistically significant results. As with the previous seminar research noted, cautions are needed in interpreting the findings. No randomized control group was used, and many threats to internal validity exist (see Garzon et al., 2001, for a detailed discussion of this project). This leads us to an examination of the current status of Freedom in Christ research.

CURRENT STATUS OF RESEARCH ON FREEDOM IN CHRIST MINISTRIES METHODS AND MESSAGE

To understand the current status of Freedom in Christ research, it will help to see what experts in religious intervention research recommend for a research strategy. In 1998, the National Institute for Healthcare Research published a volume, *Scientific Research on Spirituality and Health: A Consensus Report,* edited by David Larson, James Swyers, and Michael McCullough. In one chapter, Thoresen, Worthington, Swyers, Larson, McCullough, and Miller (1998) delineated a series of recommended general research steps for the exploration of spiritual intervention in treatment. First, a clear description of the intervention model itself is recommended. This may be found in Dr. Anderson's numerous works. Next, exploratory studies that utilize quasi-experimental designs should be done. Examples suggested include one-group pretest-posttest designs, single-subject designs, and quasi-control-group pretest-posttest designs. After these kinds of studies have suggested efficacious treatment effects, more empirically valid randomized control group studies should follow.

Why not just do some randomized control-group studies and ignore exploratory research? As alluded to in the introduction to this section, the pre-experimental and quasi-experimental types of research mentioned above have advantages and disadvantages. The primary disadvantage of exploratory, quasi-experimental research is that it cannot be used to make conclusive causal statements. Empirical, randomized control-group studies are needed for that, but exploratory quasi-experimental research does have its place in establishing an intervention's efficacy in several respects.

Martin Seligman (1995) notes why both exploratory and empirical studies are needed when investigating a technique's efficacy in psychotherapy. First, psychotherapy does not have a fixed limited session number, as randomized control-group studies do. Therapy goes on until the client improves or quits. Likewise, the case studies in this book did not have any fixed limit in sessions. Second, psychotherapy is self-correcting and makes adjustments to what is needed. In Gregory's and Mary's cases, the order of the Steps to Freedom was rearranged to fit what each client presented. Randomized clinical trials are manualized and do not make such adjustments. Third, clients in psychotherapy frequently have multiple diagnoses and problems. Participants in empirical trials are carefully screened to eliminate clients with multiple diagnoses (unless two conditions are highly comorbid, i.e., two pathological conditions existing at the same time). Thus, most empirical research doesn't generally validate treatments for the types of clients that therapists really see! The clinical cases presented in this book contained real clients with multiple diagnoses and problems.

Another advantage to exploratory research is that it is much less expensive to perform. Research-funders do not like spending the large amounts of money required to do a true experiment unless they have an indication that the experiment is worth the risk. Exploratory research helps give them an idea as to what they might find. If the research summarized on Freedom in Christ had produced no significant findings, then we could have stopped there and gone no farther. Fortunately, the research has been very encouraging.

So what can we say? Research on the Steps to Freedom is at an early stage, and interpretations of its findings must be very limited. The types of research done on Freedom in Christ so far have given some indication of external or "real-world environment" validity while sacrificing internal (causal) validity. Both types of validity are needed to truly determine efficacy. One cannot say that the various research projects on Freedom in Christ have proved the Steps to Freedom are effective. What can be said is that research has been done with several types of people normally likely to experience the Steps to Freedom—regular seminar participants, divinity students, and Christian psychotherapy clients. All of these studies have found encouraging results that suggest an association between the Steps to Freedom and improvements in mental and spiritual health. Whether that association is causal remains to be seen. What's needed now is more research with comparison groups and true empirical experiments (randomized control-group studies). Such studies will allow an assessment of whether the Steps to Freedom are causing the observed improvements.

SPEAKING AS CLINICIANS

You've read the case studies and seen the current research on Freedom in Christ; now let us talk to you as practicing Christian mental health professionals. First, we encourage you to become familiar with the message and methods of Freedom in Christ Ministries. Attend one of Dr. Anderson's seminars, read some of his materials, and consider for yourself whether this approach has merit. As many therapists already know, one of the best ways to become familiar with an approach is to actually experience it. Psychoanalysts and now even some cognitive therapists (e.g., Beck, 1995) recommend this.

Second, consider doing your own clinical research on Freedom in Christ in your practice. In addition to his regular writings, Dr.

Anderson has written several training materials available to help lay counselors become familiar with his approach. These are easily applicable to professionals. Study these materials and prayerfully consider using the Steps to Freedom with appropriate clients. Below you'll find a detailed recommended strategy for use that Judith wrote for *Christ Centered Therapy*.

STRATEGY FOR USE

We have developed a strategy that we generally follow in using the Steps as an adjunct in therapy. Consider tailoring some of these ideas as they particularly fit for you, your type of practice, and your particular client population. Our usual procedure is as follows:

1. Hear the client's story; take a brief social history and assessment.

2. Make a clinical diagnosis, and assess the degree of ego strength. A client must be motivated for change with a fairly intact ego. A severely abused client must be taken through the Steps very slowly or else all in one sitting. A fragile ego needs more work with the therapeutic relationship.

3. Establish a trusting therapeutic relationship.

4. Assess for medical problems and consider medical intervention. Sometimes the decision is made to hold off on medication until after the Steps have been completed. This depends on the degree of organic dysfunction.

5. Introduce the idea of the Steps at an appropriate time, as the Lord leads. Have the client read *Victory Over the Darkness* and *The Bondage Breaker*. Give them a Seven Steps booklet to read and review.

6. Schedule a ninety-minute or two-hour appointment in which to work on the Steps if possible.

7. Start each session with the beginning Prayer and Declaration and finish each session with Daily Prayer or the Statement of Truth. Complete the first step before the others.

8. Make notes of issues to explore further in therapy or, as the Lord leads, continue to work on a particular issue in the midst of the Steps.

9. Eventually complete all the steps.

If there are spiritual issues emanating from listening to and believing lies, then there could well be a spiritual battle for the mind. Most of us have experienced spiritual oppression simply as a result of our living in a broken world with our own personal wound-edness from the past. This is especially true for our clients who have been through significant trauma. No amount of therapy is going to free them if there is a spiritual battle for their minds unless a spiritual intervention is used. The Steps can deal effectively with this issue in a nondramatic, quiet fashion.

CONCLUDING REMARKS

Finally, as you do your own exploration of Freedom in Christ, we believe you'll find what we have—more rapid symptom reductions for many clients, increased client awareness of spiritual coping resources, and increased client satisfaction with treatment. No, we're not making "magic bullet" claims for this intervention, but we do believe it's definitely worth having in your therapist tool kit. Don't we need more overtly Christian intervention strategies in our tool kit, anyway?

Jesus Christ, our Master, is the answer. He has come to set the captives free. He is the Light and source of love that shines into the darkness of our souls, birthing hope again (1 John 1:5). We are called as wounded healers to bring hope where there is despair, light where there is darkness, and healing where there is pain. We are learning and will continue on this learning curve for our entire lives. We have paused in the midst of this process to share with you what we have found so far, with the hope that this will encourage you, stimulate your thinking, and refresh your spirits. As therapists, we all have the awesome calling of being Christ's servants for the multitude of people who are suffering from emotional and spiritual ills. Thankfully, Jesus did not leave any of us as orphans (John 14:18), but sent the Holy Spirit, the Spirit of Truth, to be with us. May the Holy Spirit guide you as you consider this ministry. We believe you'll find the Steps to Freedom to be a valuable tool that fosters the essential process of establishing our freedom in Christ. May we all "grow in the grace and knowledge of our Lord and Savior Jesus Christ" (2 Pet. 3:18 NASB), and become His freedom fighters for our clients.

"How great is the love the Father has lavished on us, that we should be called children of God! And that is what we are!" (1 John 3:1 NIV).

Notes

Part One: Introduction
1. Fernando Garzon, David Kleinschuster, Erica Tan, and Jennifer Hill, "Freedom in Christ: Quasi-Experimental Research on the Neil Anderson Approach," *Journal of Psychology and Theology*, 2001, Vol. 29, No. 1, 41–51.

2. Edmund J. Bourne, *The Anxiety and Phobia Workbook*, rev. ed. (Oakland, CA: New Harbinger Publications, Inc., 1995).

3. Edmund J. Bourne, *Healing Fear* (Oakland, CA: New Harbinger Publications, Inc., 1998), 2.

4. Neil T. Anderson, Terry and Julie Zuehlke, *Christ Centered Therapy* (Grand Rapids, MI: Zondervan Publishing House, 2000).

5. Bourne, *Healing Fear*, 5.

Chapter 2
1. For a detailed discussion on sanctification, read *God's Power at Work in You*, which I co-authored with Dr. Robert Saucy. It is published by Harvest House.

2. Anne gives a good description of what it means to "take every thought captive." Later in her letter, she says, "I just need to examine the thought according to the Word of God and then choose the truth."

3. Renouncing Satan is verbally standing against him as we are taught in James 4:7: "Resist the devil and he will flee from you" (NIV).

Chapter 3

1. In the parable of the rich man and Lazarus, we are clearly told of the great chasm that separates the living from the dead, I do not believe it was actually Sandy's mother who appeared in her dream. There is no way to know for sure, but perhaps God used Sandy's sensitivity toward her mother as a means of communicating with her and drawing her to Himself.

2. *The Seduction of Our Children* is published by Harvest House (Eugene, OR, 1991).

3. *Spiritual Protection for Your Children* is published by Regal Books (Ventura, CA, 1996).

References

Part Two: Introduction

Attkisson, C. and R. Zwick, "The Client Satisfaction Questionnaire," *Evaluation and Program Planning 5* (1982): 233–237.

Beck, A. T., G. Brown, R. A. Steer, and A. N. Weissman, "Factor Analysis of the Dysfunctional Attitude Scale in a Clinical Population," *Psychological Assessment 3* (1991): 478–483.

Boivin, M. J., A. L. Kirby, L. K. Underwood, and H. Silva, "Spiritual Well-being Scale," in *Measures of Religiosity*, edited by Peter C. Hill and Ralph W. Hood Jr., 382–385. Birmingham, AL: Religious Education Press, 1999.

Derogatis, L.R. *SCL-90-R: Administration, Scoring, and Procedure Manual-I for R.* Minneapolis: National Computer Systems, 1994.

Dobson, K. S. and H. J. Breiter, "Cognitive Assessment of Depression: Reliability and Validity of Three Measures," *Journal of Abnormal Psychology 92* (1983): 107–109.

Ellis, J. B. and P. C. Smith, "Spiritual Well-being, Social Desirability and Reasons for Living: Is There a Connection?" *The International Journal of Social Psychiatry 37*, no. 1 (1991): 57–63.

King, J., G. Hurst, and H. Parks, "Freedom in Christ Ministries Survey." Knoxville, TN: Freedom in Christ Ministries, 1999.

King, J. "Qualitative Client Satisfaction Inventory." Knoxville, TN: Freedom in Christ Ministries, 2002.

Larsen, D. L., C. C. Attkisson, W. A. Hargreaves, and T. D. Nguyen, "Assessment of Client/Patient Satisfaction: Development of a General Scale," *Evaluation and Program Planning 2* (1979): 197–207.

Ledbetter, M. F., L. A. Smith, J. D. Fischer, W. L. Vosler-Hunter, and G. P. Chew, "An Evaluation of the Construct Validity of the Spiritual Well-being Scale: A Confirmatory Factor Analytic Approach," *Journal of Psychology and Theology* 19 (1991): 94–102.

Miller, G., W. Fleming, and F. Brown-Anderson, "Spiritual Well-being Scale Ethnic Differences Between Caucasians and African-Americans," *Journal of Psychology and Theology* 26, no. 4 (1998): 358–364.

Oliver, J. and E. Baumgart, "The Dysfunctional Attitude Scale: Psychometric Properties and Relation to Depression in an Unselected Adult Population," *Cognitive Therapy and Research* 9, no. 2 (1985): 161–167.

Paloutzian, R. and C. Ellison, "Loneliness, Spiritual Well-being and Quality of Life," in *Loneliness: A Sourcebook of Current Theory, Research and Therapy*, edited by L. A. Peplau and D. Perlman, 224–237. New York: Wiley Interscience, 1982.

Richards, P. S. and A. E. Bergin. *A Spiritual Strategy of Counseling and Psychotherapy*. Washington, D.C.: American Psychological Association, 1997.

Scott, E. L., A. A. Agresti, and G. Fitchett. "Factor Analysis of the Spiritual Well-being Scale and Its Clinical Utility with Psychiatric Inpatients," *The Journal for the Scientific Study of Religion* 37, no. 2 (1998): 314–318.

Seligman, M., "The Effectiveness of Psychotherapy," *American Psychologist* 50, no. 12 (1995): 965–974.

Weissman, A. N. and A. T. Beck. "Development and Validation of the Dysfunctional Attitudes Scale: A Preliminary Investigation." Paper presented at the annual meeting of the Educational Research Association, Toronto, Ontario, Canada.

CHAPTER 8

Enright, R. D. *Forgiveness is a Choice*. Washington, D.C.: American Psychological Association Press, 2001.

Worthington, E. *Five Steps to Forgiveness: The Art and Science of Forgiving*. New York: Crown Publishers, 2001.

CHAPTER 11

Beck, J. *Cognitive Therapy: Basics and Beyond*. New York: Guilford Press, 1995.

Seligman, M, "The Effectiveness of Psychotherapy: The Consumer Reports Study," *American Psychologist* 50, no.12 (1995): 965–974.

Thoresen, C., E. Worthington, J. Swyers, D. Larson, M. McCullough, and W. Miller, "Religious/Spiritual Interventions," in *Scientific Research on Spirituality and Health: A Consensus Report,* edited by D. Larson, J. Swyers, and M. McCullough's. Washington, D.C.: National Institute for Healthcare Research, 1998.

Acknowledgments

There are no "self-made" Christians. The true children of God are born from above. "God-made" believers are spiritually alive, and when they abide in Christ they bear much fruit. They mature as their minds are renewed by the Word of God, and by overcoming the harsh realities of a fallen world. God does not save us from the trials and tribulations of life. He saves us from a godless eternity. We enter into this eternal life the moment we put our trust in Him. He sets us free from our past and works through the difficulties of life to produce godly character.

We want to acknowledge the people who have agreed to share their stories in this book. They have found their peace *in* Christ, and *through* Christ. They are in the process of overcoming the world, the flesh, and the devil. They have graciously allowed their stories to be told for the purpose of helping others. In the process of working with us, some had to relive the horror they had gone through. In our minds they are heroes of the faith. Their only motive for sharing their stories was to help others gain an understanding of how they too can be free in Christ and how the pastors and counselors can help others.

We also want to acknowledge our dear friends Ron and Carole Wormser, who helped assemble the first edition, and personally counseled some of the people in this book.

About the Authors

Dr. Neil T. Anderson was the chairman of the Practical Theology department at Talbot School of Theology for ten years. He is the founder and President Emeritus of Freedom in Christ Ministries. Neil has five earned degrees, including two doctorates. He has written many bestselling books, including *Victory over the Darkness*, *The Bondage Breaker*, *Finding Hope Again*, *Freedom from Fear*, *Getting Anger Under Control*, and *The Freedom in Christ Bible*. Happily married for thirty-five years, he has two children and two grandchildren.

Dr. Fernando Garzon is an assistant professor in the School of Psychology and Counseling at Regent University. He specializes in research on Christian interventions in psychological treatment and has written articles on Freedom in Christ research. Dr. Garzon is also an associate pastor at *Cristo Redentor* (Christ the Redeemer), a predominantly Latino church in the Virginia Beach area. He received his doctorate in clinical psychology from Fuller Seminary and is an ordained minister with the Evangelical Church Alliance. Dr. Garzon maintains a private, donation-based counseling practice.

Judith E. King is a graduate of the University of Toronto and Western Michigan University, where she received her MSW in 1985. As a clinical therapist in Grand Rapids, Michigan, Judy integrates psychological and biblical principles in her therapy, and has a special interest in research and caring for professionals in ministry. She is a member of the National Association of Social Workers (NASW), National Association of Christians in Social Work (NACSW), and The American Association of Christian Counselors (AACC). Judy is in private practice (Sonlife Associates) with her psychiatrist husband, Stephen King M.D.

If you would like more information on resources and conferences available through Freedom in Christ Ministries, you may contact them at:

Freedom in Christ Ministries
9051 Executive Park Dr., Suite #503
Knoxville, TN 37923
phone: (865) 342-4000 / fax: (865) 342-4001
E-mail: info@ficm.org
Web site: www.ficm.org